W9-BZZ-251

For a long time, scholars have generally shared the belief that late medieval authors – particularly in England and especially Chaucer – wrote for private readers. This book assembles and analyzes in depth, for the first time, an overwhelming mass of evidence that contradicts this view, as well as current orthodoxies in orality/literacy theory. In both Britain and France, literate, elite audiences continued to prefer public reading (i.e., reading books aloud in a group) to private reading, from the mid fourteenth through the late fifteenth century.

This book offers the first sustained critique of Walter Ong's *Orality and Literacy* (1982), which has encouraged medievalists to underestimate the nature and role of late medieval public reading. Using an "ethnographic" methodology, Joyce Coleman develops several schemas from the data, and applies them in analyses of texts including historical records, works by Chaucer, and works by other literary authors into the late fifteenth century.

CAMBRIDGE STUDIES IN MEDIEVAL LITERATURE

This series of critical books seeks to cover the whole area of literature written in the major medieval languages – the main European vernaculars, and medieval Latin and Greek – during the period *c.* 1100–*c.* 1500. Its chief aim is to publish and stimulate fresh scholarship and criticism on medieval literature, special emphasis being placed on understanding major works of poetry, prose, and drama in relation to the contemporary culture and learning which fostered them.

Recent titles in the series
15 *Chaucer and the Tradition of the "Roman Antique,"* by Barbara Nolan
16 *The "Romance of the Rose" and its Medieval Readers: Interpretation, reception, manuscript transmission*, by Sylvia Huot
17 *Women and Literature in Britain, 1150–1500*, edited by Carol M. Meale
18 *Ideas and Forms of Tragedy from Aristotle to the Middle Ages*, by Henry Ansgar Kelly
19 *The Making of Textual Culture: Grammatica and literary theory, 350–1100*, by Martin Irvine
20 *Narrative, Authority, and Power: The medieval exemplum and the Chaucerian tradition*, by Larry Scanlon
21 *Medieval Dutch Literature in its European Context*, edited by Erik Kooper
22 *Dante and the Mystical Tradition: Bernard of Clairvaux in the "Commedia,"* by Steven Botterill
23 *Heresy and Literacy, 1000–1530*, edited by Peter Biller and Anne Hudson
24 *Virgil in Medieval England: Figuring the "Aeneid" from the twelfth century to Chaucer*, by Christopher Baswell
25 *Sciences and the Self in Medieval Poetry: Alan of Lille's "Anticlaudianus" and John Gower's "Confessio Amantis,"* by James Simpson
26 *Public Reading and the Reading Public in Late Medieval England and France*, by Joyce Coleman

A complete list of titles in the series is given at the end of this volume

CAMBRIDGE STUDIES IN MEDIEVAL LITERATURE 26

Public reading and the reading public in late medieval England and France

Man reading book to Philip the Good and court
(1468; Flanders; Wauquelin, *Chroniques de Hainault*; Bibl. Roy. 9243 [vol. II], f. 1)

Public Reading and the Reading Public in Late Medieval England and France

JOYCE COLEMAN

University of North Dakota

CAMBRIDGE
UNIVERSITY PRESS

Published by the Press Syndicate of the University of Cambridge
The Pitt Building, Trumpington Street, Cambridge CB2 1RP
40 West 20th Street, New York, NY 10011-4211, USA
10 Stamford Road, Oakleigh, Melbourne 3166, Australia

First published 1996

Transferred to digital printing 1998

Printed in Great Britain by Biddles Short Run Books

A catalogue record for this book is available from the British Library

Library of Congress cataloguing in publication data

Coleman, Joyce.
Public reading and the reading public in late medieval England and France / Joyce Coleman.
p. cm. – (Cambridge studies in medieval literature; 26)
Includes bibliographical references and index.
ISBN 0 521 55391 1 (hardback)
1. Books and reading – England – History.
2. Books and reading – France – History. 3. Oral reading – History.
4. Oral tradition – England – History. 5. Oral tradition – France – History.
6. Literacy – England – History. 7. Literacy – France – History.
I. Title. II. Series.
Z1003.5.G7C65 1996
028'.9'0942–dc20 95–37984 CIP

ISBN 0 521 55391 1 hardback

CE

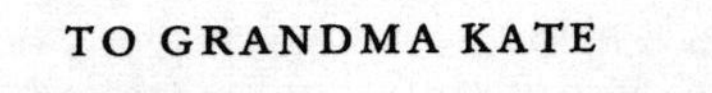

TO GRANDMA KATE

Of hem that writen ous tofore
The bokes duelle, and we therfore
Ben tawht of that was write tho:
Forthi good is that we also
In oure tyme among ous hiere
Do wryte of newe som matiere,
Essampled of these olde wyse
So that it myhte in such a wyse,
Whan we ben dede and elleswhere,
Beleve to the worldes eere
In tyme comende after this.

(Gower, *Confessio Amantis* prol.: 1–11)

Contents

Illustrations

Preface

This book is not about illiteracy. It *is* about public reading in late medieval England, but it is not about book shortages or any other technological factor that might be supposed to explain the popularity of public reading. This book is dedicated to showing that public reading was and remained popular because people enjoyed listening to books in company; that these aural audiences included the sort of literate upper-middle- and upper-class readers for whom Chaucer wrote; and that even the arrival of the Renaissance signaled not the extinction of aurality but its transmutation.

To explore the nature of late medieval aurality (defined as the reading of books aloud to one or more people), I have drawn on both historical and literary sources. Since this investigation extends across some 175 years, I have kept it focused on one form of reading material: i.e., "court-oriented," secular, vernacular writing in English. Inevitably, I have strayed into other languages – Scots, Anglo-Norman, French, and Latin – but I have been firmer about genres, excluding the drama and most romances, histories, non-recreative translations, and scholarly works of science or philosophy. I have also excluded religious reading (by religious or of religious material, whether orthodox or Lollard) and reading by or to children.

This book is not about Chaucer, but he is certainly the most important author involved, and much of the debate over forms of reading derives from a general desire among modern scholars to distance him from the perceived concomitants of "primitive orality." In fact, however, there is not much debate; while Chaucerians of all theoretical stripes are eagerly asserting that Chaucer marked the birth of English literature by writing for private readers, another, smaller group of critics are simply content to mildly acknowledge his aurality before going on to other business. No scholar has yet engaged directly with the arguments of the anti-auralists, examining either their theoretical underpinnings or the historical substance of their claims.

Since these claims tend to a notable circularity – even Chaucer's references to hearers are held to prove his "literacy," by a complicated argument I label "fictive orality" – they are difficult to refute. In attempting this task, I have moved both deeper into Chaucer's canon and outside it, to records of historical reading events and to the writings of other authors, from Chaucer's time until the early Renaissance. The results, presented in chapters 5–7, offer overwhelming evidence that far from being identified with ignorance, poverty, lack of sophistication, with bards or with minstrels, public reading was a common practice among the upper-middle- and upper-class elite audiences of both France and England until and (in modulated form) beyond the very end of the Middle Ages.

Another thing this book is not about is style. Several distinguished scholars have concerned themselves to create definitive lists of "oral" and "literate" stylistic traits, and many other scholars have confidently applied these prescriptive definitions to medieval texts. I would not say these ascriptions are always invalid, but I am certain that, as presently applied, "oral" and "literate" are very nearly invalid as categories. Too much confidence has been placed in theoretical models based on outmoded evolutionary and Eurocentric principles, and too many capabilities denied to "orality" by those unfamiliar with the relevant ethnographic and folkloristic research.

Rather than imposing universal, self-validating categories of "oral" and "literate" style on texts, we should work outwards from given texts and literary environments to develop culture-specific descriptive systems. These systems would have to recognize that modes of reception are driven not only by technology but by many other factors, both literary and social. Until such factors have been incorporated into the schematizing, and until more of the sort of inductive research offered in this book has been done, generalizations about stylistic traits would be premature, and I do not attempt here to offer any.

It may relieve tension for me to state at the beginning that the conclusion of all this pro-aurality argumentation is not that we must now read Chaucer (or his contemporaries) in some radically different way. Chaucer was and remains a sophisticated, writing poet, the father of English literature. His work remains as "literary" – in the sense of subtle, self-conscious, and ironic – as ever. The evidence assembled in this book would simply suggest that this subtle, self-conscious, ironic literature was directed primarily at listeners rather than private readers. Since these listeners were literate, educated members of the upper classes of society, the literature need not have been too imperiled by the contact.

This book begins with a consideration of the theoretical framework provided – and the fallacies encouraged – by standard orality/literacy theory; the second half searches primary historical and literary sources from the late Middle Ages for evidence of how people read. In brief, chapter 1 examines the weaknesses that have been emerging in standard orality/literacy theory as formulated by Eric Havelock, Jack Goody and Ian Watt, and Walter Ong, and as adapted to discussions of medieval culture. These have had the particular effect of suppressing recognition of such "mixed" forms as aurality. Drawing on the critiques of several social scientists – Sylvia Scribner and Michael Cole, Brian Street, and Ruth Finnegan – I argue for a more inductive, "ethnographic" approach.

Chapter 2 attempts to facilitate the discussion of aurality by developing a more precise and elaborated set of terms with which to describe the varieties and intersections of medieval literary reception. With the help of this augmented critical vocabulary, chapter 3 critiques the biases that often inform the secondary literature on the reception of medieval authors, especially Chaucer.

Chapter 4 moves on to offer a variety of observations derived from and serving to introduce the intensive data of the last three chapters. These analyses clarify the interrelationship of public and private reading, and suggest some reasons why even the most ambitious vernacular authors and their elite audiences should accept this situation happily. After this extensive theoretical introduction, chapters 5–7 offer the solid data. Chapter 5 analyzes historical reports of reading habits or events from late medieval France and the dukes of Burgundy, on the one hand, and from England and Scotland on the other. Chapter 6 offers a detailed look at Chaucer's references to audience reception and his depictions of reading. And chapter 7 reviews upper-class, non-Chaucerian, secular English literature of the mid fourteenth through the late fifteenth century, in three chronological blocks.

The evidence thus assembled strongly supports a contention that public reading survived well past the announced date of its obsolescence. The strong influences of rising literacy and improving book-technologies, including printing, were countermanded for a considerable period by a simple, persistent preference among elite audiences for the social experience of literature. Such group-listening was synonymous neither with rowdy boorishness nor with paralyzed docility – two extremes frequently mooted by modern scholars. The data suggest, rather, that those who listened to the late medieval texts surveyed here were literate, sophisticated people who participated actively both with their attention and their response. While we can never recover the full experience of such sessions, it behooves us to recognize that they took place.

I should note that all translations, unless otherwise stated, are by me. To facilitate out-of-order reading, I have added a Glossary to the end of the book that offers brief definitions of the terms introduced in the theoretical chapters. All citations of Chaucer's works are from *The Riverside Chaucer*, ed. Larry D. Benson, 3d ed. (Oxford, 1988).

The final pre-textual word goes to the colleagues and friends who have helped me in the long work of completing this book. I am deeply grateful to Sarah Carpenter, John Ellis, Ruth Finnegan, Douglas Gray, Lee Haring, Claire Sherman, and Tom Shippey for their advice and encouragement. Nancy Black, Nancy Freeman Regalado, and Evelyn Birge Vitz have been my particular academic angels, providing models of scholarship and humanity. Much-appreciated support has come from Dan Sheridan, chair of the English Department at the University of North Dakota. Alastair Minnis, Josie Dixon, Kate Brett, Alison Gilderdale, and Peter Edwards have been universally encouraging and patient in steering me through the process of publication.

Special thanks go to Gregory Warren Wilson, in whose sunny kitchen I spent a happy summer revising this work, and to Cathy Curtis and Jean Pretorius, Cheryl Foster, Moira Guthrie, Peter Marks, Hal Momma, Dinny Oliver, Fiona and Tim Porter, Lindsey Shaw-Miller, Jennifer Summit, and my brother Charles and his family – Marian, Sara, and Ethan – for all their friendship and love, for inviting me into their homes, listening to my ideas, and telling me theirs. Needless to say, while many good things came into this work from all these people, any errors are entirely my own.

I

On beyond Ong: the bases of a revised theory of orality and literacy

Over the past three decades, the study of medieval literature has been increasingly influenced by theories of orality and literacy. Concepts developed to describe the impact of alphabetic script on ancient Greece have been generally adopted and extended to describe the impact of rising literacy and advancing book-technologies on medieval Europe. The theories seem to have provided a reliable means of explaining the transmutation of English texts from the time of the *scops* through the assiduous literacy of the Ricardian period and the outbreaking individualism of the English Renaissance. At each stage, as literacy rose and orality declined, literature inscribed itself more deeply as a locus of self-awareness, irony, and conscious artifice. Chaucer, particularly, is often held to express in his writings a sophistication enabled by his newly literate, privately reading audience.

My intent in this book is to dismantle that neat schema. There is no denying the progressive rise of literacy and improvement of book-technology over the course of the later Middle Ages, nor would I seek to strip Chaucer of his sophistication or the Renaissance of its individualism. I will simply try to demonstrate that the two sequences do not harmonize as closely as is often assumed. The achievements of Chaucer and the Renaissance writers cannot represent the triumph of literacy over orality, because orality was present in force for both periods. This orality was not a contaminant detracting from literacy, a superseded mentality at war with its successor, or the inert residue of an extinct modality, but a vital, functioning, accepted part of a mixed oral–literate literary tradition. Although equated frequently with a "transitional" period of low literacy and limited access to manuscripts, aurality – i.e., the reading aloud of written literature to one or a group of listeners – was in fact the modality of choice for highly literate and sophisticated audiences, not only in ancient Greece and

Rome but also among the nobility of England, Scotland, France, and Burgundy from (at least) the fourteenth through the late fifteenth century. In these different places and times, public reading proceeded in different ways, under different auspices, and to different ends, attesting to its complexity and richness as a means of experiencing literature.

The slow growth over the fourteenth through the late fifteenth century of a more individualized, less synthetic mentality was, no doubt, related to the slowly escalating habit of private reading; but the result for this crucial period was a growing sophistication of *both* private and public reading. Even if it were true – which it is not – that aurality did ultimately die out completely, we should not use that pseudo-fact as a reason for ignoring aurality during periods in which it flourished. The habit of approaching late medieval literature with the standard oral/literate polarities ready-mapped before our faces, sure the data will fit the map, has led us down some debatable paths. If we are willing to adopt a more "ethnographic" approach, following the texts as they draw their own map for us, we will identify not a triumphal, quick-step march from "orality" to "literacy," but a long-term, intricate interdigitation of the oral, the aural, and the literate.

Because the standard theories of orality and literacy have underwritten so many "chronocentric" analyses of medieval literature, this chapter will seek to expose some key weaknesses in that argument, as formulated by the general theorists and by scholars working specifically with medieval material. In the place of these excessively rigid and prescriptive models, I will draw on the more open-ended and multimodal theories of Ruth Finnegan and other social scientists. Finally, having cleared away some of the theoretical obstructions, I will attempt to suggest the uniqueness and interest of late medieval aurality.

THE FOUNDATIONAL TEXTS OF ORALITY/LITERACY THEORY

Aurality is a phenomenon that has traditionally been marginalized by its centrality; that is, since it occupies a historical and conceptual middle space between the two poles of "orality" and "literacy," attention has rarely focused on aurality itself.[1] This is a bias built into the founding premises of the standard theory, as developed by Eric Havelock in *A Preface to Plato* (1963); by Jack Goody and Ian Watt in "The consequences of literacy" (1963) and by Jack Goody in subsequent studies; and by Walter Ong in publications (1965; 1971) culminating in his famous *Orality and Literacy* (1982).

Havelock theorized that the Greeks' invention of the first fully alphabetic script brought about a revolution in consciousness and in the means of recording cultural knowledge. Oral poets such as Homer, he claims, created compendia designed to preserve in memorable fashion the key concepts, history, and even technical knowledge of their culture. Writing meant that records could be created and, over time, checked and compared. Thus began an analytical consciousness that learned, for example, to detect contradictions in two accounts of the same event, and that could venture out past the easily memorized and assimilated to more complex and esoteric thought.

Like Havelock, Goody and Watt focused on the invention of an alphabetic script in ancient Greece, but their analysis drew as well on observations from cultures such as the LoDagaa of Ghana (among whom Goody had done fieldwork). Goody and Watt identified a "homeostatic tendency" in oral cultures, whereby "whatever parts of it [the cultural heritage] have ceased to be of contemporary relevance are likely to be eliminated by the process of forgetting" (1963, rpt. 1968: 30). The classic example is the genealogy that evolves over time to emphasize important connections and drop undesirable or irrelevant ones. Once literacy arrives and written records accumulate, however, comparison encourages a critical attitude and "a sense of change and of cultural lag" (p. 49). To this process Goody and Watt attribute the development of, among other things, logic, taxonomic classification, history, and self-awareness. To explain why some literate societies failed to develop this precise complex of traits, Goody later argued that literacy could be "restricted" by various counter-forces (1968b).

Finally, in applying the model advanced by Havelock and by Goody and Watt to later Western society, Ong added two crucial factors. The first was to assume that the consequences attendant on the introduction of writing to a nonliterate society would also affect a relatively less literate society as it became relatively more literate. Thus the emphasis shifted from "literacy" in the sense of possessing writing at all to "literacy" in a vaguer sense of how many or how well people could read.

Ong's second innovation was diachronicity. Whereas Havelock's and Goody and Watt's analyses had focused on one relatively discrete, synchronic event (the introduction of an alphabetic script to ancient Greece, or of literacy to a modern nonliterate society), Ong envisioned a cultural evolution stretching from the time of "pristine" or "primary orality" through the classical period, the fall of Rome, the early and late Middle Ages, the Renaissance, the invention of printing, the Reformation, Romanticism, the Industrial Revolution, and finally the invention of radio, television, and other electronic media, which inaugurated our current era of "secondary orality." Each stage of this long process was marked by some further intensification of the consequences of literacy. Ong's frequently invoked concept of "oral residue" served to explain any seemingly "oral" traits (such as aspects of Renaissance rhetoric) that persisted into a later stage of development; any such lag is also likely to be explained with the comment that the society had not "fully interiorized" literacy (e.g., 1982: 26).

Drawing on research done by Alexander Luria in the 1930s (trans. 1976), Ong offers a checklist that defines "oral" as: additive rather than subordinative; aggregative; redundant or "copious"; conservative or traditionalist; close to the human lifeworld; agonistically toned; empathetic and participatory; homeostatic; and situational (Ong 1982: 36–57). The history of the transition from orality to (pre-electronic) literacy is reflected in the gradual development of the contrasting "literate" qualities in individuals, cultures, and literatures.

The elegant analyses of Havelock, Goody and Watt, and Ong seem to have exposed a fundamental shaping mechanism of human culture and consciousness. Many apparently disparate events – plus the whole burst of genius we associate with ancient Greece – found a systematic and supple explanation in the mnemonic shift entailed by the introduction of the first fully vocalic alphabet. Ong's extension of this paradigm across the span of Western history gave a gratifying prominence to the Middle Ages, during which Europe climbed back from the near-total nonliteracy of the "barbaric" age through many crucial stages, climaxing in the invention of printing.

Although Jack Goody, in particular, has attempted to modify the universality of this schema (see, e.g., Goody 1968b, 1987), the master theory has remained so consistently attractive – to its originator as to others – that, as Brian Street notes, "it is ... the grand claims rather than the caveats that other writers tend to follow" (1984: 52). As reflected in the work of influential theorists of medieval orality and literacy such as Paul Zumthor, Franz Bäuml, Brian Stock, and Paul Saenger – and in research such as that presented in the anthology *Vox*

Intexta: Orality and Textuality in the Middle Ages (ed. Doane and Pasternack, 1991), which may be considered indicative of much recent work in the field – many scholars of medieval literature have accepted these theoretical structures as adequate and productive for the analysis of many different periods, languages, and genres.

CRITIQUES OF "LITERACY THEORY"

The confidence of literary scholars in orality/literacy theory may, however, be somewhat misplaced. While the theory falls in readily with the training, focus, and prejudices of such scholars, social scientists were quick to call attention to the ethnocentricity and rigidity of its categories. Only recently have literary scholars such as Gabrielle Spiegel (1991), Paul Goetsch (1991), and D. H. Green (1990, 1994) begun to echo these criticisms.

The ready reliance accorded the model by many medievalists has had dire consequences for their ability to conceptualize aurality. If aurality is to regain the importance it deserves as a long-standing, sophisticated means of experiencing medieval literature, we need to examine the inadequacies that underlie, at every step, the smooth flow of the standard theory's premises.

Polar divides

The standard theory envisions orality and literacy as two rigidly differentiated entities, each identified with an equally distinct, invariable set of cognitive and literary traits. There is little room for a conceptual middle ground between these two poles of the "Great Divide" (Finnegan 1973). Since aurality must lie, if anywhere, in this middle ground, it fits into medievalists' schemes, if at all, usually as a symptom of transition – as a residual holdover from orality or (alternatively) as a herald of literacy. In either case, it naturally attracts little attention on its own. To build a case for aurality's status as an independent phenomenon, we must disassemble the mechanisms of polarization.

According to the standard theory of orality and literacy, the advent of writing systems, or each increment of improved writing-technology, necessarily transforms the way people think and create. Moreover, these changes always run in the same direction: from the synthetic, communalizing "oral" towards the analytic, individualistic "literate." A corollary of this "technological determinism" (Finnegan 1988: 8), frequently applied in discussions of medieval culture, suggests that where increased literacy (or increments thereof) can be detected, one may assume that cognitive functions or literary sophistication also increased. Conversely, where enhanced cognition or sophistication can be detected, one may assume that some increment of literacy was the cause. Having identified a technological shift (the reintroduction of word-spacing), for example, Paul Saenger (1982) deduces that cognitive advances must have resulted. Brian Stock (1983), having identified certain cognitive "advances" (basically, an increasingly intellectual and empirical attitude toward texts), deduces that literacy must have increased. Both deductions may well be correct, but in both cases they are underdiscussed, the authors considering their deterministic premises self-evident and self-validating.

But why should the technology of writing be the only factor affecting human thinking and creativity? Critics of this assumption have noted many other possible influences: economic systems (Gough 1968); judicial, political, and religious institutions (G. E. R. Lloyd, cited in Goody 1968b: 63–71); social organization, urbanization, schooling, and the characteristics of particular scripts (Scribner and Cole 1981). Many medievalists are happy to credit Chaucer's breakthroughs to rising literacy and improving book production. But few apply that logic to the succeeding period, in which writers "remedievalized" despite an unbroken upward curve of technological gain, including the invention of printing. Those who confront the issue have to call on other factors, such as a conservatism fostered by religious persecution (see, e.g., Spearing 1985: 89).

Nor, when technology changes, does it necessarily produce effects that run in the approved direction. Finnegan points out that printing, for example, "can be – and has been – used for enlightenment *and* for mystification; for self-expression or rebellion *and* for repression; for systematic analysis and the development of knowledge on the one hand *and* for obfuscation, dogma and the propagation of prejudice and intolerance on the other." A technology's effects, she concludes, "depend on how people actually use it and how it interacts with a large number of other factors in the current situation" (1988: 163).

The weakness of the case for technological determinism can be nowhere better illustrated than in the society that the theory was generated to describe: ancient Greece. The anthropologist Brian Street (1984: chap. 2) has painstakingly unraveled Goody's logic to reveal that, even within the terms of the argument as Goody presents it, the introduction of writing did not have the global transformative effects claimed for it. At one point, for example, Goody quotes Havelock's comment that the pre-Socratics (of the sixth century BC) were "essentially oral thinkers" and, explaining this as a result of restricted literacy, claims that the true breakthrough came in the time of Plato (fifth–fourth century BC) (Goody 1968b: 3–4). But then, Street argues, the true breakthrough could not have been a consequence only of literacy: "What happened between early and later Greek society to generate these developments must have been something other than the 'intrinsic' qualities of literacy alone since literacy was present in both periods" – without, it may be noted, any of the restricting factors identified by Goody (1984: 63).

Classicists have echoed the anthropologists' objections. William V. Harris dismisses the arguments of Havelock and Goody as "woolly and grandiose" (1989: 41), concluding that "the accumulation of texts was a necessary though not sufficient condition for many of the literary and intellectual achievements of the classical world" (p. 336). Rosalind Thomas is similarly dismissive, noting "it is not enough to observe the presence of literacy without considering its uses ... there is a complex mixture of both oral and written processes which persists long after the initial introduction of writing" (1989: 30).

Besides having to interact with other social factors to achieve, if it did achieve, its startling transformations, ancient Greek literacy had the further, little-noted disadvantage of being chiefly aural. Goody and Watt themselves remark that "in the ancient world books were used mainly for reading aloud, often by a slave" (1963, rpt. 1968: 42; see also Saenger 1991: 209) – to literate, upper-class listeners, of course. No one seems to have wondered how the often-cited ability to examine, compare, and jump around in texts (see, e.g., Goody 1977: 44) can be held responsible for the intellectual advances of the ancient Greeks, when most or all of the ancient Greeks were in fact hearing their texts read aloud.

Certainly, the "professional" intellectuals and writers may well have read books privately, in order to study them and write their own. Xenophon quotes Socrates as saying "that he was accustomed to unroll the treasures of the sages of old times which they had left in books written by them, and to study and mark extracts from them with his friends" (quoted in Kenyon 1932: 21). Kenyon notes that even such reports as this (in which Socrates, though reading, was not alone) are in the minority: "it must be admitted," he says, "that the general picture which we have, both in Plato and in Xenophon, is of oral instruction and conversation, not of reading and private study" (ibid.).

Medievalists who have adopted the literacy model are accustomed to dismissing aurality in *their* period as "oral residue." The very basis of the theory they are relying on so implicitly, however, seems to offer aurality as a potential source of, or at least as no hindrance to, major cognitive transformations. Thus even the foundational case of the foundational writers fails to conform to their determinative premises. If advances in writing-technology do not automatically dictate a move towards more "literate" thought and behavior (including private reading), then it becomes conceivable that rising literacy and improved book-technology in Chaucer's period and later need not have automatically resulted in the abandonment of aurality, or public reading. Moreover, if the ancient Greeks could combine aurality with sophisticated thought and composition, it should be less of a surprise to find medieval English people doing likewise.

The tendency to link the state of writing-technology to states of human mentality is much facilitated by a homology of terminology: "oral" (nonliterate) societies are said to be "oral" (aggregative, synthetic, etc.) in character, while "literacy" (the presence or improvement of writing-technologies) supposedly brings "literate" (individualistic, analytic, etc.) traits in its wake. The semantic and conceptual equation of technology with mentality prepares us to accept technological change as a necessary and sufficient predictor of cultural transformation.

This logic was codified for many scholars in Walter Ong's master-list of "oral" and "literate" traits (see above), whose development he aligns unquestioningly with the technological progression of book-technology. Many medievalists have accepted this checklist as definitive and authoritative, and have applied it freely in their work – invoking Ong's concept of "oral residue" to explain away any apparent overlap of traits. In some cases, analyses of texts degenerate into mere exercises in imposing the list's prescriptive and self-fulfilling categories: e.g., identifying anything "aggregative" as "oral," and anything "analytic" as "literate." Even important and learned discussions of key stylistic elements (such as fictionality) supposedly unique to "literacy" turn out to be based on no stronger support than Ong's assertions.

But Ong's assertions, as it turns out, are themselves very far from strongly based. In *The Psychology of Literacy*, Sylvia Scribner and Michael Cole (1981) point out an important ambiguity in the work of Ong's key source for this list, Alexander Luria. In comparing illiterate Soviet peasants to others recently educated as part of a government campaign in the 1930s, Luria had found that the first group tended to respond to the experimental tasks "in a concrete, context-bound way, guided by the perceptual and functional attributes of things. The most schooled group, on the other hand, tended to take an abstract approach and be responsive to the conceptual and logical relationships among things" (Ong 1982: 10).

While these results fit the Great Divide view of literacy's effects, Scribner and Cole note, Luria's test situation did not allow him to differentiate the effects of various covariables from those of literacy per se. Schooling was one chief covariable – the peasants may have begun to think more abstractly because their teachers encouraged them to do so, not because literacy in and of itself always engenders such forms of thinking. Students who were taught to group words into taxonomic classes, for example, would gain skills not necessarily acquired simply by learning to write the words "dog," "cat," or "animal."

In a six-year field-study among the Vai people of Liberia, who may be literate in Arabic, English, or their own syllabic script, Scribner and Cole were able to compare the effects of nonliteracy, non-schooled literacy, and literacy learned under two different forms of schooling. They found that in each case, the effects reflected the particular nature of the script, the way it is learned, and how it is used. Abstract reasoning and other traits so often associated with the acquisition of literacy of any sort turned out to be consistently fostered among the Vai by only one form of literacy – that in English, the language learned in formal Western-style schools (pp. 242–44).

Scribner and Cole conclude by advocating "a practice account of literacy," for which

> literacy is not simply knowing how to read and write a particular script but applying this knowledge for specific purposes in specific contexts of use. Thus, in order to identify the consequences of

literacy, we need to consider the specific characteristics of specific practices. (pp. 235–37)

Scribner and Cole's work suggests that Ong's supposedly universal list of "oral" and "literate" traits in fact describes (and extrapolates from) only one specific context of literacy: that of modern Western society. Western liberal education certainly does tend to encourage analytical, logical, de-homeostatizing, and other "literate" ways of thinking. But there seems to be little basis for assuming that literacy alone, however acquired, will invariably produce similar effects – or that nonliterates are necessarily denied them.

Critics of standard orality/literacy theory have documented many instances of traits skipping freely across the notional boundaries drawn by the theorists. Finnegan notes that the nonliterate Limba, of Sierra Leone, "possess and exploit abstract terms and forms; and they reflect on and about language and have media for standing back from the immediate scene or the immediate form of words through their terminology, their philosophy of language and their literature" (1988: 55).

Finnegan also offers many illustrations of oral compositions that demonstrate the traits generally declared possible only for written texts. An Eskimo poet, for example, seems as conscious of his creative processes as Mallarmé: "I wonder why / My song-to-be that I wish to use, / My song-to-be that I wish to put together, / I wonder why it will not come to me?" (p. 64). A Tikopian (Western Pacific) islander ironically parodies the language of religious converts by declaring, "My mind is dark / Why don't I abandon it?" (p. 67). Oral poetry achieves esthetic distance, Finnegan notes, via special castes of poets or special poetic languages, the offsetting of critiques onto animal protagonists, and special performance conventions (p. 165).

Scholars who eagerly analyze the *Iliad*'s formulas, lists, and heroic type-characters as the pattern of primary orality are usually rather silent as to the *Odyssey* – whose wily hero tricks Polyphemos by labeling himself "No one" yet cannot resist shouting out his real name as his ship pulls away; who has himself tied to a mast so he can hear the Sirens; who alone of his crew escapes swinehood; and who when shipwrecked would rather trust a broken piece of raft than a goddess' magic veil. How does all this rampant individualism square with what Ong calls "the pristine aggregative, paratactic, oral-style thinking perpetuated in Homer" (1982: 28)? Yet the *Odyssey* is just as formulaic as the *Iliad.*

Folklorist Barbara Babcock identifies the condescending assumptions inherent in the standard view of oral composition as a "myth of primitive narrative." This approach, she explains, "postulates that oral or folk narrative is simple, natural, and direct – uncontaminated by the devices, digressions, and structural complexities of the modern, written tale. Most importantly, it regards oral narrative as uncomplicated by the latter's conscious forms of self-commentary" (1977: 63). Babcock responds to this myth with many examples of "metanarrative" commentary by performers of oral genres and of the implicit recognition of fictionality incorporated in such figures as the trickster (p. 74). As R. Narasimhan (1991) and others have pointed out, the elaborate "mnemotechnic" system developed to preserve, in oral tradition, both the *Rigveda* and an extensive critical apparatus demonstrate that orality is no bar even to literary scholarship.

Thus oral cultures, procedures, and texts seem capable of individualism, self-awareness, irony, metalanguage, fictionality, fixity, and even scholarship and criticism – suggesting that while writing may indeed promote or otherwise affect these capacities in many ways, it does not create them. "It seems from the evidence," Finnegan concludes,

> that there is in fact no one kind of literature or literary style that always follows from orality, nor is the effect of literacy on oral processes necessarily to bring about radical changes in either form of composition or literary style. For this, as for other postulated characteristics of literacy or of orality, generalized conclusions have been based on instances from only a limited number of situations and cannot be taken to be universal. (1988: 159)

Just as "oral" cultures may exhibit many "literate" traits, so too do many "literate" cultures exhibit "oral" traits. Odysseus' anomalous "oral" individualism, for example, is counterpointed by the "literate" communalism of premodern Chinese and Indian elites. "The individualization of experience and the liking for privacy," Kathleen Gough concludes, "do not seem to me necessarily to characterize literate society in general ... In both China and India, the main body of literati evidently conformed rather strictly to the mores of their class and were discouraged from unwonted expressions of individual experience" (1968: 82).

"Oral" fixed texts can be counterpointed against "literate" fluidity. In his fieldwork in Iran, Brian Street found that the writtenness of the texts the *mullahs* expounded merely disguised a creatively selective and reinterpretive process reminiscent of oral-formulaic poetry. "The authority and apparent fixity of the written tradition in such religions [Islam and Hinduism]," he notes, "is the very characteristic that provides scope for individual mediators to offer their own interpretation as the authoritative one" (1984: 135). One might extend Street's observations to the readings of the Bible offered by various Christian sects and preachers.

Even statistically ranked lists of research results, one of the most sacrosanct of "literate" paraphernalia (cf. Goody 1986), may change as much across a series of printed citations as any *griot*'s genealogies do in oral presentation. Barry O'Neill (1994) has compiled almost 250 printed variants of a pair of lists contrasting the top problems of American public schools in the 1940s and 1980s. The contents, their number, their ranking, the source cited, and the date assigned the second list vary continuously, reflecting the current concerns of the writers, the editors, and the audience addressed.

Nor is the written text necessarily more "autonomous" than the oral. As the sociolinguist Deborah Tannen points out, anyone who has tried to learn a word-processing program from the manual supplied by the manufacturer should have outlived the illusion that literacy enables decontextualized communication (Chafe and Tannen 1987: 398). Homer is clear, John Halverson notes; Heidegger is opaque: "In general, there is no empirical or theoretical reason to think that written prose in itself is any more explicit or less in need of interpretation than oral poetry" (1991: 624).

A few medievalists have made equivalent arguments dissociating "literate" traits from literacy or from evolutionary presuppositions. Carl Lindahl's extensive analysis of the discourse patterns underlying many of the Canterbury tales led him to assert that Chaucer's "particular uses of irony, assumed by some to constitute his greatest poetic achievement, have few literary antecedents but a great many oral parallels" (1987: 13). Mary Carruthers notes that de-homeostatization – the recognition that the past differs from the present – was not, as usually claimed, a late medieval development. Rather, she says, "the division of 'modern' from 'ancient' was first formulated at the beginning of the Middle Ages. It simply does not seem to have been thought to be of paramount importance" (1990: 193).

The sweeping generalizations about "oral" and "literate" traits favored by advocates of the Great Divide dissolve, on examination, into much more muted, relativistic statements. Both "orality" and "literacy" seem liable to forms of thought or composition one could characterize as aggregative, redundant, empathetic, or traditional, just as they both seem capable of encouraging analytic, precise, abstract, or individualistic ideas and texts. The story becomes one not of vast new cognitive powers released by the one magus-force of "literacy," but of the interaction of that one considerable force with other social forces to preserve, augment, create, or mutate both "literate" and "oral" traits in a culture.

Any model necessarily oversimplifies, some scholars might respond; some degree of overlap between categories is inevitable and does not constitute a disproof of the entire theory. The lack of fit we have been tracing, however, derives not from the general sloppiness of things but from the untenability of the two mechanisms invoked to explain the radical dichotomy of traits.

The premise behind the first mechanism is that creativity in oral cultures is dominated by the need to preserve information. Havelock considered data-storage the underlying function of oral epics such as Homer's. For Ong, who extends Havelock's argument, the "psychodynamics of memory" becomes the literary equivalent of natural selection: in an oral society, textual complexity and individuality are selected against in favor of the more rememberable communal and formulaic. Features such as rhyme, meter, and even the love of the "heroic and marvelous" are reduced to mere mnemonic devices. Ong explains, for example: "With the control of information and memory brought about by writing and, more intensely, by print, you do not need a hero in the old sense to mobilize knowledge in story form" (1982: 70–71). With equal conviction, Ong echoes Havelock's citation, as a sample of an oral-style navigational manual, of a passage from Homer that mentions, in full, a ship, a crew, a hecatomb, and a captain (p. 43).

Obviously, any ancient Greek captain who knew no more than this about sailing would have foundered as quickly as Ong's argument. Technical knowledge in oral cultures is generally passed on by instruction, from master to apprentice – without, usually, any recourse to epic formulas. Such genres may indeed preserve cosmogony or history, and features such as rhyme and meter are probably crucial in helping singers remember their songs. But it seems condescending and reductionistic to assume that oral cultures are precluded from creativity, and oral poets from individual artistry. The persistence of rhyme, meter, heroes, and other "oral" traits long beyond the advent of literacy are testimony to their esthetic appeal, independent of technological dicta. Their occurrence within oral cultures is thus not as merely passive indicators of mnemonic pressures, nor does their presence preclude the co-presence of supposedly "literate" traits, whether or not these can be held to promote memorization.

The second mechanism generally cited to explain why "orality" is synthetic and "literacy" analytic is the possibility the latter offers of comparing texts. Comparing recorded versions of the same event induces readers to develop a critical mentality, notes Havelock; Goody and Watt explain how oral cultures insensibly update their texts, while in literate ones old records and books can teach readers that the past differs from the present.

Both points are valid to an extent, but both again seem determined on underestimating the "oral." Even in a nonliterate society one would often *hear* variant reports of events, as well as different performances of the same text. If listeners cannot make esthetic judgments, how do certain individuals within such societies ever achieve the status of poets or orators? Members of oral cultures can gain a sense of the past simply through living their lives – remembering their own earlier years and significant events they'd witnessed. Do the *griots* who modify genealogies do so as helpless victims of homeostasis, or because they know their patrons will reward them for their editorial efforts? Nor is it accurate to imply that literate historians are any less subject to bias. Would we expect a Frenchman and an Englishman, say, writing today about the Hundred Years' War, to produce substantially identical accounts?

The preceding discussion has sought to undermine the pillars of the Great Divide. The technology of literacy seems not, upon examination, to guarantee a mentality of "literacy"; the mentalities of "orality" and "literacy" do not seem to align in a very predictable way with the technological states of orality and literacy; and the mechanisms that supposedly generate those alignments are in practice neither exclusive nor reliable.

The typology endorsed by what she calls the "strong" model helps, says Ruth Finnegan, "to make sense of complex data but at the cost of over-simplifying and so distorting. For how useful is this binary typology when it turns out that most known cultures don't fit?" (1988: 141). The theory encourages us to see orality and literacy as unitary phenomena – always the same everywhere – and to focus only on the differences, the Great Divide, between them. It thus blinds us to the fact that there may be as much difference within nonliterate and literate societies as between them. Finnegan describes, for example, two different oralities:

> the Limba [of Sierra Leone], in spite of their capacity for abstraction in certain directions, have not developed anything like the complex and systematic symbolic scheme worked out by, say, the Dogon [of Mali]. But the difference here cannot be put down to literacy – for the Dogon are equally non-literate. (p. 56)

Brian Street (1984), on the other hand, gives an example of two different literacies interacting within one Iranian village. Men learn in the "maktab" (religious school) to read Islamic texts in Arabic; some of these then go on to apply these skills to commercial transactions conducted in Farsi (whose alphabet is almost identical to that of Arabic). "In the change from one literacy to another," Street concludes, "some of the skills previously acquired are appropriate and can be adapted to the new literacy, while others may atrophy and, without relevance or function, be forgotten" (p. 155).

One price of polarization is to obscure, or erase, such intra-modality differences; the only variety that theory could accommodate would be the progressive stages of orality giving way to literacy or of literacy experiencing the transforming effect of improvements in writing-technology. These seem dull, reductionistic options compared to the lively variations and crossover influences that become visible when we abandon technological determinism and place events within a larger cultural context.

In contrast to the "strong" theory of orality and literacy, Finnegan advocates a "weak" theory that sees literacy "not as an effective cause, but as an enabling factor: something which *can* facilitate particular forms of cognitive development, etc., but does not of itself bring them about" (1988: 160). This "more modest approach" to the categories of orality and literacy suggests that scholars search not "for opposing pure types of cultures as wholes, but rather for *specific* characteristics or consequences likely to be associated with orality and with literacy" (p. 146).

Finnegan emphasizes one particular aspect of the picture that emerges from this complexified enterprise: the potential for the long-term coexistence and interaction, in a society, of different kinds of oral and literate literature and thought. "This kind of mixture is and has been a common and ordinary feature of cultures throughout the centuries," she notes, "rather than the 'abnormal' case implied by the ideal types model" (p. 141). Similarly, Brian Street comments: "The reality of social uses of varying modes of communication is that oral and literate modes are 'mixed' in each society" (1984: 4).

Within the technological determinism of the Great Divide theory, mixed states of orality and literacy are conceived of as necessarily transient and unstable. Since writing obviates the need for oral forms of mnemonic storage, it is assumed that any period of mixedness will pass as soon as society sorts itself out and recognizes the superior features of literacy. But the newer theorists argue that such mixtures *can* be stable – not in the sense that they will never cease or change, but that they are not fated by their very nature to a short duration. In arguing for the stability of mixed states, Finnegan and others are accepting that the choice of modalities reflects other influences besides (or in addition to) the search for efficient data-storage. In looking at such situations, the scholarly impulse should not be to enforce a preemptive classification or hierarchy of "oral" and "literate," but to recognize and accept the situation's fundamental "mixedness" and to evolve modes of analysis suited to its "ethnographic" reality rather than to superimposed, essentialist polarizations.

Evolution and the march of literature

By extrapolating the polarizations and determinisms of orality/literacy theory across the span of Western history, Walter Ong gave a crucial role to the Middle Ages. He has been rewarded with many citations from medievalists eager to apply his formulations to the literature and culture of their chosen periods. Yet the fallacies inherent in the theory as enunciated by Havelock and by Goody and Watt were only intensified by Ong's historical model.

In diachronizing the Great Divide, Ong chose an unfortunate model of historical process: Darwinian evolutionism as adapted by the first anthropologists, who conceived of human society as passing from savagery (the age of magic) through barbarianism (the age of religion), to civilization (the age of science). This evolutionary thrust was preserved by classifying phenomena that persisted from one stage into the next as "survivals."[2] Based as it is on this heavily goal-oriented, teleological model, Ong's story always has to be the *extinction* of one mode in favor of the other; *evolution*, not coexistence or covariation. Since this evolution has the status of a natural force, there is no need to provide any more sophisticated conception of how it proceeds than the unexplicated mechanism of "interiorization."

Although the evolutionary schemas popular in earlier literary histories have been falling out of fashion, Ong and his followers preserve the system in nearly its original form. Once a more efficient storage mechanism – writing – has become available (and has been sufficiently "interiorized"), orality – the less efficient solution – will drop away, just as nature selects the more favorable biological adaptation. Any hangover from one state into the next is dismissed as "residual orality" or "oral residue" – that is, a survival. "Habits of thought and expression inseparable from the older, more familiar [oral] medium," Ong explains, pseudo-scientifically, "are simply assumed to belong equally to the new until this is sufficiently 'interiorized' for its own techniques to emerge from the chrysalis and for those more distinctive of the older medium to atrophy" (1965: 26). This residue has no more power to define its matrix than do fossils in rock strata, or than did "primitive" spiritualism in "civilized" Victorian London.

How long, one wonders, can it take to emerge from a chrysalis? Over the course of *Orality and Literacy* (1982), Ong invokes "oral residue" or "residual orality" to explain "oral" traits in "English style in the Tudor period and even much later" (p. 115), the Douay Bible of 1610 (p. 37), "the age of Romanticism or even beyond" (p. 41), the historical writings of Thomas Babington Macaulay and of Winston Churchill (pp. 41, 158), near-contemporary Soviet political rhetoric (pp. 38–39), and "regressive genres" such as the Western (p. 154). At a rough count, this gives residual orality a run of some 500 years; if we started counting with the Greeks' invention of a fully alphabetic script, the span would be more than 2,500 years.

Ong's occasional acknowledgment that some cultures "have known writing for centuries but have never fully 'interiorized' it" (1982: 26) doesn't seem a sufficient explanation for this consistent non-extinction of orality – unless he would be willing to include

Western society among those recalcitrant cultures. The persistence of "oral" traits despite repeated announcements of orality's demise suggests that orality might more profitably be conceptualized as an active, functional element of Western culture.

In imposing an evolutionary schema over the polarized, Great Divide conception of orality and literacy, Ong has inspired a literary history that proceeds in a series of uncomfortable lurches. Since orality and literacy are conceived of as essentially different and mutually incompatible states, they can exist historically in only three different relationships:

1 orality in the complete absence of literacy;
2 orality in transition to literacy;
3 literacy having extinguished (all but residual) orality.

The basic story told by orality/literacy theorists is the story of stage 2, how the literate overtook the oral. Extended over three centuries of ancient Greek history, this made an exciting and initially plausible sequence. Extended from the fall of Rome to the present day – some 1,500 years – the sequence begins to sag a bit in the middle. What Ong in fact presents us with is repeated announcements of the advent of stage 3, each duly attended with some unshakable residue of orality. Long before that persistent residuum has been scrubbed away, radio has been invented and we find ourselves entering the age of secondary orality.

In one way, any detailed examination of an individual historical period within Ong's overarching evolutionary vision has less trouble. The author can simply retell the basic stage-2 story, concluding with stage 3, the proportional decline of the oral in favor of the literate. Put end to end, of course, these studies pose more of a problem: the heightened "literacy" with which each hopefully concludes somehow re-emerges as the "orality" with which the next one begins. Since there is only one event to record – the eternal synchronic moment when literacy prevails over orality – as a diachronic, teleological narrative orality/literacy theory can only produce perpetual recapitulations of that one moment. Orality, with its concomitant trait-set always being eroded by ever-rising literacy and ever-improving book-technologies, is the dying and reviving god of orality/literacy theory, perpetually slain only to be resurrected in order to be slain again.

For an example, we can follow a sequence of accounts describing critical advances in medieval literacy:

Rosamond McKitterick: "the [eighth- to ninth-century] Carolingian period [was] one in which fundamental transformations and adjustments concerning the function and future of the written word took place" (1989: 5);

Brian Stock: "[T]hroughout the eleventh and twelfth centuries an important transformation began to take place ... oral discourse effectively began to function within a universe of communications governed by texts" (1983: 3);

Eugène Vinaver: the rise of romance in the twelfth century meant "the birth of a world in which vernacular writings were to share with Latin texts the privilege of addressing the reader through the medium of visible, not audible symbols" (1971: 4);

Dolores Warwick Frese: Marie de France's "Bisclavret" and "Arthur and Gorlagon" (late twelfth century) are "poetic fables concerned to represent the prolonged and often anguished phase of adjustment attending the cultural shift from orality to literacy" (1991: 187);

Jeffrey Kittay: "The twelfth and thirteenth centuries are significant not because somehow writing was imposed unilaterally during that time, but because *an interstitial space not fully resistant to innovation was discovered*" (1988: 227, emphasis in original);

John Fisher: "It was the tension between the oral residue and the literary initiative in [the] poems [of Chaucer et al.] that students of style are beginning to examine most carefully" (1985: 248);

Walter Ong: "Of course, long after the invention of script and even of print [mid fifteenth century], distinctively oral forms of thought and expression linger, competing with the forms introduced with script and print" (1967: 22).

On this showing, literacy – while hovering near triumph from at least the eighth through the fifteenth century (and "long after") – never *quite* made it from stage 2 to stage 3.

Of course, the obvious response would be that each historical period shows not a complete replacement of orality by literacy but a shift of relative dominance. Histories like those cited above direct our attention to the key points at which some technological or cultural innovation moved Western society one notch closer to the literate pole. Certainly such histories have great interest, and I do not mean to discount their value in general, or the integrity of the particular studies cited above. But if the "fundamental transformations" McKitterick associates with the written word in the eighth century were still "competing," as Ong says, with oral forms "long after" the invention of print, then clearly orality and literacy were *functionally interacting* over almost a millennium, including the whole of the later Middle Ages.

How much sense does it make, therefore, in examining some small slice of that millennial span, to dismiss its oral manifestations as "transitional"? The only relevance of situations defined as transitional is as evidence of transition – i.e., of the residual persistence of orality or of the incipient victory of literacy. Such terminology persistently deflects attention away from the mixedness of the situation we are actually looking at, onto some future, projected, long-distant literate resolution. This inability to focus on the period at hand and to conceptualize relatively stable, mixed forms of orality and literacy has had a major impact on the conceptualization of medieval aurality. It also, as discussed above, relegates to "transitional" status the form of reading from which, if the theory is true, the ancient Greek intellectual revolution actually emerged.

THEORISTS OF MEDIEVAL ORALITY AND LITERACY

Many medievalists have accepted as self-evident the polarizations and evolutionism of orality/literacy theory. To them, the advent of literacy (to an individual or, at sufficient if undefined levels, to a society) means that people are reading privately, that authors are writing for private reading, and that people, texts, and the culture in general begin exhibiting "literate" traits. Any indication from an author that he knew that he was writing and that his work would exist in a bound manuscript is considered sufficient to establish that he expected to be read privately. Any indication from such an author that he expected his bound book to be read aloud is quickly explained away – either as a brief transitional phase or as a form of "oral residue," the author's deliberate or unconscious carry-over of literary forms now rendered obsolete by literacy. As such, although the text's apparent aurality may be briefly acknowledged, it tends to fall quickly out of critical focus.

Such evolutionary and deterministic rationales have undermined the attempts of many theorists to identify or describe the operation of medieval aurality. If they note it at all, they tend to assume that such "mixedness" reflects the degree to which literacy (and the essentialist traits associated with it) has or has not yet transformed the "oral" mentality and literary style. Franz H. Bäuml, for example, cites Goody and Watt in equating the oral performance of literature (within a literate society) with illiteracy and social disadvantage. Like many other medievalists, Bäuml marks aurality for rapid obsolescence by associating it with minstrels, who supposedly took to the practice as literacy sapped the audience for their memorial performances (1980: 244–45).[3]

Brian Stock does acknowledge, and is often cited as acknowledging, a mixedness, or "interdependence," of oral and written traditions within his period. He notes, for example, that the change in turn-of-the-millennium European society "was not so much from oral *to* written as from an earlier state, predominantly oral, to various combinations of oral *and* written" (1983: 9). Once into his discussion, however, he imposes a strict evolutionary frame onto this mixedness. The docile conformities of "orality" – into which Stock conflates the oral delivery of texts, oral tradition, folklore, superstition, and illiteracy – give way to the autonomies of "literacy," as evidenced in the heretical "textual communities" led (usually) by clerics who read and expounded the Bible or other religious text to a group of listeners. Although such readings mixed orality with literacy, it is literacy that gets the credit for the resulting cognitive transformation. Stock's "mixedness," therefore, merely freezes a moment in the evolution from old to new.

Even within the frame of his argument, however, it is not clear what was particularly new about the phenomenon Stock describes. Clerics had been, or been supposed to be, literate, and had been reading and expounding the Bible to listeners, well before the millennium. Heresy, of course, dates back nearly to the origins of Christianity. Autonomy might indeed have risen during Stock's period, but his contention that "literacy" deserves the credit rests only on the circular logic of technological determinism (cf. McKitterick 1989: 1).

Similarly wishful thinking underlies Paul Saenger's (1982) widely cited arguments for the prevalence of not merely private but silent reading among the late medieval laity. Having made a good case for some degree of silent reading in the schools and monasteries of earlier centuries (pp. 383–86), Saenger goes on to claim that "in the mid-fourteenth century, the French nobility began to accept the same practice of silent reading and composition for vernacular literary texts." To substantiate this statement, he notes that Charles V of France commissioned translations and "was the first king to assemble a true royal library ... In miniatures, he was painted seated in his library reading with sealed lips in silent isolation" (p. 407).

Saenger never doubts that reading behavior is driven solely by technological factors: i.e., that anyone lucky enough to be literate and to have a book, in the late Middle Ages, would want to read it privately. Yet in fact, for all his undoubted literacy and bibliophilia, Charles V is one of the best-attested public readers in the Middle Ages (see chapter 5; and Sherman 1995), and his favorite reader was his librarian, Gilles Malet (Christine, *Fais*, 2: 63).

Saenger's two other sources of evidence are equally frail. Those who commissioned translations were as or more likely to employ someone like Malet to read them aloud as to read them privately. Writing as late as 1447, for example, Jean Wauquelin addressed his translation of *Annales illustrium principum Hannoniae* "à tous oans et lisans" ("to all the listeners and readers") (quoted in Doutrepont 1909: 415). The frontispiece to volume 2 of this translation (Bib. Roy. 9243, f. 1) shows a functionary reading the book aloud to the man who had commissioned it, Philip the Good of Burgundy (see frontispiece to this book).

Finally, while Charles is certainly shown reading privately in two miniatures (see figure 7 and Sherman 1969: figs. 6, 8), his sealed lips are no guarantee that he is reading silently. The lips of the public readers and lecturers in many other illuminations are equally sealed (see, e.g., figures 5–6, 8–9). This is so even when a scroll containing the person's words is floating by his or her mouth. Lips are shown unsealed only when people are singing (as in the illustrations of the Office of the Dead, a common element in books of hours).

This excursus into the primary evidence may suggest the fallacy of equating the presence of books with the extinction of "orality." Offering a sympathetic assessment of a 1990 collection of Stock's essays, Gabrielle Spiegel noted:

> In his reliance on Goody and Ong, Stock is, to some extent, a prisoner of his pioneering status in the historical investigation of the shift from orality to literacy ... Goody's reification of oral culture as tradition-bound, homeostatic, unanalytic, and consensual has

> perhaps had too long a run among historians, and certainly it has been abandoned by most anthropologists. (1991: 481–82)

The same cautions apply as well to Bäuml and Saenger. Not only their essentialist approach to modalities but their facile invocation of the evolutionist "transitional" model reflect what Spiegel may be rather optimistic in considering an outdated theoretical bias.

It would be unfair to leave this section without acknowledging the medievalists who have shown considerable, dogma-free tolerance for aurality. Michael Clanchy's impressively detailed *From Memory to Written Record* (1979) set a still-unmatched precedent in demonstrating the complex, far from straightforward effects of literacy over the period from 1066 to 1307. Noting that the thirteenth-century English preferred to listen to rather than read documents, for example, Clanchy recognizes that "this was due to a different habit of mind; it was not because the recipient was illiterate in any sense of that word" (1979: 215).

The literary historian R. F. Green notes of fourteenth- and fifteenth-century France and England: "It is quite clear that not only kings but also their courtiers regarded the public reading of such things as moralized histories and improving stories as an enjoyable and worthwhile pastime" (1980: 100). Some Chaucerians have taken the master's aurality as their critical premise (Kolve 1984; Lindahl 1987; Bowden 1987) or maintained a consciousness of it throughout their criticism. As long ago as 1972, A. C. Spearing warned his colleagues:

> Until the very end of the Middle Ages books were usually written to be read aloud to a group; and it takes some effort to recall that precisely this fact puts the twentieth-century literary critic at a severe disadvantage in dealing with medieval literature. (p. 17)

Finally, the Germanist D. H. Green has recently been developing the first focused and explicit discussion of medieval aurality of which I am aware. Focusing on twelfth- and thirteenth-century texts, Green argues for what he calls "the intermediate mode of reception, widespread in the Middle Ages, in which a work was composed with an eye to public recital from a written text, but also for the occasional private reader" (1990: 277; see also 1994: esp. chaps. 7–8). Green specifically resists preemptive interpretations by colleagues that effectively suppress this "public recital" in favor of the "private reader."

These strong voices, however, have as yet had little influence on the area of my primary focus, late medieval English literature. What might have developed into a dialogue has continued, by and large, to be dominated by the self-confident monologue of those who equate "literature" with "literacy."

VIEWS ON CHAUCERIAN ORALITY AND LITERACY

The intersection of the teleological thrust towards "literacy" with the inconveniently frequent references to hearing in their texts has inspired scholars of medieval English literature to evolve what could be described as a "yes, but" approach to aurality. The phenomenon occurs particularly in relation to Chaucer, a poet whom many critics are eager to protect from the negative implications with which they have surrounded "orality."[4]

Yes, Chaucerians will acknowledge, Chaucer refers to hearers, but he's more interested in readers since he was an avid reader himself (Christianson 1976/77); yes, Chaucer probably performed his poetry to friends or patrons, but he also wrote for readers beyond his immediate audience (Mehl 1974); yes, Chaucer addresses listeners, but this (only) reflects his indebtedness to the minstrel tradition (Burrow 1971), or represents his deliberate fostering of a "myth of storytelling" (Payne 1963; Brewer 1966; Pearsall 1976); and (more recently) yes, Chaucer mentions hearers, but the really interesting thing about it is how postmodern this makes him sound (Patterson 1989). Discussion moves off in pursuit of the "but" argument, leaving in its wake only a footnote citing what the scholar usually identifies as a short list of works on the (vaguely conceived) oral delivery of Chaucer.

Although this "aurality reference" often suggests that a multitude of auralists are baying at Chaucer's heels, in fact only a few titles turn up more than once, and these in fact say very little about late medieval aurality, as distinguished from "orality" broadly (and vaguely) understood.

Of the seven most-cited texts, the most thorough coverage of the topic comes in Ruth Crosby's "Oral delivery in the Middle Ages" (1936), which is also the earliest. Of its twenty-two pages, about seven canvass an impressive array of primary sources to demonstrate that most medieval authors addressed a listening audience. The rest of the article lists the stylistic traits that Crosby finds reflective or indicative of oral delivery (pp. 100–6). Crosby's follow-up article of

1938 ("Chaucer and the custom of oral delivery") repeats the procedure with Chaucer, identifying his references to (and depictions of) listening audiences, then surveying his works for examples of her aural traits. In both these essays Crosby, like many of the people to follow her, pays little attention to and makes little distinction among the various forms of oral delivery, including minstrel performance, reading aloud, and recital by the author. Although only the latter two, of course, are possible performance formats for Chaucer's poetry, the chief source of the observations in her 1936 article seems to be romances.

In "Chaucer's art in relation to his audience," Bertrand Bronson (1940) covers basically the same territory as Crosby's Chaucer article, advancing, rather more elegantly, the considerably more worrisome assertion that Chaucer wrote primarily with his own performance in mind.

H. J. Chaytor, in *From Script to Print* (1945; rpt. 1967), certainly does accept oral delivery as the primary vehicle for late medieval literature, although he mentions Chaucer only a few times, peripherally, and does not bother much about which form of oral delivery is involved at any given time. In fact, most of Chaytor's discussion concerns troubadors and minstrels, tending to contrast the conditions pertaining to their twelfth- through early fourteenth-century texts with those prevalent in the sixteenth and later centuries. The later fourteenth and the fifteenth centuries are generally conflated with the earlier Middle Ages, and public reading with minstrel performance under the rubric "recitation."

The two other books in the short list, Mary Giffin's *Studies on Chaucer and His Audience* (1956) and Bronson's *In Search of Chaucer* (1960), are both rather slight affairs. Giffin offers elaborate historical reconstructions of the possible occasions and original audiences for four of Chaucer's poems. Some of these speculations are pegged to Chaucer's performance of these pieces before certain audiences. These speculations seem not to have entered the critical canon; they are not even referred to in the notes for the relevant poems in the *Riverside Chaucer* (Chaucer 1988). Bronson indulges in even less substantiable fantasies about Chaucer's thought processes in composing his works, referring in passing to the poet's probable performance of them and the stylistic constraints this imposed. At most, these two books offer some insight into how Chaucer may have presented his own work to his first audience. Neither throws much light, however, on possible later aural reception of Chaucer's work, or of other contemporary literature.

Finally, A. C. Baugh's "The Middle English romance: Some questions of creation, presentation, and preservation" (1967) presents a coherent and well-argued case for the oral performance of the romances. Baugh speculates briefly about whether minstrels ever read romances aloud (pp. 21–23), but concentrates, in this as in his other works (e.g., 1950, 1959), on memorial performance. As interesting as his work is, therefore, it contributes relatively little to a reference list based on literature that was recited or read aloud.

As purged, that list becomes remarkably short. Only Crosby's two articles and Bronson's 1940 essay can fairly be cited as "about" the aural performance of literature in Chaucer's time. These three works were all published over the short five years from 1936 through 1940, over a half-century ago. Most of the other, more recent texts sometimes cited in "aurality references" turn out, on inspection, to contain some preliminary discussion of medieval aurality. Most then proceed, however, to concentrate on other issues: the inscribed audiences of *Troilus and Criseyde* (Mehl 1974), for example, or manuscript histories (Brunner 1961) or Chaucer's grounding in medieval grammatical theory (Irvine 1985). Beryl Rowland (1981, 1982) offers only a rather speculative and unsympathetic discussion, assuming that Chaucer's oral performance of his own texts necessarily sapped them of their "literariness."

Why do the majority of current writers on late medieval literature remain content with this very wobbly citation list of old or marginally relevant discussions, and unreceptive to more sophisticated recent approaches? As long as orality and literacy are kept separate, sequential, and ill defined, scholars will continue to identify aurality, as conflated with "orality," with many traits from which admirers of Chaucer naturally wish to distance him. Discouraged by the theory's extreme polarizations from distinguishing among varieties of orality, some scholars tend to identify "oral delivery" with oral tradition or folklore, with peasants and illiterates, with galumphing minstrel rhymes and podgy little stock formulas. Chaucer's self-consciousness and irony, the complexity of his devices, and the obscurity of his intentions are felt to place him in the world of the literate, private reader as surely as do his patchwork of literary borrowings and his self-description as an inveterate reader.

Fortunately for those subject to severe cognitive dissonance on the issue of Chaucer's aurality, the Great Divide framework that creates the conflict also provides the cure. Inasmuch as anti-auralists can associate aurality with (oral-formulaic and memorial) orality, they can discount its relevance to Chaucer, who obviously has little in common with bards, *scops*, and *guslari*, and only a distant relation to minstrels. On the other hand, since Chaucer's aurality is predicated on a written text, scholars can choose to emphasize the literacy and literariness this implies. Attention shifts to fourteenth-century literacy rates, to Chaucer's use of written sources, or to his awareness of himself as an author.

Thus even though the rising interest in orality is beginning to generate articles assessing the "orality" of later medieval writers (see, e.g., Brewer 1988; Harwood 1990), these discussions tend to degenerate into tail-chasing attempts to pin a wide variety of oralities and literacies down within Ong's essentialist guidelines. Rarely do these scholars formulate and consistently apply the idea of aurality to their texts.

THE PRACTICE OF AURALITY

Having survived my extended defense of the uniqueness and importance of aurality, some readers might by now be justifiably impatient to know what exactly I think aurality was, and what was so unique about it. In advance of the extensive data to be reviewed in later chapters, I would here offer some theoretical considerations about this model-breaking modality.

It is undeniable that, at their poles, "orality" and "literacy" describe distinct forms of literary experience. Bards composing extemporaneously in crowded meadhalls and authors writing in studies for armchair readers operate in radically different environments. Moreover, it is clear that, in England, the one environment gradually developed into the other. It makes little sense, however, to carry into an investigation of that process a model based on "orality" and "literacy" as they manifest themselves in their most extreme forms. What one finds in later medieval England, at least, is a state of acute mixedness, manifested both in the voiced textuality of the read-aloud manuscript and in the interactions of that mode of reception with private reading as ascribed by authors to themselves or to their audiences. Aurality, in particular, combined the two poles of "orality" and "literacy" in a unique way whose implications cannot properly be perceived if most of the critical energy is devoted to pulling aurality into line with a superimposed Great Divide.

Aurality is distinguished from "orality" – i.e., from a tradition based on the oral performance of bards or minstrels – by its dependence on a written text as the source of the public reading. Although writing for performance, the author had time to compose the text at his own pace and alone, knowing that it would be preserved in written form and that this written form would visibly dominate the group experience, in a way that no oral or memorial author's text could do. The audience's awareness of the book before them entailed an increased awareness of the fixity and authority of the text, and of the author's role as mediator of the traditions that text represented. Such awareness promoted (as the authors did themselves) the reputations of individual, named writers. Knowing that their texts were stored in books, these authors and audiences were more conscious of the interplay among the texts of these and other books. Since many audience members were literate, they would have a sense of familiarity with books and the handling of books; and they could listen in the knowledge that at another time they might, as D. H. Green says, "withdraw into privacy with the text and study it with as much critical leisure as was available to the author in preparing it for his recital" (1984: 292).

These consequences of writtenness are familiar from many theoretical explications (although few consider aurality as a separate phenomenon). Less familiar are the consequences that follow from the written text being read aloud. What distinguishes public from private reading (i.e., what distinguishes aurality from "literacy") is that the former defines literature as a social event. However many intertextual echoes and rhetorical personas might be operative within a privately read text, and however many extra neurons are employed in voicing as opposed to silently perusing it (see Saenger 1991), the experience of reading a book by oneself differs materially from that of sharing it with others.

The presence of these others can greatly condition the text as its listeners experience it (see Coleman 1995: 70–79). The aural situation carries over from orality a significant proportion of what folklorist Richard Bauman calls the "emergent quality of performance." Bauman notes that this quality "resides in the interplay between communicative resources, individual competence, and the goals of the participants, within the context of particular situations" (1977: 38). In a bardic or minstrel performance, everything from the choice of genre and of text, along with many decisions about the emphases within and the length of the text, would be subject to a feedback process (p. 42). The text, and the event, would be different with every performance. In this empowering situation, the audience could customize the experience to their mutually negotiated sense of what defines their group identity in the particular circumstances of the moment – even if that is that they are a bunch of drunken louts shouting down the performer!

All such events would share in what Bauman calls "part of the essence of performance, that it offers to the participants a special enhancement of experience, bringing with it a heightened intensity of communicative interaction" (p. 43). Traditional "oral" traits such as formulas, rhyme, and repetition contribute to this intensification precisely because of their culture-affirming familiarity. With the addition of the performer's skills as composer, actor, singer, and/or editor (of the text as he or she performs it), the event can become a deep affirmation of the group's sense of self and togetherness – rather as, today, audiences may leave a performance of some fundamental text of our culture – *Hamlet* or Bach's *St. Matthew Passion* – united in a feeling of sorrow or exhilaration.

The degree of potential audience investment in an oral/aural experience is suggested by a sermon of Jean Gerson, delivered on Good Friday, 1403. "When a singer of romances, or of *gestes*," says Jean,

> relates the words and deeds of a good prince who was fair to look upon, vigorous in battle, courteous, gentle, and debonair in victory, he is willingly and sweetly heard and listened to; and when he comes to the hero's death, there is neither man nor woman so hard-hearted as not to start applauding and crying, especially those who are of his blood and his lineage. (quoted in Ferrier 1956: 97)

Gerson's point is that Christians should react even more strongly to the story of Christ's passion, since they are all of his blood and heritage. Owst paraphrases an English homilist who makes a similar point about explicitly aural reception, complaining: "One who is left unmoved by the story of Christ's Passion read in the Gospel for Holy Week, is stirred to tears when the tale of Guy of Warwick is read aloud to him" (1961: 14 n. 14). Figure 3 demonstrates the sort of reaction these preachers would welcome; hearing the Bible read in his monastic refectory, the monk (in the words of the manuscript's illustration program) "cannot contain himself, but, moved with a great love, strikes his finger on the table and cries out: 'It's true, it's true'" (quoted in Monks 1990: 146). Such accounts give us an idea of the kind of "deep play" involved in group hearing, the emotionality it accessed, and the identifications it fostered.

Obviously, in comparison to a purely oral performance, a public reading is constrained by the use of a written text – although, of course, the initial choice of that text, and of which part to read out, is subject to negotiation. Even after the text has been selected, however, there is considerable scope for Bauman's "emergent quality," in the performance skills that the reader deploys and in the responses and interpolated comments of the audience. In the present day, live audiences tend to develop a "group personality," laughing together at some lines of a play one night, for instance, and together, again, at different lines the next night. Alert actors, or performers of any kind (including lecturers), learn to recognize each audience's inclinations and to play to them. It is not hard to imagine a similar phenomenon affecting even the reading aloud of a written text in the late Middle Ages, especially as the audience would feel free (if the behavior of Chaucer's pilgrims is any indication) to speak up in praise or criticism of the reading as it progressed, or even to stop it altogether. Such a group dynamic could, for example, evoke from the reader either a straightforward or an ironic presentation of *Troilus and Criseyde*, or of particular characters within it.

The presence of this reader is obviously another element that distinguishes aurality from "literacy." This mediating agent between the author and the audience could add many elements of performance and interpretation. A skilled reader could, for example, recreate voices more accurately than most private readers could "hear" them with their mind's ear. That such dramatization was an accepted aspect of aurality is suggested by the grammarian Diomedes' definition of *lectio* (or public reading) as "an artful rendering, or the various recitation of each kind of writing, preserving the dignity of persons and expressing the character of each mind" (quoted in Irvine 1985: 857–58 n. 23). The Reeve's Tale read by someone who could reproduce the class, dialectal, and gender distinctions of the protagonists' voices would be a richer experience than almost any private reader could attain today, or even in Chaucer's time.

The audiences of such readings, whether literate or not, would certainly have been, in W. F. Bolton's useful coinage, "audiate." That is, they were experienced hearers, possessing both competence in the matter and manner of traditional oral and aural literature as well as a "quite remarkable facility for maintaining their attention and for grasping matters of individual detail or overall structure" (1970: xvii). Listening with other people created the opportunity for these competencies to be pooled, for discussion of the text and the topics or reminiscences it aroused. I hypothesize in chapter 4 that specula principis were written in the hope that they would promote just such discussions. Chapter 5 reviews the considerable historical evidence that French and Burgundian nobles sponsored public readings of commissioned texts as an effective form of dynastic propaganda. These sophisticated functions, aimed at the very upper reaches of society, rely on the publicness of public reading for their success.

Finally, and most crucially for its persistence, aurality offered the basic advantage, as it was perceived, of a shared, enjoyable, social experience. Historical and literary reports consistently associate British public reading with festive occasions and relaxation, often including other diversions such as harping and singing (see chapters 5 and 7). Listening to texts was "solace & gamen / In felawschip when thai sitt samen [together]" (Mannyng, *Chronicle*, lines 9–10). The shared experience of a text could further promote the sort of emotional release and group affirmation suggested by Gerson and his English colleague, a gain reinforced by the opportunity to exchange comments on the text and its performance.

Nor was this pleasure confined to the less educated or less intellectual. Several medieval theorists evoke a sort of phenomenology of reading in which modalities and senses, profit and pleasure, are inextricably mixed in the reception of elite Latin texts. In a typically synesthetic passage, Geoffrey of Vinsauf counsels that "the final labor [of poetry is] to see that a voice managed discreetly may enter the ears of the hearer and feed his hearing, being seasoned with matched spices of facial expression and gesture" (trans. Kopp: 36). Richard de Bury similarly mingles sensory channels: "But the truth that shines in books," he says, "seeks to manifest itself to every impressible sense; to the sight when it is read, to the hearing when it is heard, and moreover commendeth itself in some sort to the touch, while suffering itself to be transcribed, collated, corrected, and preserved" (trans. Taylor: 9). Both the rhetorician, speaking of poetry, and the bishop, speaking of scholarly and religious texts, involve public reading in a rich and sensual experiential mix that helps explain the persistent attractiveness of high-context – performed, social, shared – aural reception.

Public reading, therefore, is like and not like private reading, and like and not like bardic or minstrel performance. To insist that this unique and complex phenomenon can be viewed only as a subform of orality or literacy is like treating all greens as shades of either blue or yellow. It's a valid procedure if you're trying to investigate primary colors, perhaps, but not conducive to further understanding of green itself. As a method of analysis it seems destined to distort the very subject it purports to be analyzing.

CONCLUSION

There is no question that, over the course of Western history, literacy rose and its technologies improved, nor is there any question that these events had many important consequences or that excellent histories can be and have been written tracing these developments. There are, however, serious problems with histories that adopt the distorting premises of "strong" orality/literacy theory. With primary value and focus always on the end-product – what Kenneth George calls the "inscribed modern" (1990: 19) – such histories become a teleological progression from less to ever more desirable intellectual states. Oral traits persisting after their expiration date are dismissed as survivals or residue. Other influences conditioning the operations of orality and literacy are ignored or minimalized, allowing literacy to emerge as the single effective force. Thus the histories become self-validating: orality gives way to literacy, because any orality that does not, doesn't count. As the following chapters will illustrate, this assumption plays an important role in many commentaries on medieval literature.

The preceding critique has, hopefully, exposed some of the flaws in such historical constructions. Yet many literary critics continue to embrace the Great Divide uncritically, perhaps because the literary and intellectual history that results from its premises seems in many ways compatible with the natural interests and foci of such critics. To people who spend their life with written texts, it makes sense to write history as the story of the emergence and dissemination of writing, and to single out literacy as the agent of human efflorescence, the catalyst for many or most of the major intellectual advances of the species. The emphasis placed in modern culture on literacy skills, and the corresponding denigration of anything associated with illiteracy, is often carried over unthinkingly into a strong prejudice for a literary history written as the triumph of literacy over orality (see Clanchy 1979: 183). Is it far-fetched to suggest that the critics who take this approach are rewriting history in their own image? Ong's version of orality/literacy theory seems almost to be another case in point that "literate" society may exhibit such "oral" traits as homeostatization and an inability to distinguish self from statement. The story of the eclipse of orality by the strong sun of literacy is a modern-day scholar's creation myth; its end goal is the form of reticulated self-awareness that maximally characterizes present-day critical reading and writing.[5]

2

Taxonomies and terminology: the pursuit of disambiguity

One reason that evolutionary and polarizing premises inform so much of medieval theory and criticism, and that aurality is so consistently bypassed, is the paucity and imprecision of the vocabulary available for discussing medieval literary reception. Before we can move freely in the conceptual space opened up by the anti-Great Divide arguments of Finnegan and Street, we need to generate a disambiguated, less biased set of terms to describe what we will find.

This chapter will address two large areas of ambiguity: first, the multiple meanings impacted into the modality terms "read," "orality," and "literacy"; and, second, the confusions caused by equating the domains of modality and mentality, e.g., by assuming that "oral" equals "synthetic" or that "literate" equals "autonomous." In each case, I will seek to disambiguate, by defining vague terms more precisely and by introducing some new ones. In the last section, I will go on to explore some implications of these new terms.

DIFFERENTIATING MODALITIES

The first task is to define a collective term to designate the various channels by which medieval literature was composed, communicated, and received – other than as "stages" or "phases" of literary "development" or "evolution." I will employ either of two words for this purpose. "Format" is a value-free, pragmatic term that can be used to describe phenomena all down the line: dictation is a compositional format, minstrel recitation a performance format, reading to oneself a reception format. As a more theoretical collective term I will use "modality," which may include one or more formats in adumbrating the cultural implications that build up around a particular pattern of reception. "Format" describes the pragmatic event, "modality" the event, or set of events, as a cultural phenomenon.

The following sections will discuss first the formats and then the modalities pertinent to medieval English literature, trying to nominate and describe them in an unbiased, nonevolutionary framework.

Texts composed in performance with the help of standard formulas and themes, as described classically by Milman Parry and Albert Lord (see esp. Lord 1960), are often called "oral-formulaic." Within English literature this is the province, obviously, of bards or *scops*. Works composed without writing and memorized for delivery with few or no improvisatory additions could be called "oral-memorial," while texts written with the use of traditional formulas could be called "written-formulaic."

Texts composed in writing but presented orally from memory would be "memorial" – whether the performer learned it from a manuscript or from hearing another performer. To the degree that the surviving texts exhibit apparent improvisations overlaid on the "standard" wording, they could be considered "memorial-formulaic."

"Public reading" and "private reading" should be clear enough as designations, with "public" carrying the sense of social, shared reading – reading aloud to one or more people, not just to oneself. "Private reading" would mean reading to oneself, whether muttering the words or absorbing them in silence. An alternate term for "public reading" is "prelection," a useful word I borrow from John of Salisbury, who borrowed it from Quintilian. John uses it to distinguish between the teacher's reading to the students, which he calls "praelectio," and the student's reading to himself ("lectio") (*Metalogicon*, ed. Giles, p. 56; for a translation, see McGarry 1955: 65–66). The English form "prelection" – along with "prelect" and "prelector" – appears in the *Oxford English Dictionary*, with citations from 1586 through 1907 giving the same general meaning as John: reading aloud within an academic setting. It is a slight and hopefully permissible extension of meaning to include reading aloud within domestic and other settings as well.

The word "prelect" will prove particularly helpful in desynonymizing the trickiest word of all in both the primary and secondary literature – namely, "read." Standing alone in a medieval text – as in "Many speken of men that romaunces rede / That were sumtyme doughti in dede" (*Laud Troy Book*, lines 11–12) – does it mean "read to oneself" or "read aloud"? Are you speaking of these doughty men *after* you've (privately) read about them? Or are the reading and the speaking visual and oral constituents of the same act – reading aloud?

Medieval usage had no problem attributing the activity of reading to what we would consider, perhaps, the passive listener: Criseyde tells Pandarus, for example, "This romaunce is of Thebes that we rede," when it was not she but her maiden who was actually holding and prelecting the book (T&C 2: 100).

In many cases a plain "read," which one might assume from the context to designate a private reading, develops a notably aural connotation further on in the passage. One Scottish scribe apologized for any miscopying by asking his "worthe readeris":

> Quhen ye it reid, ye help it thar ye may,
> Sillabis or wordis heir suppois that I
> Throw negligence I haue lattin pas by ...
> (Hay, *Buik of King Alexander*, lines 19,346–49)

The scribe is asking his readers not just to forgive his mistakes but to "help" the text, presumably by supplying these missing syllables and words in performance.

If the medieval "read" seems often ambiguous, surreptitiously aural, or unconcernedly bimodal, the modern scholar's reading of that "read" usually places it in a strictly "literate" context – i.e., interprets it automatically as evidence of private reading. Paul Christianson, for example, in an article on "Chaucer's literacy," cites as an instance of "contemporary references to private reading" (1976/77: 126 n. 4) Gower's/Amans' comment that

> Fulofte time it falleth so,
> Min Ere with a good pitance
> Is fedd of redinge of romance.
> (CA 6: 876–78)

Christianson's assumption, presumably, is that this is a voiced private reading – yet nothing in the text specifies whether Amans' ear is fed by his own voice or, as is surely equally likely, by that of a prelector. Perhaps Gower also thought the "worldes eere" (CA prol.: 10) to which he directed his *Confessio* would simply be hearing the private mutterings of the world's tongue. But he certainly provided an unambiguous reference to public reading of romances (to a literate audience) in Amans' declared willingness to obey his lady when "hir list comaunde / To rede and here of Troilus" (CA 4: 2794–95).

In such a context, I would suggest that we simply do not have enough information to decide whether Gower, in the passage quoted by Christianson, meant that Amans was reading privately or publicly. Perhaps he meant that Amans did either or both, depending on the circumstances. To annex every uncontextualized "read" to private reading is to perpetuate a chronocentric *petitio principii* – assuming what we are ostensibly setting out to prove. If, in investigating Chaucer's "literacy," one assumes that every "read" means "read privately" (and, perhaps, that every "hear" is mere "residue"), then clearly one will discover Chaucer to be a very "literate" author.

We have thus distinguished four major formats of medieval English literature: oral-formulaic, memorial, prelectate or publicly read, and privately read (which would have two subformats of voiced and silent). The corresponding modalities, or cultural matrices within which these modes of reception operate, might be listed as "orality," "memoriality," "aurality," and "literacy."

The middle two terms are relatively straightforward. "Memoriality" designates the format and implications of delivering vernacular literary texts largely from memory. In the context of this book it will usually designate minstrel performance, although it would apply as well to the recitation of written poetry or orations.

"Aurality" could be a rather ambiguous term, as all "oral" literature is heard through the ear (Latin *auris*). Since no bad effects seem to proceed from this semantic overlap, however, I will continue to use "aurality" in the more limited sense of literature experienced through public reading. Many medieval texts invoke both hearing and reading as reception channels, e.g., Chaucer's prayer to "hem alle that herkne this litel tretys or rede" (CT 10: 1081). Although the word "read" in such statements could mean "read aloud" or "read privately," the latter meaning is clearly possible, and in any case all written literature was clearly *available* for private reading. One might describe this situation, in which authors wrote for an audience that might read their text publicly or privately, as a form of "bimodality." To some extent I will perpetuate an ambiguity by often using "aurality" to describe the bimodal literature of late medieval England. By calling bimodal texts "aural" I am emphasizing the neglected yet often dominant portion of their bimodality, and I hope that no confusion results.

Confusion over "orality" and "literacy," however, seems impossible to avoid. As common as the words are, their precise meanings, whether standing alone or in relationship to each other, are endlessly

Chart 2.1: *Taxonomies of "orality" and "literacy"*

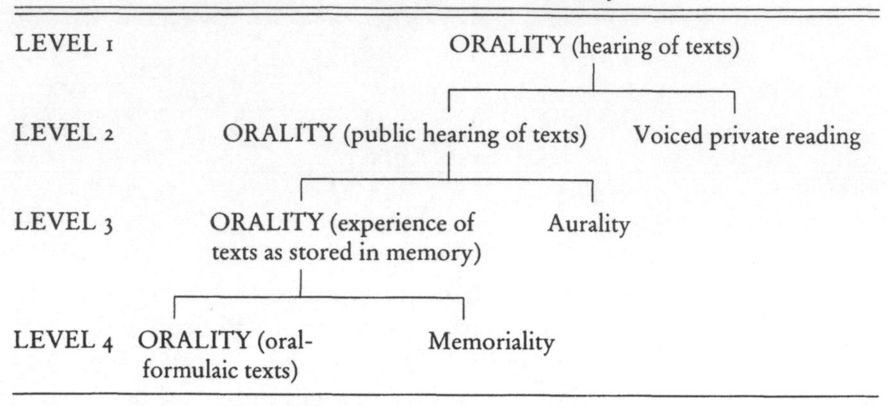

shifting. If we are to assume that they designate mutually exclusive denotative fields, the following contrast-pairs are possible:

Orality = the hearing of texts[1]
Literacy = the silent reading of texts

Orality = the public hearing of texts
Literacy = the private reading of texts

Orality = the experience of texts as stored in memory
Literacy = the experience of texts as stored in writing

In fact, each term is used at various times to mean all these things. These relationships can be presented in two taxonomic diagrams (chart 2.1).

In the same way that "plant" as opposed to "bush" comes under the heading of "plant" as opposed to "tree," which comes under the heading of "plant" as opposed to "animal" or "mineral," so both "orality" and "literacy" simultaneously designate phenomena at different taxonomic levels. The potential confusions are many, and the potential is often realized. A description of public reading as "oral," for example, may result in the dismissal of the format as archaic, because "oral" literature, in the sense of *oral-formulaic* literature, or of oral-formulaic and memorial literature, *was* archaic by the time under discussion – although public reading, in fact, may not have been (cf. D. H. Green 1990: 271–72). Similarly, it is very easy to conflate "literacy," in its level-1 sense of the experience of texts as stored in writing (which includes prelected texts), with "literacy" in its level-2 sense of the private reading of texts (which excludes

Chart 2.1 cont.

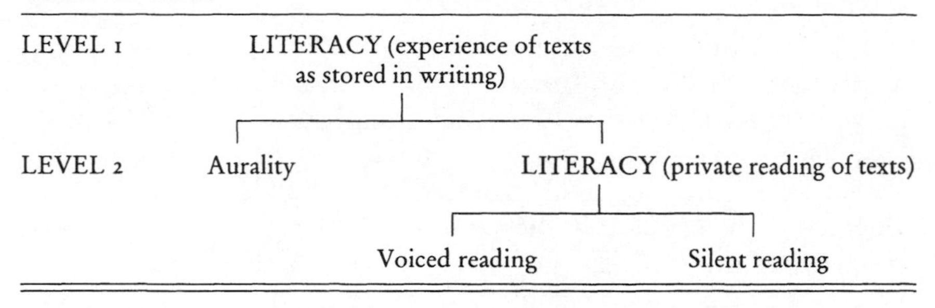

prelected texts). Some progressive relationship might actually exist between the two levels, but surely it should not be enforced via an unexamined taxonomic homology.

A still more fundamental source of confusion appears when we contemplate the contrast-pairs (e.g., "the hearing of texts" vs. "the silent reading of texts") used to generate the two diagrams of chart 2.1. These mutually exclusive categories are the definitions that the Great Divide model demands, by insisting on the mutual exclusivity of "oral" and "literate." If these categories were really so separate, however, then each should generate its own chart, with no elements repeated. Yet there are two elements that appear in each chart: namely, voiced private reading and aurality. The demon of "mixedness" seems to lie hidden within the very logical structures of the Great Divide.

A descriptive system need not be composed of strict contrast-pairs, however; intersecting denotations are quite acceptable as long as their intersections are recognized and incorporated into the scheme. In this and the following two sections, I will attempt to set out a terminology that will allow for considerable overlap, as the connecting lines in chart 2.2 will illustrate. At the top level of my scheme I would preserve "orality" and "literacy" as broad general (and overlapping) terms, in their common, not rigorously contrasted sense of "the hearing of books" and "the reading of books." These terms designate the cultural presence, operation, and potential of, on the one hand, orally experienced texts and the oral or audiate skills of speaking, remembering, and listening; and on the other hand, written texts and the literate skills of reading, remembering, and writing. In these two senses, orality and literacy have coexisted in Western culture since its inception, and still do. One of the areas in which they coexist most intimately, of course, is in the reading aloud of written texts, that is, aurality.

A level below "orality" and "literacy" in my modality hierarchy would come the level of "aurality," which would be linked by a line to each superior category. But what would stand on either side? If "aurality" is the reading aloud of written texts to at least one other person, we need to think about what (besides "orality" and "literacy") we could call the experience of texts with no books involved, or the experience of texts with no other people involved. What can we do toward naming and explaining that first entity, texts without books?

The first step is to renounce the negative formulation. The people who listened to oral epics or minstrel romances did not sit there wishing they had a written copy of the text (and/or the ability to read it); as noted above and in chapter 4, all the evidence is that they were happy to "sitt samen [together]" in "felawschip" as the performance unfolded. After casting around a good deal in search of a viable term, I would suggest the word "peroral," which *Webster's* defines as "occurring through or by way of the mouth." This term picks up the familiar designation of this literature as "oral" while acknowledging the specifically bookless nature of this orality (as opposed to the book-employing orality of prelection) through the prefix "per-," which serves to intensify the force of the morpheme it precedes. (*Webster's New Collegiate Dictionary* defines "per-" as "throughout; thoroughly.") Thus "peroral" communicates the idea "thoroughly, or completely [i.e., booklessly], oral." While "perorate" and "peroration" have distinct, not quite relevant meanings, we may institute the term "perorality" as the modality term for "peroral."

Having cobbled out a word to go on the left of "aurality" in my modality chart (2.2), I now need a word to go on the right, designating "books read alone." This word could be quite useful in disenabling a prevalent, and pernicious, ambiguity in the use of "literacy" and "literate." Many scholars assume that learning to read instantly converts people into private readers; "rising literacy" often functions as a shorthand equivalent of "the increased habit of private reading." This semantic coziness leaves no room, obviously, in which to conceptualize the prelection of texts to literate listeners.

The potential confusions are aggravated by the use of "literate" to mean "able to think abstractly," as well as "educated" or "cultured."

Stir all these connotations together, and you get the not uncommon assumption that once literature is understood as written, or once enough people learn to read, all but the insignificant and the illiterate promptly abandon all public forms of experiencing literature, while simultaneously indulging in a great deal of book-handling *and*, not coincidentally, blossoming out into high degrees of intellectual and literary sophistication. Since the present book is dedicated to proving the existence of literate listeners, as well as the potential sophistication of listeners whether literate or not, I obviously consider this another area needing disambiguation. The task, however, is daunting.

In trying to generate a word for "reading books alone" or "private reading," I found that most of the obvious root-words (especially the "eye" ones) already carry other meanings[2] or produce excessively awkward neologisms. My best suggestion is the term "dividual," which the *Oxford English Dictionary* defines as "That is or may be divided or separated from something else; separate, distinct, particular." This seems to capture the sense of a non-social, individualized, and potentially individuating reading experience. A "dividual" reader would be one who chooses to read privately; a "dividual" text would be written for such reading by a "dividual" author. The bimodality peculiar to late medieval English literature could be described as combining aurality and "dividuality" – i.e., tolerating either a public or a private reading. Aurality would also overlap with dividuality in the area of voiced private reading.

Putting all of the above considerations together, I would offer chart 2.2 as an overview of the modalities relevant to medieval literature in English. As suggested above, overlap is part of the system, operating between modalities both at the same level and from one level to the next. Horizontal overlap might ideally be presented as intersecting Venn circles, but it is easier to present, as here, using horizontal lines with an arrow at either end. Vertical overlap is indicated by converging lines running to the upper-level modalities.

As opposed to chart 2.1, in which the labels "orality" and "literacy" occurred at almost every level of generalization, chart 2.2 offers a distinct terminology at each level. Clarity thus becomes, if not inevitable, at least conceivable. Moreover, orality and literacy, as construed here, are free to interact in a range of phenomena, rather than being so relentlessly, inaccurately, segregated that, as with chart 2.1, they cannot even be made to fit into the same diagram.

Chart 2.2: *Transmission and reception modalities of medieval English literature*

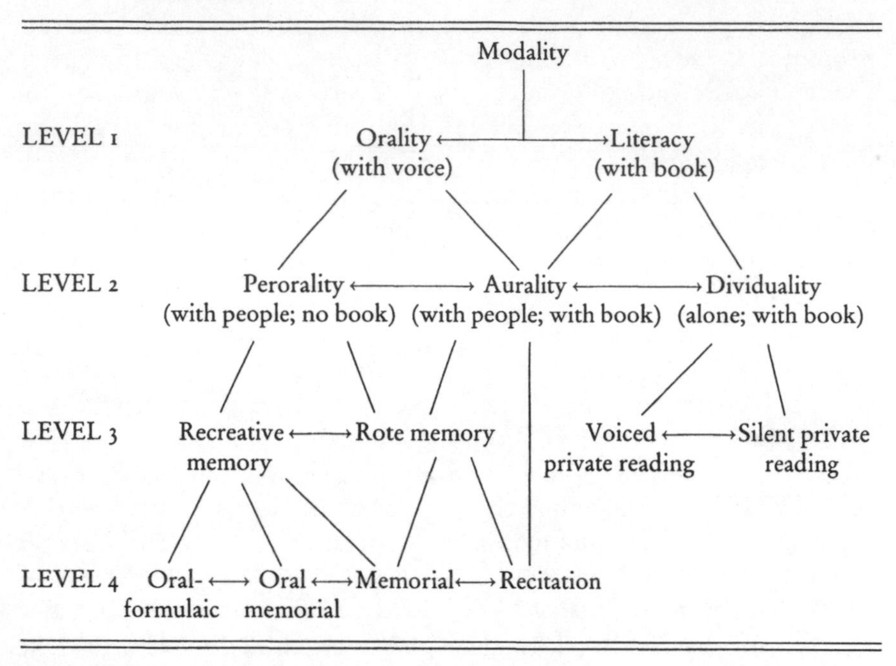

DIFFERENTIATING DOMAINS

We now have some idea of what we mean when we say "oral" and "literate," at least when we are talking about literary modalities. These meanings align fairly well with the "technological" sense of "oral" as not involving (or possessing) writing and of "literate" as having and using writing. But the clearer the literary and technological senses of these two terms become, the more problematic is the common usage of them to designate mentalities – i.e., synthetic versus analytic, concrete versus abstract thinking, and so on. The previous chapter has demonstrated that these categories, so confidently aligned with "oral" and "literate" by Goody and Watt and by Ong, in fact seem to distribute themselves freely across the spectrum of technological or literary modalities. Similarly (although I will not be discussing the issue in detail here),[3] the traits of literary style commonly identified as "oral" and "literate" seem very little inclined to remain firmly identified with "oral" and "literate" texts.

"Strong" literacy theory encourages a hierarchy of assumptions about these various domains: e.g., that rising literacy (a technological innovation) will lead to greater numbers of private readers (literary-modality), which will encourage more critical thinking (mentality), which will promote textual traits such as authorial irony (literary-stylistic). Every one of these four steps can be described as involving "literacy" – and since the events tend to be described with the same words, the sequence of events naturally seems seamless. But what words do we use if we would claim that the ability to read did *not* always result in greater skepticism or a choice of private reading, or that irony existed *before* the reading levels rose?

To desynonymize, we need, again, to disambiguate. Thus, to represent the mentalities identified by Goody and Watt and by Ong with orality and literacy, I would suggest two linguistic terms that designate different ways in which sentences construct meaning. An "exophoric" sentence can be understood only if one knows the context or situation from which it emerges: e.g., "No I don't." An "endophoric" sentence provides all the necessary information within itself: e.g., "William Caxton was the first printer in England." The exophoric carries (*pherein*) or refers you to the surrounding environment, the endophoric directs you within. Although they are jargonistic, the terms have the advantage of neutrality: they attach no value judgments, suggest no specific mechanisms, and imply no chronological or hierarchical relationship.

The exo/endophoric distinction seems to capture the essential element of the erstwhile opposition between "oral" and "literate" mentalities: the degree to which a society, individual, or text is immersed in or can conceptualize a separation from its immediate context. These new terms exist on a continuum, not as polarized opposites, so that societies would be described only as relatively one or the other. To each category could tentatively be assigned a set of traits (see chart 2.3), similar to those variously identified with aspects of oral and literate, non-Western and Western, "traditional" and "modern" culture.

The alignment of these traits in two lists in no way implies that they are absolutes or that they do not miscegenate – rather, the contrary. With the technological link removed – so that "oral" traits are not preordained to consort with orality, nor "literate" with literacy – we are free to map the distribution of cultural mentalities without presupposing what we may be seeking to prove: their relationship to orality and literacy. Thus we could look at ancient

Chart 2.3: *Exophoric and endophoric mentalities*

Exophoric	Endophoric
Language	
Contextualized	Decontextualized
Concrete	Abstract
Embedded	Distanced
Context-bound	Context-free
—	Formal metalanguage
Restricted code	Elaborated code[4]
Relationship of self and other	
Communal	Individual
Assimilative	Autonomous
Synthetic	Analytic
Conservative	Iconoclastic
Collective	Idiosyncratic
Traditional	Innovative/Original
Public	Private
Unselfconscious	Self-conscious
Anonymous	Self-identified
Group-directed	Self-directed
Communal recreation	Individual genius
World view	
Homeostatic	De-homeostatized/Possessing a sense of the past
Myth	History
Magic	Science
Personalized	Impersonal
Proverbial wisdom	Formal logic

China, as Gough (1968) portrays it, as a literate society with an exophoric sense of self but an endophoric sense of time and space. While this does not tell us why the traits are distributed as they are, the disambiguation of "literate" in this context at least allows the question to be posed, or the situation to be described, more clearly.

The perils of an un-disambiguated approach to late medieval literature can be well illustrated from a recent article. Any educated fifteenth-century reader of the Wife of Bath's Prologue, argues Susan Schibanoff (1988), would have recognized her distortions of St. Paul. Anyone who actually needed the Ellesmere glosses for the purpose suggested by Graham Caie (1976) – as a warning not to accept these distortions – would have to be

> uneducated, what we would call illiterate or nonliterate ... Thus Caie's putative audience would mostly consist of what I call "old" readers, not of the "new" educated and private readers of manuscripts whose emergence was well under way during Chaucer's era. (Schibanoff 1988: 75–76)

Schibanoff unhesitatingly equates the "new" with the *educated*, and the "new" and educated with the *private*, reader. Inasmuch as she does accept that public and private reading coexisted in Chaucer's period, she conceptualizes not coexistence but transition, the emergence of the "new" (improved) reader, and bases her interpretations of the Wife of Bath glosses on that reader's supposed reactions. The "old" reader, although present, is irrelevant – because due for extinction – and his or her reactions do not, therefore, figure in Schibanoff's constructions.

Later in her discussion, however, Schibanoff apparently inverts her own categories by identifying Alison of Bath herself as a "new" reader:

> Because her reading differs so much from the conventional reception of this antifeminist material [in Jankyn's book], she emblematizes the new reader par excellence even though, ironically, Alison appears to be an ear-reader, not an eye-reader. Her literal act of taking the book into her own hands demonstrates the power of new reading and dramatizes her female textuality. (p. 104)

What could have led Schibanoff into the manifest self-contradiction of first defining the "new" reader as an educated, private reader and then labeling as "the new reader par excellence" a certainly uneducated and probably illiterate public (or "ear") reader? I think that she falls into this particular solecism due to the impoverishment of the evolutionary, polarized vocabulary she endorses. Because the standard Great Divide theories aggregate desirable traits such as Alison's interpretive autonomy under the rubric of "literacy," which it identifies as the evolutionary successor of "orality," Schibanoff is naturally led to equate autonomy ("literacy" as mentality) with the ability to read ("literacy" as technology), with private reading ("literacy" as modality), with "newness" – with a probably illiterate auditor of an old-fashioned public reading.

If, on the other hand, Schibanoff had been able to conceive of autonomy as an "endophoric" trait, she could have queried its relationship to literacy and to periodization. There is, after all, nothing new about being a woman, nor do women need to be literate to resent misogyny.[5] Femaleness must always have nurtured divergent, and therefore possibly endophoric, responses to the mainstream, male-dominated culture. Alison herself claims to reject orthodox doctrines because these doctrines misrepresent and malign her sex – although there is no reason to doubt (within the scope of Chaucer's fiction) that she derived much of her facility in text-chopping from her "aural literacy," as the intelligent auditor of Jankyn's prelections and commentary. There is no contradiction in describing Alison as an uneducated, probably illiterate woman encouraged by her native self-esteem, plus her husband's (inadvertent) coaching, to the endophoric act of questioning clerical views of women.

Having a set of terms that disengage mentality from technology should help release the grip of the latter on the former, problematizing relationships that have hitherto often been, often inaccurately, accepted as self-evident.

If the exophoric is not always "oral," nor the endophoric always "literate," we are suddenly faced with the possibility of two sorts of orality and two sorts of literacy. To start with the latter, we might distinguish between exophoric and endophoric literacy. Exophoric literacy (or, in syncopated form, "exoliteracy") would be a use of literacy skills that functioned to reinforce an assimilative relationship with one's intellectual or cultural environment. Situations that contradict the premises of standard orality/literacy theory – e.g., that of educated, modern citizens of Western societies endorsing fundamentalist readings of the Bible – can be easily explained as instances of exoliteracy.

Richard Hoggart's sensitive account of the effects of university training on a scholarship boy from a working-class background offers another example of present-day exoliteracy. Such a student, he wrote in 1957,

> tends to over-stress the importance of examinations, of the piling-up of knowledge and of received opinions. He discovers a technique of apparent learning, of the acquiring of facts rather than of the handling and use of facts ... [O]f other forms [of initiative] – the freely ranging mind, the bold flying of mental kites, the courage to reject some "lines" even though they are officially as important as all the rest – of these he probably has little. (p. 297)

The literacy identified with the "bold flying of mental kites" and the challenging of received opinion would be endophoric literacy (or "endoliteracy"). It manifests the endophoric trait of autonomy, just as the scholarship boy's desire to assimilate to his environment is a classically exophoric trait.

With this distinction in place, we can recognize that the sort of "literacy" invoked in "strong" orality/literacy theory – the liberating factor said to have created Chaucer's allegedly "new," critical, sophisticated audiences – is what we have described as endoliterate. Yet in fact, much of the literate culture of medieval England would be better described as exoliterate.

Medieval students, like the Arabic-learners among the Vai studied by Scribner and Cole (1981; see chapter 1), were taught by rote, and by reading and memorizing highly valued cultural texts (beginning, in medieval England, with prayers, psalms, and liturgical devotions). Those who went on to further studies would read morally improving Latin texts and learn the "colors" of rhetoric but would not be encouraged in the endophoric habits of individualized, analytic engagement with tradition (Orme 1973). As writers they would be expected to imitate, and to translate across languages, not to explore their own budding subjectivities (cf. Lewis 1964: 211). The *ars dictaminis* consisted in the educated imitation of good models. Only at the university level were some forms of critical thinking encouraged – although, even there, heavily constrained by the demands of orthodoxy.

As Mary Carruthers has demonstrated, the emphasis on memory and imitation was an intrinsic part of the learned Latin culture of the Middle Ages. Paraphrasing Hugh of St. Victor, she notes: "The 'dicta et facta memorabilia,' exemplary deeds and words of others impressed into our memories like a seal into wax, shape our moral life in shaping our memories" (1990: 71). The result was in large part, she continues, "a 'self' constructed out of bits and pieces of great authors of the past" (p. 180).

Obviously, texts that a certain high-status group of people all memorized with considerable initial effort (impressing them in their memories like a seal into wax), that they perceived as bearers of key cultural values and models, and that they constantly sought to integrate into their daily life and thought, would exert a powerful communalizing, synthesizing, and homeostatizing influence. In short, they would encourage an exophoric literacy. Since medieval

Englishmen did not receive the same sort of education as modern Westernized people, and as Luria's Soviet peasants, it is not to be expected that they and their literary expressions would conform to the essentialist lists that Walter Ong compiled based, in large part, on Luria's research.

Realizing the exophoric tendencies of medieval culture explains an often unaddressed paradox of orality/literacy theory as applied to medieval English literature. If technological literacy (along with improved book production, private rooms, or whatever other technological factors) deserves much of the credit for the endophoric revolution known as the Renaissance, why did that revolution take so long to arrive? For centuries there had been near-universal literacy and good access to books in England's two universities, as well as in the Inns of Court, among clerics, and in the upper echelons of government and society. When it did arrive, the Renaissance emerged not from any newly literate sectors of English society but from precisely those groups that had been literate for generations: princely and episcopal patrons, university scholars, lawyers, and government officials (Weiss 1957). What happened was not (just) a change from less to more literacy, or from fewer to more books, or even the invention of printing; all of these factors, somehow, interacted with others to change the *nature* of literacy (and orality): from (relatively) exophoric to (relatively) endophoric.

Of course, in saying this I may seem to be begging the question: are we in any better position to explain this crucial transition just because we now have two new bits of jargon? Well, I would answer, we are in a *somewhat* better position. At least we can now ask how the endophoric shift was related to rising literacy – instead of asking, in effect, how increased literacy was related to rising literacy. Not surprisingly, the question was previously so tautological that it tended not to be asked at all.

If literacy is not always endophoric, neither is orality, or aurality, necessarily exophoric. One medieval example of endophoric aurality is the Wife of Bath's idiosyncratic reaction to her husband's favorite book; another might be the illiterate eleventh-century audiences mobilized into heresy by the clerical prelections described by Brian Stock (1983). Ruth Finnegan has collected many examples of oral literature that manifest endophoric traits such as irony and fictionality (1988: chap. 4; see chapter 1).

Certainly, literacy augments critical functions, through the various mechanical advantages of being able to manipulate texts, make notes, and so on. Yet, as pointed out in chapter 1, possibly the most crucial endophoric breakthroughs in Western history – those which developed during the heyday of classical Greece – emerged from a cultural climate in which the predominant format of reading was prelection. Erich Auerbach held the Roman habit of reading texts aloud directly responsible for the *oversophistication* of later Latin literature (1965: 243–47). Aurality in the English Renaissance took on such endophoric forms as Gabriel Harvey's co-readings of Livy with various patrons and fellow scholars (Jardine and Grafton 1990), or Roger Ascham's readings of Demosthenes with Queen Elizabeth (*Schoolmaster*, p. 7) (see chapter 5).

One particular form of orality that had always borne a relatively endophoric character was rhetoric. Perhaps because of its potential to unsettle the customary arguments about orality's deficiencies, this connection has rarely been made. Even Walter Ong, who has written extensively about rhetoric and considers it a form of oral residue (e.g., 1971; 1982: 109; 1984: 3–4), has not tested his essentialist characterizations of oral mentalities against the writings of the rhetoricians. These authors were all talking, of course, about the oral recitation or prelection of texts written in Latin, the high-status language used only by highly literate and educated men.

Rhetorical orality accommodates many supposedly "literate" traits. Irony is communicated, according to the thirteenth-century rhetorician Boncompagno of Signa, by a speaker's gestures. If we cannot see his gestures (or even, presumably, if we can), "we shall detect an ironic intention by the presence in what he says of *manifestum delictum et immunda conscientia* (manifest evil and impure belief)" (quoted in Spearing 1976: 35). Complexity is considered not only viable but even useful in aural reception. In discussing amplification, Geoffrey of Vinsauf (bet. 1208–13) claims: "it is a step onward when, since a statement merely hops through the ears if the expression of it be abrupt, a substitute phrasing is made for it in the form of a long sequence of statements, and a difficult sequence at that" (*Poetria nova*, trans. Kopp: 42). Geoffrey welcomes originality in the description of a beautiful woman, noting that otherwise such passages may often be "trite and outworn" (p. 55).

Scholars have had some difficulty conceptualizing the possibility of endophoric aurality. H. J. Chaytor, for example, explains the failure of medieval vernacular writers to follow the rhetoricians' "elaborate rules" by the fact that the writers "wrote for recitation, and for recitation at intervals of time" (1945, rpt. 1967: 4). If centuries of rhetoricians are to be taken at their word, however, their rules were always aimed at works written for recitation.

As puzzling to literary evolutionists as the endophoricity of medieval rhetoric is the orality of Renaissance rhetoric. "What may at first be startling," notes Arthur F. Kinney,

> but is nevertheless essential to understand, is that philosophy was displaced by rhetoric among humanists and humanist educators ... Tudor humanists formulated a plan of lessons centered on the trivium of the *ars disserendi*, or the arts of speaking correctly, speaking well, and arguing well. Together such verbal studies would lead men toward individual perfection while also training them to be ideal citizens through reasoning by Aristotelian *pisteis* (modes of persuasion). (1986: 7–8)

Renaissance educationalists thus intensified the endophoric potential of rhetoric, firmly assigning it the job of generating the new, humanistic sense of self that by evolutionary logic should have appertained to the private study of the easily available, printed editions of the rediscovered classics.

Walter Ong, himself a student of rhetoric, has had little success in explaining the modality mismatch represented in endophoric orality. On the one hand, he acknowledges the "literacy" of medieval rhetoric, crediting it to the rhetoricians' bookishness: "The exquisitely analytic oral disputations in medieval universities and in later scholastic tradition into the present century were the work of minds honed by writing texts and by reading and commenting on texts, orally and in writing" (1982: 105). On the other hand, he discounts the orality of Renaissance and later rhetoric by invoking the inevitable survivalist framework: "Over the centuries, until the Age of Romanticism, ... explicit or even implicit commitment to the formal study and formal practice of rhetoric is an index of the amount of residual primary orality in a given culture" (p. 109). Ong's rhetorical *sic et non* leads only to the weak conclusion: "As the paradoxical relationships of orality and literacy in rhetoric and Learned Latin suggest, the transition from orality to literacy was slow" (p. 115).

A more supple model for describing such intersections of bookishness and orality resides in the anthropologists' idea of multiple literacies and oralities. The high Latin tradition of the rhetorical manuals, simply, represents a different form of orality than, say, the "romanz-reding" and *geste*-singing described at Havelok's coronation (lines 2328–29), or than the prelection of romances in Criseyde's paved parlor. Released from the insistence that orality is only ever one kind of thing, that it exists in radical opposition to literacy and books, and that it matches up with a precise list of cognitive traits, we can describe this rhetorical tradition as a highly endophoric and book-involved orality. As such, its persistence as a viable cultural expression "into the present century," as Ong acknowledges, represents not a "paradox" but, simply, evidence of the persistent relevance of a certain kind of verbal dexterity.

CONCLUSION

It is hard to speak, or think, clearly if no words exist to describe what you are trying to talk about. This chapter has been devoted to developing a language with which to discuss public reading. A great part of that effort consisted of developing a language that did *not* discuss public reading – i.e., in unpacking the many disparate meanings conglomerated in the words "oral/orality" and "literate/literacy." By substituting an open-ended, freely overlapping description of these modalities for the previous rigidly polarized and in fact inoperable taxonomic model, and by liberating mentality from its factitious servitude to technology, I hope to have "saved the phenomena" in a more workable, productive way.

3

A review of the secondary literature

In chapter 1, I explored the biases built into the Great Divide and evolutionary paradigms adopted by the "strong" literacy and orality/literacy theorists. Chapter 2 offered a vocabulary designed to enable a more precise and unprejudiced discussion of modality relationships. The present chapter will employ that vocabulary in examining how the depleted perspective of "strong" theory has blinkered discussions of late medieval English literature. Since that literature has always been assessed for its role in the development of literary discourse, I will start with the critical responses that I feel reflect a questionably apt reliance on the Ongian evolutionary model of orality and literacy.

EVOLUTION AND THE MARCH OF LITERATURE, PART 2

As described in chapter 1, the unilinear evolutionism long discredited by anthropologists and eschewed as well by many literary theorists has found a new niche in literary studies under the aegis of orality/literacy theory. Within the model of the march of progress, evolution discarding less efficient solutions as it refines and perfects for the future, the history of medieval English literature is often written as an evolution from primitive/oral to sophisticated/dividual.[1] One rather startlingly explicit invocation of the Victorian antecedents of this pseudo-scientific approach is the recent remark:

> Literary inventions and discoveries carry the very same importance as those of science. Informing us about the world, they dazzle with equal brilliance. If I imagine, say, Chaucer transplanted in that other world, he would most resemble Darwin, encountering for the first time those giant turtles – nature's exotics – in the Galapagos islands. (Sanders 1991: 111)

Driving this purported literary evolution are various interconnected, broadly conceived "technological" events such as the adoption of English as a high-status language, rising literacy, improved technologies of book production, and a rising middle class.[2] Out of some intersection of these influences emerged the Galapagean Chaucer, signaling the advent of true literature – i.e., of literate authors writing for private readers – until with Caxton we emerge into the state of grace represented by the fixed text. Aurality, reduced to a "transitional stage," is identified as either (or both) a "survival," "residue," or "vestige" of "orality," or/and a proxy for the "literacy" to which it was destined to give way.

Some scholars are quite prepared to admit that late medieval English literature was sometimes read aloud. People had to read aloud to each other, these writers point out, because many people were illiterate and because manuscripts were scarce; but the situation improved as literacy rose, paper became available, scribal production increased, and houses incorporated private rooms that encouraged private reading. This "deficiency theory" depicts prelection as the make-do phase of early literacy – a stand-in for the fuller literacy that would take over from it as soon as social conditions and technology allowed.

Deficiency theory allows scholars uncomfortable with public reading to declare it defunct as soon as they can point to traces of technological or educational improvement. Little attention is paid to the evidence that literate people with good access to manuscripts often chose to have them read aloud. Scholars of medieval literature are prone to the "eureka" topos, by which they eagerly identify some single technological factor – most commonly "rising literacy" – as allegedly inaugurating the new age of authors who write self-consciously and in critical dialectic with their tradition, expecting to be read in an interiorized, thoughtful fashion by solitary readers.

Eugène Vinaver is in the mainstream of the eureka tradition when he trumpets the rise of romance in the twelfth century as

> the birth of a world in which vernacular writings were to share with Latin texts the privilege of addressing the reader through the medium of visible, not audible symbols; through words intended to be read, not sung or even recited; and with this went a radical alteration of the very nature of literary experience. The change heralded our modern world in much the same way as St. Ambrose's silent approach to his text heralded our reading habits. (1971: 4)

For Janet Coleman, rising literacy was the sole cause of major cultural and literary innovations in the *fourteenth* century. "The strikingly brief period of transition," she says,

> from a society that consisted for most people in essentially traditional and oral values to a society where literacy was no longer unique brought about the achievements of a Chaucer on the one hand, and the alliterative revival in prose and verse on the other. (1981: 161)

Paul Saenger (1991) finds his eureka in a more esoteric source: "the reintroduction of word separation in the early Middle Ages by Irish and Anglo-Saxon scribes" (p. 210). The importance of this event "was great," he claims, for it

> freed the intellectual faculties of the reader, permitting him to read all texts silently and, therefore, more swiftly and in particular to understand greater numbers of intellectually more difficult texts with greater ease ... [S]eparated written text became the standard medium of written communication of a civilization characterized by superior intellectual rigor. (pp. 210–11)

Donald Howard credits the advent of private reading to a rather later event, the introduction of paper:

> If they had not been so rare, if the materials had not been so expensive, books wouldn't have had this "public" quality. Of course the rich always had some books they could read by themselves (if they could read), and the monasteries and schools had libraries; but all would have been different if only books could have been cheaper. That is why the introduction of paper into Europe in the twelfth century is one of the most important events in European intellectual history – compared to it, the printing press was only gadgetry. (1976: 64)

H. J. Chaytor would disagree with the "gadgetry" remark; in an often-quoted statement, he advocates a different monocause: "The question is sometimes asked," he notes,

> when did the middle ages come to an end? They ended, so far as their idea of literary style is concerned, with the invention of printing. (1945, rpt. 1967: 82)

Derek Brewer, however, gives a good deal of weight to the fourteenth-century fashion for withdrawing rooms. "The significance of such better homes," he notes,

> was that they allowed for private reading not only by day but at night, in the warm if dim light of a candle (which Chaucer says left his eyes bleary). Private reading to oneself is very different from hearing songs and stories in hall. Silent reading demands an individual, not a group, response, more solitary but more thoughtful. (1982: 21)

The effect of Brewer's rather confusing discussion is that the endophoric revolution – the advent of solitary, thoughtful reading – is pinned to a satisfyingly "hard" architectural evolution.

By explaining "orality" as the by-product of technological deficiencies, and crediting the advent of dividuality and endoliteracy to the removal of those difficulties, these scholars both endorse a reductionist view of modality shift and distort the primary evidence. They simplistically apply to the literary sphere the same reciprocal law of technological determinism that Brian Stock and Paul Saenger applied in their discussions of cognitive "advances" (see chapter 1), assuming that any visible "advance" in literary technology (literacy rates, book production) must bring an "advance" in literary practice (dividual reading, endophoric reading), while behind any visible (or alleged) advance in literary practice must lie an advance in literary technology. Scholarly discussions of modalities are likely to become an exercise in imposing this template, reading evidence into the blanks in the record, and ignoring the contradictory evidence that is there.

As we will see in later chapters, medieval historical and literary texts provide abundant proof that public reading maintained its popularity long after the rise in late medieval literacy rates and the advent of word-separation, paper, private chambers, and even print. While illiterates might have listened because they had no choice, and the book-deprived to share out the goods, the evidence shows that many literate members of the upper classes – even those renowned for their libraries – *chose* to listen to books. According to everything they say, they did so because they enjoyed and felt they benefited from the experience; the only technological problems the primary literature tends to recognize are scribal distortion, the need to translate out of Latin or French, and the variability of English dialects.

While technological (and other) changes may have helped, gradually, to change the relative popularity of different modalities, it is far too simplistic to consider any such shift a transparent reflection of technological change. The innate futility of such an approach reveals itself in the citations above, where a chorus of eurekas arises over a notably disparate collection of single causes. More important than the exact cause any scholar pinpoints seems to be the urgent sense that something important changed, and that something technological must have been responsible. Any of the usual suspects will do to provide the sought-after relief of reaching the "new."

The deficiency theory, as applied to medieval literature, moreover ignores the fact that any form of creative expression exists within a social-technological matrix and is subject to change if that matrix changes. The fact that silent movies were rendered passé by sound recording has not prevented scholars from hailing many silent films as classics. Neither the people who created those movies nor the audience who enjoyed them are denigrated for participating in a soon-to-be-outmoded artistic experience. Why is such a defeatist attitude adopted towards public reading – which, unlike silent film, continued as a creative medium long after its evolutionary successor, private reading, had appeared on the scene? As the film example suggests, after all, we have never *not* been in a transitional era.

The evolutionary framework, and the emphasis it places on technological constraints, imply that any evidence of orality persisting into the age of "literacy" is anomalous. To deal with that anomaly scholars have resort to the concept used by the first anthropologists (see chapter 1) to explain curiosities such as the persistence of "savage" witchcraft in civilized Victorian England: namely, survivals. Like rock strata or like the fossils found within them (to recall the concept's antecedents in Lyell's geology and Darwin's biology), cultural survivals preserve into a later age the inert vestiges of a bygone, superseded era.

Scholars, thus, tend to explain the presence in a late medieval text of such traits as formulas, redundancy, or references to the hearing of literature, all associated with a hazily conceived orality, as the carry-over into a new modality of habits formed within the old. References to hearing audiences are considered no bar to identifying a text as intended for private reading – because, by evolutionary logic, its textuality defines the text as post-oral. The most influential recent exponent of this survivalism is Walter Ong, who persistently invokes the idea of "oral residue" (see chapter 1) to explain, among other things, "oral" elements in medieval texts.

The vocabulary used in discussing alleged carry-overs from orality often reflects the Victorian idea of survivals and that idea's pseudo-scientific antecedents. Dieter Mehl, for example, argues that *Havelok* represents "a distinctly literary product and this means that the social occasion has become, as it were, fossilized" (1974: 174). Ronald Waldron finds in fourteenth-century poetry "the remains of an oral technique embedded in written literature" (1957: 794) and notes: "We might naturally expect this intrusion of oral-formulaic features into written poetry to take place in periods when general literacy was increasing" (p. 793). Here, formulas are embedded in written literature like fossils in strata, or intruded like volcanic magma – despite the fact that references to hearing, as well as a certain amount of redundant, formulaic language, would be perfectly relevant and functional in works written to be read aloud.

The logic of survivalism underwrites a common strategy for bypassing late medieval aurality, particularly but not only in the works of Chaucer. "Fictive orality" explains away aural elements in a text as holdovers from the days of minstrel performance, preserved either inadvertently or in a deliberate attempt to foster in a privately reading audience a sense of the happy, bygone days of live performance (what might be called a *nostalgie de la bouche*). Either explanation dissolves the functional aurality of the late medieval author into a fictionalized orality. The actual aurality invoked in these texts may be flickeringly acknowledged but soon disappears into a preemptively polarized sense of the "oral"; all that remains is the aggressively dividual.

The fictive orality argument may have been launched by J. A. Burrow, in his classic *Ricardian Poetry* (1971). "Chaucer was an intensely bookish poet," Burrow wrote,

> and in his metropolitan circles the new age of widespread literacy and the mass-production of books had already dawned. In his *Canterbury Tales*, accordingly, the older face-to-face relationship between narrator and audience, the relationship characteristic of an age when books were scarce, is internalized and fictionalized; and the corresponding features of style are thus accommodated and given a new justification within the poem's fiction, to which in turn they lend strength and authenticity. (p. 36)

The first premise of this argument should by now be familiar: technological progress – higher literacy and more books – was enough to ensure the obsolescence of orality among metropolitan sophisticates. Chaucer's response, the logic goes on, was to fictionalize the performance situation identified with the outgoing format of minstrel poetry. In this way he, apparently, retains for his book-isolated readership the "strength and authenticity" of the oral experience.

This attractive argument depends, however, on an untenable premise. Orality in the form of minstrel recitation (memoriality) may have been in decline by Chaucer's time; but orality in the form of public reading (aurality) was not. By invoking the deficiency theory and conflating aurality (the oral modality he does *not* mention) with minstrel performance and oral tradition, Burrow deprives Chaucer's aural phraseology of pragmatic effect. With no listening audience needing clear transitions, enjoying the author's direct address, or giving rationale to the many aural reception-phrases ("as ye shall hear," "as ye have heard devise," and so on), Burrow must interpret such traits as a mock-orality, a sophisticated, self-conscious adaptation of a forgone stylistic.

Protected by its elisions, the premises of fictive orality keep it completely self-enclosed: anything that points to aurality can be dismissed as fictional, because it is based on a discarded reception format. "On the whole," says Derek Pearsall, for example,

> it can be taken as a general rule that references within a romance to a listening audience do not provide a certain indication of the actual mode of delivery, since some dramatization of the author–audience relationship is characteristic of nearly all literature. On the other hand, references to the written text and the private reader are not likely in a romance designed for performance, since they are not appropriate to the dominant relationship. (1976: 61)

Pearsall's smooth polarizations only work, however, by excluding the possibility of a read-aloud romance, in which references to writing would be quite appropriate. References to the author's or translator's professional reading would be equally unsurprising, and references to the recreational reading of the audience or other people would most likely be format-neutral – there are almost no unambiguous references to *private* recreational reading in medieval English literature.

With the advent of postmodernism and the widespread valorization of artificiality, the fictive orality argument has become almost an accepted "fact" about Chaucer. Some authors seem to admit frankly that they are pursuing it not because it is the more accurate but because it is the more interesting or "relevant" viewpoint. "There is no doubt," says Dieter Mehl,

> that Chaucer belongs to a tradition of oral poetry, that he is essentially pre-Gutenberg, and that serious critical distortions result if we read him with the kind of expectation that the European novel from Richardson to James Joyce has helped to create. But it has also been observed that this particular audience at the court of Richard II is, for us, only a piece of historical fiction. Whatever reality it may have had for Chaucer, for us it can never be more than an abstract reconstruction which does not really affect our experience when we read Chaucer. (1974: 173)

Mehl then goes on to offer a frequently cited reading of *Troilus and Criseyde* based on the assumption that Chaucer inscribes a hearing audience in the text, in order to provide an enjoyable illusion for privately reading audiences. Does Mehl thus mean to imply that Chaucer rejected his own contemporary reality in order to produce a simulation of that reality for *us*, six hundred years later? Ruth Crosby seems to have anticipated Mehl's arguments thirty-six years before he made them. "Although Chaucer used his verse-tags and stock expressions with artistic skill," she wrote, "we cannot say that his aim in doing so was to create in *us* the illusion that we are listening rather than reading. His aim was to hold the interest of a fourteenth-century English audience that actually would be listening" (1938: 432).

Fictive orality has also been spreading beyond the Chaucerian canon. Evocations of prelection in the poems of the Alliterative Revival, says Thorlac Turville-Petre, for example, represent "a convention which has a *literary* function, ... part of the fiction created by the poet" (1977: 37–38). Alain Renoir agrees that the authors of the *Nibelungenlied* and *Sir Gawain and the Green Knight* invoked "oral-formulaic elements [to] lend the poem an air of archaic legitimacy" (1986: 131).

How can we escape, supposing we want to, from the circularity of the fictive orality argument? If all evidence of orality (or, more precisely, aurality) is fictive, and any evidence of reading is not only factual but co-opted to dividuality, how can we recoup any space for the read-aloud book? The attempt to do so is one major thrust of this book: chapters 5–7 will argue the factuality of aurality from historical sources, from an extended analysis of Chaucer's references to reception formats, and from within so many other literary texts that, bar some century-long, multi-author conspiracy, the idea of fictive orality collapses under the weight of aural reality.

Some scholars who concede the factuality of Chaucer's references to aural performance go on to impose either or both of two amendments (variations on the "yes, but" arguments described in chapter 1). The first says that while Chaucer did envision such performance for his earlier poems, he gradually, as he reached artistic maturity (and moved away from the court), evolved towards writing for private readers. The second amendment claims that while Chaucer expected to and perhaps did perform all or some of his poetry himself for his first audience, he expected equally that his later audiences would be reading his work privately.

Attempts to sustain the argument that Chaucer telescoped within his own writing career the crucial oral-to-literate transition can lead to a kind of pretzel-logic. After all, in what are actually or very nearly his last written words, Chaucer addresses his retraction to "hem alle that herkne this litel tretys or rede" (CT 10: 1081). If such references are accepted as proof of aurality in earlier works, how would one justify rejecting them in later contexts? Paul Strohm does his best to show that Chaucer migrated away from aurality over the course of writing *Troilus and Criseyde*. "The immediate, aural audience presupposed in the opening books," he says, "is replaced by a more remote 'redere' (v.270), with the aural audience not to reappear until late in the poem (v.629, 637)" (1989: 56). This is hardly an all-out victory for "literacy," with a possibly format-neutral reader popping up once near the end of the poem, ostensibly "replacing" the aural audience – which reappears a mere 359 lines later!

Few advocates of the "first audience" argument are as categorical as Bertrand Bronson, who declared that "Chaucer wrote for the ends of social entertainment and he wrote always from the point of view of one who himself in person would be giving that entertainment" (1960: 66). Yet they are ready to admit, and imagine (often based on the famous frontispiece to the Corpus Christi manuscript of *Troilus*), the idea of Chaucer performing to an audience of friends or patrons (e.g., Brewer 1978: 162–63); the exact composition of that audience, for various poems or periods, is a subject of considerable discussion. In itself, this idea of Chaucer's first audience is an interesting topic with, probably, a good basis in fact.

For those uncomfortable with Chaucer's aurality in general,

however, the first-audience idea provides an attractive escape clause. Chaucer read or recited to his first audience, they agree; but he also wrote for people beyond that audience. Why else would he worry about scribes mismetering his poetry (T&C 5: 1793–96), or contemplate his status relative to Virgil, Ovid, Homer, Lucan, and Statius (T&C 5: 1789–92)? And this further audience, of course, consists of private readers – since that is the only alternative to Chaucer's own oral performance. Paul Strohm supposes that Bukton, Scogan, and other of Chaucer's friends who would hear him read "must share his attention along with a larger audience of imagined page turners, encountering Chaucer's work beyond his control" (1989: 51). Dieter Mehl admits initially that "Chaucer's poetry was written for a live performance, not for the study" (1974: 173). But he goes on to say:

> When, in the Prologue to the *Canterbury Tales*, he warns the reader of what is to come and asks him to skip a story if he does not approve of it, he is obviously not talking to the courtiers listening at his feet, but rather to the anonymous reader of one of the many manuscripts that were soon to circulate. (p. 174)

I would agree with Strohm and Mehl that Chaucer wrote for an audience beyond his immediate circle; but why must that audience have consisted of private readers? Chapter 6 will demonstrate that Chaucer invites his audience, throughout his works and throughout his career, to *hear* what he has written; his use of "read" is either identified with professional literary or scholarly reading, or is format-neutral (that is, it does not select between private and public reading). After all, Chaucer consigns *Troilus and Criseyde* to posterity with the words:

> And red wherso thow be, or elles songe
> That thow be understonde, God I biseche!
> (5: 1797–98)

"Read or sing" is a variant (based on church services, which were literally read or sung) on the familiar bimodal phrase "read or hear."

That Chaucer was unconcernedly projecting into the future the aurality he was used to in his present is further substantiated by a similar but more explicit passage from Christine de Pizan. In her *Livre de la paix* (1413), she addresses not only Louis de Guienne (son of Charles VI) but also other, unknown readers-to-be:

> Because in the future when this present book, if God wills, may have been distributed and read in many places, for books carry on in the world as if perpetually because of the multiple copies that are usually made of them ... (ed. Willard, p. 71)

Having clearly, and optimistically, envisioned her book's textual perpetuity, Christine goes on to admonish Louis and these "other hearers" (*autres oyans*) that its content is true, "and you who hear it can believe it" (p. 72). Thus, writing later than Chaucer, in a more serious genre, and for a more sophisticated court, Christine shows no doubt that the ear will prove as "perpetual" as the book.

Under scrutiny, many medievalists might admit that the evolution they like to trace from bards to minstrels to Chaucer (whose writings are often equated with "real" literature) is an approximation disguising a shift in relative concentrations, not an all-out succession of literary species. They might even accept the presence and force of the continuing references (by Chaucer and writers up to a century after his death) to a listening audience. Stretch them this far, however, and their elastic is bound to snap back with the invocation of survivalism: these references to listeners may have been there, but if so they were either a literary game played by authors who really expected to be privately read, or addresses to the exponents of a moribund modality. In either case, the argument is justified on purely evolutionary grounds: aurality was on the decline, it was superfluous after the advent of private reading, and thus could be invoked only in terms of its incipient senescence. The chronocentric perspective of such scholars tends to confer validity only on what they recognize and value in their own period.

Yet a hundred years after it had supposedly been supplanted by private reading, aurality was still popular and acknowledged – and documented in the historical record. Since people enjoyed and valued the experience of reading together, it should be no surprise that they did not abandon the practice the moment that an alternate modality became technically more feasible. If as a private reader you gained the power to flip around in your copy of Chaucer (and why would you want to, if you were an ordinary, nonscholarly reader?), you sacrificed the warmth, companionability, interactivity, and social-cultural reinforcement of a shared reading. The fact that such reading was increasingly (though never totally) supplanted, beginning at the very end of the Middle Ages and carrying on to the present, is irrelevant to discussion of literature produced before that decline began.

POLAR DIVIDES, PART 2

Intrinsic to the doctrine of literary evolution is the rigid Great Divide polarization of "orality" and "literacy." Only if these are maintained as radically discrete phenomena can any evidence of the latter be considered proof of the former's obsolescence. The depth of the feeling that the two modalities cannot possibly coexist, other than in a fleeting relationship of evolutionary transition from one to the other, emerges in both older and more recent scholarly writings on medieval literature. Faced with the teeming aurality of the primary texts, such authors defend their polarized turf either by co-opting aurality to one pole or the other, or simply by refusing to notice its presence at all.

The best possible illustration of the preemptive deletion of aurality (as opposed to its conflation with orality or literacy) concerns a line that has become the *locus classicus* for birth announcements of the new, post-oral age: the famous "leef" passage with which Chaucer introduces the Miller's Tale.[3] Those who would be offended by the rough language, Chaucer suggests, might wish to

> Turne over the leef and chese another tale.
> (CT 1: 3177)

This line has raised the eureka topos to the status of a hallelujah chorus. "The illusion of fictional oral narration" in the *Canterbury Tales*, writes Paul Christianson, for example,

> is to be only ironically allowed to mask for the private reader, free to "turne over the leef and chese another tale," a recognition of the essential artifice and the accompanying sense of achievement, pleasure, and artful time spent that is inherent in literacy. (1976/77: 115)

Robert Kellogg agrees that the passage offers "one of the great freedoms of being readers rather than auditors." It suggests a new-found power of "choosing the tales in our own order, skipping, comparing, cross-referencing, omitting and re-reading" (1977: 655). Tracing Chaucer's personal evolution from "oral" to "literate," Derek Pearsall notes that with the *Canterbury Tales*, "There was now, for the first time, a general expectation of private reading built into the work as a whole, in several allusions, both in tales and links."

As support Pearsall cites, among others, line 3177 of the Miller's Prologue (1985: 296).

One might think that faith in the dividuality of the leaf-turner would waver among those who paid any attention at all to line 3176 of the Miller's Prologue. Not wanting to falsify his matter, Chaucer begins his warning:

> And therfore whoso list it nat *yheere* ...
> (CT 1: 3176; emphasis added)

Yet even so astute a scholar as Paul Strohm does not hesitate to state, while citing both lines, that Chaucer was writing for

> a reading audience, which will draw its conclusions in private, away from any possibility of Chaucer's intervention. To such readers, encountering his poetry through the medium of a bound manuscript, he refers in the Prologue to the *Miller's Tale*:
> ... whoso list it nat yheere,
> Turne over the leef and chese another tale. (1989: 65)

The control Chaucer ascribes to his audience implies, to every scholar in my "leef" collection, only one possible reception format: private, endoliterate reading. The association between page-turning and (private) reading is so strong that it doesn't need statement, and is not available for refutation. Imbued as they are with this belief, the writers quoted here deal with the prominent, stressed "yheere" of line 3176 by not citing it, by ignoring it, or by dismissing it as an illusion of a fiction (that is, as what I have called "fictive orality"). The word that Chaucer does *not* use, "read," dominates the readings of the passage; amidst the excitement and the assumptions, the single, stubborn word "yheere" is deprived of all resonance.

Yet the "yheere" line is inextricably bound into the if–then logic of Chaucer's statement: *if* you don't want to hear the tale, he says, *then* turn over the leaf. A truer reading of the passage would have to accept that somehow, in Chaucer's mind, hearing and page-turning coexisted. Even scholars who have come so far as to acknowledge both halves of the statement, however, honestly fail to see how they can be reconciled. Jörg O. Fichte's comment is that "obviously two modes of reception are blurred here ... the author momentarily confuses the communicative situation" (1988: 124). And Carl Lindahl can only conclude: "The fact that these two phrases are juxtaposed in the *Canterbury Tales* gives some idea of the problems such [internal] evidence presents" (1987: 159). The eureka chorus may drop to an unhappy mutter once the "yheere" sinks in, but the idea of leaf-turning listeners remains inextricably oxymoronic.

Perhaps, however, that is only because we have accepted too passively the idea of the oral audience's passivity – of their supposed inability to affect the experience they were having. Evoking the manners "we know ... best from the theatre or concert hall," V. A. Kolve assumes that medieval listeners would

> submit to a process strictly controlled by a reader/reciter who, on behalf of the poet, exercises a maximum power over their experience of the whole ... Chances are, for instance, no one will interrupt, or leave before the end. (1984: 15–16)

To this restrained environment Kolve contrasts the private reader's freedom to "read slowly or quickly, one time or many times, from beginning to end or in any other sequence that seems attractive: 'turne over the leef and chese another tale'" (p. 17).

But what happens if we suspend our assumption that medieval audiences sat through prelections as meekly as modern audiences sit through plays and concerts? Or if we shift the comparison to a more informal setting, say an audience at a folk club hearing a favorite local singer? In the latter environment, a fair amount of interplay and negotiation between audience and performer would be quite normal. Indeed, even the folk club comparison fails to reflect fully the power of the medieval listener. In almost every description of recreational prelection I came across in which the prelector was somehow identified, by name or by role, the prelector was of lower status than at least one member of the audience. Maidens read to their parents or their mistress, priests or authors read to their patrons, lovers read to their lady, household retainers read to the monarch. Where the prelector is not identified, the sense is usually that he or she would be at most a peer of the audience's, rarely in the superior position of a performing artist today.

Along those lines, it is not hard to construct a scenario that gives equal weight to both features of the "leef" passage. Instead of a private reader flipping pages she doesn't want to hear, could Chaucer not be thinking of an audience who might instruct a prelector – or of a prelector who might himself decide – to skip a portion of the text? Thus if Criseyde, for example, had not wanted to hear some particular part of the *Siege of Thebes* – because she considered it indecent, or boring, or for whatever other reason – she need only have said, "Don't read that bit. Go on to the part about x"; and her maiden would have complied. Precisely the same action would have brought the same result in any medieval English households where the audience decided against hearing the Miller's Tale. Or the prelector could have decided, on his or her own authority, to turn the page. Or the entire group might have laughed and called for the reading of the Miller's Tale to begin forthwith. Or there might have been a spirited argument, with some later surreptitious private reading by the pro-Miller's Tale faction.

The manipulability of the written book is juxtaposed with its audibility in just this way by another fourteenth-century writer, Robert Mannyng of Brunne. Having instructed the audience of his *Handlyng Synne* (1303) to "lestene & lerne wan any hem [the book] redys" (line 118), he goes on to explain:

> Whedyr outys thou wylt opone the boke,
> Thou shalt fynde begynnyng on to loke.
> Oueral ys begynnyng – oueral ys ende,
> Hou that thou wylt turne hyt or wende.
> Many thynges ther yn mayst thou here;
> Wyth ofte redyng mayst thou lere.
> (HS: 121–26)

Mannyng envisions his audience not only turning a leaf but turning and "wending" their way through the entire book. Yet he combines this hot-fingered textuality with explicit invocations of the audience hearing and listening to the contents. The only explanation is that he expected the prelector, in consultation with the audience, to skip around in the book, reading out rubrics, presumably, until he and they found a section they wished to read together.

This "emergent" or negotiated quality of public reading (see chapter 1) is particularly vivid in the case of Chaucer's other famous aural reader. Alison of Bath had no trouble in determining what was to happen with the leaves of the book she was "passively" hearing, and no shyness about interrupting the prelector: when she saw that Jankyn "wolde nevere fyne / To reden on this cursed book al nyght," she "plyght" three leaves "Out of his book, right as he radde" (CT 3: 788–90). Jankyn was trying, one might say, to transfer to his hearth-side the sort of academic prelections he would have experienced as a student at Oxford, where the higher-status lecturer read and expounded great books to his silent, subordinate audience. As a husband, he was (technically) of higher status than Alison, he was reading from a florilegium of auctorial texts, and his audience was even less enfranchised than a university one, being female and (probably) illiterate. Jankyn had the book, the "read" verbs (nine of them in the Wife's description, CT 3: 669–793), and the voice; but, as he discovers, in a setting that his listener ultimately interprets as more proper to recreational reading, none of these sources of control avails a prelector who will not read cooperatively with his audience. As the Host comments to the Monk, in seconding the Knight's interruption of his tale:

> "For certeinly, as that thise clerkes seyn,
> Whereas a man may have noon audience,
> Noght helpeth it to tellen his sentence."
> (CT 7: 2800–2)

The clash of auralities set in motion by Jankyn's disregard of this clerkly doctrine suggests that another modality tangle may be contributing to modern scholars' inability to reconcile hearing and page-turning. The sort of literacy many scholars find in the "leef" passage is the sort of literacy they exercise as professional academics: "skipping, comparing, cross-referencing, omitting and re-reading" (Kellogg 1977: 655). This is how we read if we are writing a lecture, article, or book on the text(s) in question; it is not how recreational readers would approach a book, six hundred years ago or now. We know that two classes of medieval "professional" readers did engage with Chaucer in a relatively critical, comparative way: i.e., glossators and fellow authors. Unless we are prepared to argue that this is the audience for whom Chaucer primarily wrote, however, we must ask ourselves why the ordinary reader or hearer of Chaucer's time would *want* to engage in the study-group maneuvers envisioned by Kellogg. Many of the less ambitious text-manipulations practiced by modern recreational readers were equally available to medieval audiences: the latter could skip tales by telling the prelector to turn the leaf, or could recover forgotten details by asking the group to remind them, or the prelector to page back and find out.

It is far from clear, in any case, that even medieval academics read in the nose-to-book mode their modern successors celebrate in Chaucer (and themselves). "For surely, you don't think," exclaims Hugh of St. Victor *c.* 1130,

> that those who wish to cite some one of the psalms have turned over the manuscript pages, so that starting their count from the beginning they could figure out what number in the series of psalms each might have? Too great would be the labor in such a task. Therefore they have in their heart a powerful mental device, and they have retained it in memory, for they have learned the number and the order of each single item in the series. (quoted in Carruthers 1990: 263; see also quote on p. 83)

Some scholars might argue that the syntax of Chaucer's direct injunction – "whoso list it nat yheere, / Turne over the leef" – implies that the reluctant listener and the page-turner must be the same person. But one could argue as well that the social melding promoted by public reading blurred the bounds of such agency. Criseyde herself signals the potential strength of this role-elision when she tells Pandarus, "This romaunce is of Thebes that *we* rede" (T&C 2: 100; emphasis added). Here she ascribes to her entire group what might be considered the activity of only one, the maiden who was actually holding and prelecting the book. Criseyde goes on to explain that "*we* han herd how that kyng Layus deyde" and that "*we* stynten at thise lettres rede" (T&C 2: 101, 103; emphasis added), including the prelector among the hearers and extending the decision to halt the reading – which must have proceeded from her – to her co-readers. If Criseyde had ordered any pages skipped, would she not have explained her action similarly: "we turned over the leaf and chose another tale"?

My interpretation of lines 3176–77 of the Miller's Tale may not be the correct one, but it certainly takes the unusual step of accepting the lines as they stand, rather than preemptively suppressing the first and imposing a possibly factitious dividuality and endoliteracy onto the second. Alternate interpretations should at least account for the "yheere" of line 3176, and without the biased circularity of the fictive orality argument – i.e., without assuming that "oral" traits appearing after the advent of "literacy" cannot be evidence of "orality," because "orality" disappears upon the advent of "literacy."

Outright denial of orality's persistence is one common means of reassuring oneself that it has disappeared, or fallen into desuetude. Another frequently seen behavior is conflation, which deals with the persistence of orality by preemptively assigning its late medieval form, aurality, to one pole or the other of the Great oral–literate

Divide. Much abetting any such tendency is the terminological and conceptual poverty, noted in chapter 2, that subsumes a wide variety of phenomena and meanings under the overburdened terms "orality" and "literacy" (cf. D. H. Green 1990: 271–72).

In their attempts to discuss aurality, scholars thus often end up switching back and forth between formal recitation by authors; non-authorial, domestic prelection or recitation; memorial performances by minstrels and jongleurs; extempore oral performance by bards; oral tradition or folklore; and even speech. There would be nothing wrong in discussing a wide variety of formats, of course – if they were clearly distinguished, and the move from one to the other recognized as a change of focus. But very often these disparate entities are lumped into one undiscriminated mass, and points made about one incontinently applied to another. Such confusion will be promulgated even by scholars who, at another point in their text, unambiguously state that much medieval literature was read aloud. Once their attention is on a broader context, however, or once the stakes have risen, they revert to their "default settings."

The end result is often that prelection is marginalized by being conflated into less relevant categories. If reading aloud is somehow assimilated to minstrel performance or oral-formulaic composition, it can be relegated with these less relevant formats to mere background in readings of canonized writers such as Chaucer, the *Gawain*-poet, or Malory. With the aural phraseology thus deprived of pragmatic effect, scholars can interpret aural traits as literary conservatism, or as oral survivals, or as a nostalgic evocation of a defunct stylistic. The most important and influential example of such reasoning is Burrow's "minstrelism" theory, which (as explicated above) equates Chaucer's aural phrases with minstrel tags. By nullifying the living tradition that generated these phrases, Burrow can redefine them as fossil remnants or Chaucerian game.

A more recent trend involves a conflation of aurality, oral-formulaic orality, and actual speech patterns. This sort of confusion hinders Jörg O. Fichte in his intelligent discussion of hearing and reading in the *Canterbury Tales* (1988). The confessional prologues of the Wife of Bath and the Canon's Yeoman, he argues,

> try to imitate the form of free-flowing, live speech. Characteristic of this mode of speech are the following features: asseverations; addresses directed to the audience, such as warnings, pleas for

> silence or attention, apostrophes and rhetorical questions; repetitions; loss of one's train of thought and the recovery of one's argument; *occupatio* and the inexpressibility or inability topos. All of these rhetorical devices serve to create the impression of an oral communicative situation in which a speaker confronts his audience directly. (p. 122)

Most of the traits Fichte ascribes to "free-flowing, live speech" are formal markers rarely found at the more informal end of the oral spectrum. His list, in fact, seems based on Crosby's (1936) and/or Bronson's (1940) compilations of traits characteristic of orally delivered literature, mixed with some rhetorical devices and a couple of Ernst Robert Curtius' (1953) literary topoi. All of these are properly identified not with speech but with forms of oral or aural literature. Fichte – who does not exclude aurality as a reception mode for Chaucer – nonetheless undervalues its influence on the *Canterbury Tales* by failing to distinguish the aural traits present because Chaucer actually anticipated a hearing audience from the "oralizing" traits inserted to bolster the illusion of a fictional performance and audience.

As noted in chapter 1, there has been a recent surge of scholarly work on late medieval "orality." The usefulness of such work is almost invariably undermined, however, by its reliance on the premises of standard orality/literacy theory. The confusions that result are at times acute. Britton J. Harwood, for example, in a recent article on "Dame Study and the place of orality in *Piers Plowman*" (1990), has no other framework in which to view academic prelection than as a form of "orality," which he has no other explanation for than as the transitional vestiges of the movement towards "literacy." Dame Study represents, Harwood says, "the teaching voice" of the medieval schools, and he has to admit that academic orality was a vigorous and, of course, book-based phenomenon throughout Langland's era – although he does what he can to blame its survival on the scarcity of study-texts pre-printing (p. 9). But since he knows (citing Stock, primarily) that "orality" is characterized by the absence of cognitive traits such as abstraction, interiority, individualism, a sense of history, and a separation of self and subject (pp. 3–5), obviously Dame Study's orality must be equally impoverished. But if an ability to abstract and analyze was not to be found among fourteenth-century scholastics, where was it to be found?

Instead of faulting his reductive model for this lack of fit, however,

Harwood searches for softer forms of academic orality that seem to suit it better. He identifies Study, accordingly, with the *lectio divina*, "whether heard in the lecture room or meditated as *sacra pagina*," and links this orality with a prelapsarian (i.e., pre-"literate," or pre-quite-so-literate) mystical oneness that sounds more "oral" (pp. 10–12). The fact that one achieves this mystical orality by close reading of a written text is glossed over in Harwood's conclusion that the Study episode

> recovers for illiteracy a place within the very heart of reading ... The immediacy of preliterate communication is recovered as the integrity of reader and text within the idea that the tropological level of Scripture becomes fully realized only when the reader internalizes it as a change of life. The orality to which the "lewed" are condemned becomes, in the Study episode, not a cause for anxiety, but the oral reading of a text, the first stage of *lectio divina*, and a necessary condition for textual understanding. (p. 13)

Harwood thus collapses elegantly into a great pile of oralities, in which the long-standing reading habits of the most educated men of Langland's period are explained as a "recovery" of a "preliterate" stage (of unannounced but necessarily considerable antiquity), and identified blandly with the complete illiteracy of the completely uneducated. Harwood cannot but go around in circles, bumping over absurdities, because his premises forbid him to recognize, first, that orality (like literacy) can have a plurality of forms, whose traits cannot be predicted from an essentialist checklist; and second, that orality did not become problematic with the advent of literacy, but in fact had coexisted and continued to coexist with it throughout the Middle Ages.

While some scholars have met the evidence for aurality by conflating it with less prevalent or less relevant forms of orality, others have felt equally at home conflating it entirely into literacy. Filed under "orality," aurality slips back and away down the evolutionary timeline, leaving the field clear for the triumph of "literacy." Filed under "literacy," on the other hand, aurality is swept up into the march of literary progress – leaving the field clear for the triumph of "literacy." As with the claims that oral traits prove nothing while literate traits prove that people are reading privately, the logic of this argument is decidedly of the "heads I win, tails you lose" variety.

As a complement to Burrow's conflation of aurality with minstrels, we can note Janet Coleman's statement that in the fourteenth century "the former role of the minstrel, the singer of tales, was gradually being replaced by the private reader or the raconteur, who read what someone else had written" (1981: 56). Coleman here enforces the sense of orality's pending obsolescence by conflating two very different classes of oral performer: the mid to late medieval, (primarily) memorial minstrel and the early medieval, extempore epic composer. To this category she opposes the private reader, with whom she identifies the "raconteur" – who, since he is said to "read what someone else had written," must be equivalent to what I have called the prelector. Aurality thus appears, home and dry, on the anti-oral, anti-minstrel shore of the Great Divide.

Coleman phrases her comparison in these terms, using the unusual word "raconteur," in order to frame her upcoming interpretation of a well-known passage in the mid fourteenth-century *Winner and Waster*. In a grumpy comparison of a better *then* to a decadent *now*, the poet laments the decline of "makers of myrthes that matirs couthe fynde" in favor of beardless boys who "can jangle als a jaye and japes telle" (ed. Trigg, lines 20, 26). While at first glance the contrast seems to be between two sorts of oral performers and genres, the temptation to read the *then* as "oral" and the *now* as "literate" is too strong. Coleman declares, accordingly, that the passage records "the replacement of the minstrel by the poet" (1981: 56). At a later point, she phrases the contention even more starkly: "*Wynnere and Wastoure*," she says, "is quite clear about the distinction between minstrel performers and creative poets who write their own works c. 1350" (p. 124).

As with Chaucer's "leef" passage, where the present "yheere" was overwhelmingly ignored in favor of an absent "read," here a "maker" whom the text insistently associates with creativity is identified with minstrels, a class that the critic specifically excludes from creativity, while creative, writing poets are conjured out of a text in which writing is never mentioned by supposing that the jangling child is reciting or prelecting "the poetry of others" (p. 56).[4] The logical acrobatics are necessary, because the only way literacy can be read into the text's "now" is by interpreting the boy's performance as a prelection, and by conflating prelection into "literacy." While reversing Burrow's polarities, Coleman thus arrives at the same endpoint: the imposition on late medieval multimodality of what Ruth Finnegan describes as the "apparently unidirectional and 'natural' progress based on 'ascending' technologies of communication" mandated by the evolutionary model of literature (1988: 160).

A more direct way to disenable aurality as an independent literary modality pivots off of the hall-to-chamber evolution evoked in Dame Study's famous complaint in *Piers Plowman* (B 10: 96–102). "We may suppose," says Alain Renoir,

> that a poem designed to be read aloud to a small elite audience in the quiet privacy of elegant quarters – say, the way the "romaunce ... of Thebes" is read aloud to Criseyde and her friends in Chaucer's *Troilus and Criseyde* – will use rhetorical devices different from those found in a poem designed to be delivered before a large and heterogeneous crowd at a marketplace. In many respects, the former situation is tantamount to a silent reading by a single person, even though the reading takes place aloud. (1986: 118)

Apart from a reference in the late thirteenth-century romance *Havelok* to festivities including "romanz-reding on the bok" (line 2328), the surviving evidence suggests that reading aloud was always a domestic, small-scale occasion (see chapter 4). To equate such public reading with private reading, therefore, collapses it entirely into dividuality, begging the question of its status as an independent phenomenon. Moreover – given the communalizing and other effects of listening in a group (see chapter 1) – the transition from shared to solitary reading seems at least as crucial an event as the putative decrease in the mere size of the hearing audience. Thus the equation of small audiences with literacy and sophisticated literature seems a piece of special pleading designed to regain for literacy and private reading the ground claimed by the proponents of aurality.

CONCLUSION: THE "LITERACY COMPLEX"

Why should scholarly discussion stumble repeatedly over a fact already well known – and often acknowledged elsewhere within the same critical work? Why should the pioneering work of Ruth Crosby remain, after over fifty years and after an avalanche of orality studies, the only full-scale consideration of aural reception? Through the sort of misreadings and misinterpretations that we have been examining, scholars tend to massage medieval literary history into a particular shape, telling themselves, over and over, the same exciting bedtime story – the one about how minstrels gave way to poets, the ear to the eye, orality to literacy, roistering listeners to quiet, serious readers, blind following of tradition to self-consciousness and creativity. The marginalization of prelection seems to derive most often from an impulse to set as early a date as possible for the advent of "serious literature" within medieval England, and from a persistent misconception, in service of that impulse, of the aural. The feeling, apparently, is that to be real, worthwhile, analyzable literature, to be a *text*, Middle English literature must be completely identifiable as "written" or "literate."

I call this the "literacy complex" because, as in a psychological complex, the presence of any one element tends to activate an entire set of associations. Thus we have seen scholars hailing the rise of literacy or the introduction of paper or the assertion of autonomy or the turning of pages or the jangling of children as proof of the arrival of "literacy" in all its modern splendor. The literacy complex completely colonializes prelection, to the point of eliminating it from discussion.

In place of the "strong" orality/literacy theory of Goody, Ong, and others – and in place of generations of critical underestimation of aurality – we must begin exploring the prolific space opened up for us by "weak" modality theories such as Finnegan's and Street's. The "mixedness" they have found in the cultures they discuss is equally and easily discoverable in the late medieval period in England. We will find it the moment we allow ourselves to trust what our texts tell us – reading them not uncritically, but informedly and in collaboration with other contemporary records. It is present not only within the relatively narrow confines I have set for this book – within secular, court-oriented literature in English – but in many other texts read in many other contexts and in at least two other languages.

In fact, admitting aurality into literary history makes relatively little difference to how one goes about literary criticism. We can still do close readings of Chaucer's or other poets' work – because the work *was* written; the only problem is with manuscript divergences, not with the factitious inability of listeners to have appreciated sophisticated references and patterning. Aural poets' use of formulas can be seen to have had a practical basis – giving their listeners some familiar wording to ease their comprehension. But, as many analyses of oral literature have established, the fact that formulas have a practical function doesn't mean that an author cannot deploy them to artistic effect – which Chaucer and the *Gawain*-poet, for example, do. In fact, aurality is not the big bad wolf that critics seem to think it is; it doesn't diminish the great writers or their audiences in any way to place them in a context of bimodal rather than of private reading. To recognize the true cultural matrix in which these writers work removes a sort of scholarly neurosis in regard to what are considered the polluting effects of aurality. It doesn't close any critical doors; it may open a few; it merely reasserts a basic and too often neglected reality about late medieval literature.

4

The social context of medieval aurality: introductory generalizations from the data

The present chapter makes a bridge between the theory of the preceding three chapters and the intensive data of the following three. With the perspectives enabled by the reformulation of standard orality/literacy theory, this chapter will present some general introductory observations about aspects of late medieval literary culture. These emerged gradually over the course of setting out and analyzing the evidence about reception in chronicles and other historical writing and in literary authors from Chaucer to Caxton, and thus reflect the "ethnographic" methodology I have adopted in approaching my texts.

I will begin this chapter by setting out some of the principles applied in that methodology, and then by reviewing some pertinent background data in order to address certain persistent misconceptions about the chronological trajectory of aurality.

THE METHODOLOGY FOR AN "ETHNOGRAPHY OF READING"

The kind of research presented in the following chapters may perhaps best be described as an "ethnography of reading" – on the model of Dell Hymes' (1962) "ethnography of speaking" and Keith H. Basso's (1974) "ethnography of writing."[1] The mandate of an ethnography of reading would be to describe the interactions of authors, traditions, texts, and audiences as closely as possible within certain clearly spelled-out boundaries of time, place, language, genre, social class, and any other relevant category. In such an enterprise, members of the culture under study are further "understood to be themselves active participants in such model building and so their social and linguistic 'grammars' have to be taken into account also" (Street 1984: 69).

Such ethnographic precision becomes desirable once we discard unitary, essentialist conceptions of orality and literacy. I tried not to apply to my data any wholesale, extrinsic assumptions about modalities, and I would not expect the observations I derive from those data necessarily to apply to literatures in other times, places, or languages. Some may, some may not; it becomes an interesting exercise to examine such correspondences or the lack of them. More importantly, scholars can begin to compile similarly precise descriptions of other modality environments. The cumulation of such studies over time will enable what sociolinguists call "comparative generalization" (Hymes 1962), identifying trends and influences across the domain boundaries (including time) used to structure the research. Any "evolutions" discerned in such analyses will probably be more complex than the unilinear, teleological model often imposed on the data by standard orality/literacy theorists.

Some medievalists have begun to call for such descriptive studies. Evelyn Birge Vitz, for example, notes: "What I think we will have to do is take up works case by case, examining carefully the ways in which they belong to – embody – one or both of these [oral and literary] traditions" (1987: 300). Similarly, Carl Lindahl has echoed the social historians' claim that

> the systematic use and linkage of records can yield a more representative and ultimately more vivid view of medieval life than that provided by a collection of dramatic but haphazardly assembled vignettes. This precept, now considered a truism by historians, has yet to influence Chaucerians, who continue to use the *potpourri* approach to provide historical background. (1987: 4)

There are several things that ethnographies of reading would not do. They would not, for one thing, mix times and places together too freely. Ambrose's silent reading, for example (Augustine, *Confessions* 6: 3), is often and freely compared to Chaucer's, regardless of the miles and the millennium that separate the two. Rather, the fourth-century Ambrose is seen as participating, with Chaucer and all of medieval Christianity, in a universal, atemporal Latin culture that transcended particular times and places. Such an intellectualist approach tends to ignore the "specificity of literacy" (Scribner and Cole 1981: 107) and the uniqueness of the cultures within which even the most intellectual of writers and readers necessarily lived (cf. G. Olson 1982: 24). This is not to say that Ambrose's reading has nothing to do with Chaucer's, necessarily. But it would be interesting to see a discussion that takes their very different historical situations into account and that attempts to bridge the chasm separating them with, for example, later commentaries on Ambrose's reading habits.

Another questionable practice, from the current viewpoint, is to juxtapose isolated cases, attributing observable differences to the texts' relative "orality" and "literacy." Comparing the *Livre de Caradoc* with *Sir Gawain and the Green Knight*, for example, one scholar recently concluded that the latter poem's greater complexity and depth illustrates the superiority of "literate" (or "recursive") rhetoric (Troyan 1990). One might as well declare that men are better writers than women because *Crime and Punishment* is a better novel than *Jamaica Inn*. As Lindahl suggests, the advantage of a more ethnographic approach is that its generalizations derive from a larger, and therefore potentially more reliable, database.

Similar problems arise when passages are isolated from their textual environment, or texts from their generic or historical environment, for display as trophies of the "literate" revolution. As discussed in the previous chapter, one of the most flourished of such trophies – Chaucer's suggestion that we "turne over the leef" (CT 1: 3177) if the Miller's Tale would offend us – loses its glitter the moment we contextualize it so much as to remember the preceding line: "And therfore whoso list it nat yheere." Nor, of course, would it be any more viable to extract references to hearing while ignoring those to reading. The ethnographic methodology suggests that all texts be viewed and evaluated in context. Thus, for the present research, I looked in my medieval texts not just for references to hearing, or to reading, but for any sort of reference to reception. Having collected what I could find, I then analyzed how these references functioned together within the immediate textual and the larger literary environment. As will appear below, this procedure uncovered what seems a characteristically medieval, patterned, and persistent interaction of textual "reads" and "hears" – an insight that would have had difficulty emerging from a research methodology based on trophy-hunting.

The aim of this book is to explore the forms of reading employed for late medieval court-oriented secular literature in English. Religious and scholarly reading are excluded, as are drama and the more popular romances. I concentrate on England and "English" reading but refer often to Scottish texts; generalizations about Britain and "British" reading include both England and Scotland. Chapter 5 includes a comparative discussion of reading in France and the duchy of Burgundy.

My chief sources are the literary texts themselves, including some historical writings such as chronicles but excluding documentary records. By focusing on "court-oriented" literature (i.e., works written by authors associated with the court or addressing issues of national interest), I am able to assume that the potential audience consisted of upper-middle- and upper-class individuals, most of whom would be literate (see Thrupp 1948: 161; Orme 1973: 34).

My procedure with Chaucer and other writers through into the late fifteenth century has been to read everything they wrote (except in Lydgate's case, where I read a sample), looking for any dramatizations of, invocations of, or references to modes of experiencing literature. The most productive hunting-ground, naturally enough, was the "metatexts" – the prologues, epilogues, and rubrics with which authors framed their texts. Analysis of the chronological distribution of reception statements, phrases, and verbs has engendered a variety of conclusions about how authors conceived of their relationship to their sources and their audiences, and about changes in reading patterns over the last century or so of the Middle Ages in England. The first stage in these various investigations was to collect the "raw data" and analyze them. The second stage, which forms the basis of the discussions presented in this book, was to organize the data according to the patterns that emerged as most meaningful.

The nature of my database and analyses raises the important question: can the texts be believed? Many aspects of medieval literature were purely conventional and cannot necessarily be taken at face value. Prologues, for example, often include a range of standard topoi: the author describes the lovelornness that set him to writing, excuses the rudeness of his composition or translation, prays to God or Mary, asks his readers to correct his errors, praises his sources and patrons, and recommends his text for reading or hearing. Are we to believe that all late medieval English writers were grovelingly modest incompetents perpetually nursing broken hearts? Obviously not.

A distinction can be made, I believe, between the author's various self-dramatizations and his comments on more practical issues, such as scribal error, translation processes, and expected reception formats. Certainly, critics of all persuasions do take many such references at face value. The pro-literacy Chaucerians often cite his comments on dialectal variation in the epilogue to *Troilus and*

Criseyde (5: 1793–96), and of course place complete credence in the leaf-turning he describes in the prologue to the Miller's Tale (CT 1: 3177). Any references to reading are accepted calmly as evidence of (private) reading (see, e.g., Christianson 1976/77).

While it is possible that metatextual and other references to reading are pure reportage and such references to hearing mere convention, it is equally possible that both sorts of references are reality-based. The refusal to credit the "hears," after all, derives largely from the technological determinism of the standard orality/literacy model, which assumes that "orality" became obsolescent as soon as there were enough literate people and enough texts that everyone could read privately. If it is true, as argued in this book, that the preference for the social experience of literature preserved the popularity of public reading long past the technological watersheds, then it becomes at least *feasible* that the texts and metatexts genuinely mean what they keep on saying. Such a hypothesis follows Occam's venerable advice against multiplying entities needlessly, and is supported by both historical evidence and the co-occurrence of *non*-conventional phrases invoking aurality. Moreover, as the following chapters will reveal, this hypothesis seems to yield consistent and meaningful results until the late fifteenth century, where the evidence begins to peter out and its interpretation to become more difficult.

We must, finally, recognize that in interrogating the texts we are hearing an informed but not a disinterested testimony. We will discover, in short, what the authors thought was happening; and while that is important to know, it does not always give the whole story. Nonetheless, the basic outlines that can be gleaned from examination of the literary texts are confirmed by historical reports of British and French reading.

THE ETIOLOGY OF AURALITY

Before moving into discussion of the late medieval period in England, it will be useful to review and, perhaps, set to rest several persistent misconceptions about the historical and functional sources of aurality. As background to their comments on Chaucer, in particular, some scholars make statements about reading practices and minstrels that are based on rather naïve evolutionist assumptions. In this section I will examine the evidence provided in the primary material concerning three interrelated concerns: the identification of aurality with the "transitional" stresses of the late fourteenth-century rise in literacy; the role of minstrels as prelectors of books; and the perceived role of "deficiency" (illiteracy and lack of books) in determining the modality by which texts were received.

From the "march of literature" point of view, it seems clear that Chaucer marks the emergence in English of writing authors and privately reading audiences – a configuration previously confined to the elite Latin tradition. The vernacular tradition previous to Chaucer is ascribed to minstrels and memorial performance, with some hazy conception of public reading as an interim modality carried on by minstrels trying to keep their jobs or in households lagging behind the mainstream in literacy or reception preference.

Rather than being a later, "transitional" development, however, aurality (or bimodality)[2] was a popular format for the reception of secular texts in Latin, Anglo-Norman, and English for centuries before Chaucer. I will briefly review here the reports I have come across concerning public reading in that period, first of Latin and then of vernacular material.

An early reference to aural reception comes in William of Malmesbury's *Gesta regum anglorum* (1125). Praising Earl Robert of Gloucester, a natural son of Henry I, William claims:

> You foster letters so, that while you are busy with the weight of so many duties, nonetheless you steal a few hours for yourself, in which you can either read yourself, or listen to readers. (ed. Stubbs, p. 519)

Since William was writing in Latin, he must have expected Robert either to be able to read that language, or to have readers who could translate for him.

Even in this very early report prelection is not associated with technological deficiencies, since the earl was clearly literate (at least as William presents him) and would presumably have had little trouble obtaining books. His behavior falls more into the "habit of mind" framework suggested by Clanchy (1979: 214); for Robert, public reading is a neutral, unstigmatized companion format with private reading, both conceived as pleasant ways to pass time stolen from official duties.

At the end of the twelfth century Giraldus Cambrensis not only describes Archbishop Baldwin of Canterbury graciously "reading or hearing attentively" Giraldus' *Itinerarium Kambriae* (1191; *Opera* 6:

20), but records "publishing" his *Topographia Hibernica* in 1184 or 1185 by prelecting it at Oxford on three successive days (*Opera* 1: 73). The premier rhetorical handbook by an Englishman, Geoffrey of Vinsauf's *Poetria nova* (bet. 1208–13), a Latin text advising on the composition of Latin poetry, assumes throughout that that poetry will be heard. He offers this law to poets:

> let not the hand be in a rush toward the pen, nor the tongue be on fire to utter a word; commit not the management of either pen or tongue to the hands of chance, but let prudent thought ... suspend the offices of pen and tongue and discuss long with itself about the theme. (trans. Kopp: 34)

The famous bibliophile Richard Aungerville de Bury, bishop of Durham, was as bimodal a reader in 1344 as Archbishop Baldwin in 1191. In *Philobiblon* he comments, using the episcopal "we": "we were constantly delighting ourselves with the reading of books, which it was our custom to read or have read to us every day ..." (trans. Taylor: 71).

If the Latin tradition in England seems to have embraced aurality from the early post-Conquest period through the time of Chaucer's birth, it is not surprising to discover that the two vernaculars were equally committed to hearing books. In the Anglo-Norman *Roman de Rou* (bet. 1170–83), Wace advocated prelection of texts such as his own for Norman nobles in danger of forgetting their ancestors' deeds:

> Men ought to read books and *gestes*
> And histories at feasts.
> If writings were not made
> And afterward read and recounted by clerks,
> Many would be the things forgotten.
> (pt. 3, lines 5–9)

In the Fairfax-manuscript version of the *Cursor mundi* (*c.* 1300), the author explains that he has translated his text because "Frenche rimes here I rede / Communely in iche a stede" (lines 237–38). Similarly, in his *Chronicle* (1338), Robert Mannyng of Brunne complains that the books "That we of hym [Arthur] here alle rede, / There [France] were they writen ilka dede / Writen & spoken of Fraunces vsage" (lines 10,969–71). By the fourteenth century, serious English authors were increasingly motivated to translate texts from French because, they felt, the francophone audience was growing too elite and restricted – while remaining nonetheless firmly aural.

Reports of English-language prelection begin turning up in romances at the end of the thirteenth century, just about when English-language romances begin turning up (see Newstead's chronological list in Severs 1967: 13). The coronation ceremonies in *Havelok* (*c.* 1280–1300) include mock-battles, wrestling, stone-putting, harping, piping,

> Leyk [game] of mine, of hasard ok,
> Romanz-reding on the bok.
> Ther mouthe men here the gestes singe,
> The glevmen on the tabour dinge.
> (lines 2327–30)

Other romances pick up the French fashion of depicting attractive young female prelectors (e.g., *Li Chevaliers as deus espees* [early 13th c.], lines 4249–73, 8951–53). The late thirteenth-century *Sir Tristrem* notes that Ysolde "gle was lef to here, / And romaunce to rede aright" (2d fytte, st. 13; ed. Scott, p. 204). Similarly, *Ywain and Gawain* (*c.* 1325–50), a translation of Chrétien de Troyes' *Yvain* (*c.* 1180), preserves Chrétien's scene of a young girl reading to her parents (Y&G: 3084–94; *Yvain*: 5364–74).

One authentically native evocation of female prelection occurs in a Harley lyric that Brook names "The fair maid of Ribblesdale" and dates to *c.* 1314–25. The author, having ridden to Ribblesdale in search of "wilde wymmen" (line 2), praises his choice by claiming:

> Heo hath a mury mouht to mele [speak],
> with lefly rede lippes lele,
> romaunz forte rede.
> (lines 37–39)

If prelection in these romantic contexts is associated with the celebration or contemplation of female beauty, other texts associate it with apparently all-male festivities, in which the hearing of idle tales or heroic romances forms a popular (in both senses) culmination to bouts of social eating and drinking. Robert Mannyng of Brunne notes in *Handlyng Synne* (1303) that he undertook to English his source for "lewed men ... / That talys & rymys wyle blethly here / Yn gamys, yn festys, & at the ale" (lines 43, 46–47). Mannyng hopes his devotional manual will prove spiritually profitable to these men, not by diverting them to private reading and meditation, but by inducing them to listen together to his book rather than to their usual tales and rhymes. While it is unclear how those texts would have been performed, Mannyng certainly expects his book will be prelected: "Lestene & lerne wan any hem [the book] redys" (line 118), he advises; "Many thynges ther yn mayst thou here; / Wyth ofte redyng mayst thou lere" (lines 124–25).

Mannyng makes a similar set of comments about his *Chronicle* (1338), which he translated so that Englishmen ignorant of Latin and French could "haf solace & gamen / In felawschip when thai sitt samen [together]" (lines 9–10). While he speaks of his own writing and that of his sources (e.g., lines 12, 71), he consistently expects his audience to hear his text (e.g., lines 16, 120).

From the twelfth through the mid fourteenth century, therefore, readers in Latin, French/Anglo-Norman, and English show a consistent affinity for public reading. While I have not attempted to assess the status of other modalities, it is clear that "orality" or memoriality did not evolve over this period towards aurality (as an interim or proxy stage for "literacy"), because aurality was present from the start for all three languages. It functioned in a variety of ways for a variety of audiences, just as (as chapters 5–7 will show) it continued to do during and after Chaucer's lifetime. What emerged over the earlier period was not aurality but the use of English.

Many medievalists associate public reading with minstrels, as in J. A. Burrow's conclusion that *Gawain and the Green Knight* was intended "for recitation to a listening audience" during "the minstrel period" (1973: 357). This equation reinforces the sense that prelection is a transitional phase, an episode in the minstrels' decline from recreative memorial performers to musicians.

Of the material we have reviewed above, however, only *Havelok*'s "romanz-reding on the bok" – placed as it is in a context of multiple amusements, including the no doubt professional singing of *gestes* – may be interpreted as a probable reference to minstrel prelection. In other cases where the prelectors are either specified or can be inferred, they are:

authors (Giraldus; Geoffrey of Vinsauf's students);
priests (the Latin readers to Archbishop Baldwin, Bishop Richard, and, probably, Earl Robert, as well as Wace's Anglo-Norman clerks);

daughters of noblemen (Ysolde and the damsel in *Ywain and Gawain*);
or "wilde wymmen" (the fair maid of Ribblesdale).

Mannyng and the author of *Cursor mundi* do not say who was reading the French rhymes and romances they were always hearing, nor does Mannyng mention who might read *Handlyng Synne* to the "lewed men." The prelectors in these cases might have been minstrels. Mannyng's vehement denunciation of professional memorial performers – "disours," "seggers," and "harpours" (lines 72–110) – suggests, however, that he anticipated plain, nonprofessional prelectors for his own work.

This small sample, therefore, reveals a variety of prelectors, of whom only one is fairly obviously a minstrel. Where the prelector's status is unclear, the data do not encourage an immediate assumption that he or she was a minstrel. That this is the situation coming up to the time of Chaucer may not surprise those who assume that minstrels took up prelection as the demand for their memorial skills dropped. The material surveyed from Chaucer's period through the late fifteenth century, however (see chapters 5–7), provides no examples whatsoever of minstrel prelectors. Instead, it reveals more of the same kinds of nonprofessional performers: authors, priests or clerks, and maidens (although, alas, no more wild women), with the addition of valets de chambre, feudal subjects, lovers, husbands, and peer-group members.[3]

Literary evolutionists assume that people read publicly because many of them were illiterate, and because even those who were literate had restricted access to books. These factors certainly affected audiences, and they may account for the habit's origin, but the "deficiency" explanation is one that rarely occurred to a medieval writer. In the texts reviewed above, the deficiencies seen as constraining reading behavior were not illiteracy but "lewedness" – i.e., ignorance of Latin or French – and not the scarcity of books but the scarcity of English-language texts. Even when the listener was illiterate, as in the later cases of the fictional Wife of Bath or the historical Margery Kempe, no sense of apology or inadequacy attends on the description of public reading. Far from being humble, grateful auditors of the enfranchised reader's voice, the Wife violently "edited" her husband's reading material while Kempe, characteristically, emphasizes how much their joint reading sessions benefited the *prelector*, causing "hym to lokyn meche good scriptur & many a good doctowr whech he wolde not a lokyd at that tyme had sche ne be" (ed. Meech, p. 143).

Later authors note some other technological constraints: one thinks immediately of Chaucer's worries about dialectal variation, the mis-metering of his poetry (T&C 5: 1793–98), and Adam scriveyn's *lapsus calami.* A didact such as George Ashby was certainly ready to advise that royal children "be lettred right famously," so that they might learn reason and discretion (*Active Policy*, line 648). Even Ashby, however, writing *c.* 1470, does not insist on private reading; in an earlier passage he had associated the same virtues, reason and discretion, with "Who that herith many Cronicles olde" (line 204).

The context into which both early and late reports of medieval prelection consistently put that behavior is not any form of deficiency but, rather, a highly valued and enjoyed sociability (cf. Coleman 1990b). As in the famous dictum from Horace's *Ars poetica*, this sociability "miscuit utile dulci" (line 343; "blended profit with pleasure"; quoted in G. Olson 1982: 20). Public reading might have the immediate practical profit of enhancing the listeners' physical and mental health, according to the medieval medical theory explicated by Glending Olson (1982). It also provided a more theoretical kind of profit in the form of instruction and wise counsel. A rubric in Sir Gilbert Hay's *Buke of the Governaunce of Princis* (1456), for example, notes: "Here declaris the noble philosophour how it efferis wele to kingis and princis to have and ger rede before thame oft tymes alde ancienne noble stories the quhilkis encrescis thair wisedome and mendis thair lyfis" (ed. Stevenson 2: 103). This view of chronicles as sources of "ensample and doctrine of gude lyfing" (p. 75) is a major factor in reports of French and Burgundian prelection, as the next chapter will demonstrate. As the section on "Public reading and the public sphere" below will discuss, a similar rationale informed much of the theory behind fifteenth-century British specula principis (of which Hay's *Buke* is an example).

The testimonies to the *dulcis* side of public reading are manifold. "Men yhernes rimes for to here, / And romans red on maneres sere [various]" (lines 1–2), notes the prologue to the Cotton version of *Cursor mundi* (*c.* 1300):

> Sanges sere of selcuth rime,
> Inglis, frankys, and latine,

> To rede and here Ilkon is prest [each one is ready],
> The thynges that tham likes best.
> (lines 23–26)

"Sir John Mandeville," in the early fifteenth century, explains that "men seyn all weys that newe thinges & newe tydynges ben plesant to here" (ed. Hamelius 1: 209). Hoccleve's suggestion that Prince Hal could "desporten hym by nyght" in reading his *Regement of Princes* "yf your pleasaunce it be to here" (1411; lines 1903, 2127) is supported by historical reports of James I of Scotland spending the last night of his life "att the playing of the chesse, att the tables, yn redying of Romans, yn syngyng and pypyng, in harpyng, and in other honest solaces of grete pleasance and disport" (1437; Shirley, "Dethe," p. 54). The *Wars of Alexander* (frag. C; *c.* 1450) invokes a similarly gregarious scene with its opening statement: "When folk ere festid and fed fayn wald thai here / Sum farand thing efter fode to fayn thare hert" (lines 1–2). As V. A. Kolve has remarked, "hearing a tale in company was one of the great ceremonial pleasures of medieval society, and it was valued at all levels – by kings as well as commoners, by monks and lay, by 'lernyd and lewyd'" (1984: 14).

As far as my research uncovered, late medieval British texts almost never associate recreational prelection with illiteracy (as inability to read at all, rather than as inability to read Latin or French). I came across one isolated exception, the prologue of the late romance *Partonope of Blois* (second quarter 15th c.), which does seem to assign private reading to the "letteryd" and some degree of ignorance and naïveté to the "lewed" who can only hear their texts (see chapter 7). Yet the *Partonope* author, prescient though he may be, is far outvoted in his time-period and after by authors who continue to assign reading and hearing indifferently to their audiences. The sense of a socially weighted distinction between the two modalities seems not to reappear and gather force until the early sixteenth century. In 1513, for example, Gavin Douglas apostrophized his translation of the *Aeneid*:

> Now salt thou with euery gentill Scot be kend,
> And to onletterit folk be red on hight,
> That erst was bot with clerkis comprehend.
> (*Eneados*, "Ane exclamatioun," lines 43–45)

Around 1537 John Twyne introduced a translation of *The History of Kyng Boccus and Sydracke* by counseling "euery man to rede this boke / or [those] that cannot rede to geue dylygent eere to the reder"

(p. 2). Douglas' and Twyne's hierarchical formulations contrast with Caxton's habitual, indifferently bimodal address to, e.g., "alle them that shal rede or here" his book (*c.* 1484; *Royal Book*; in Blake 1973: 136). Their remarks suggest that aurality began in the early sixteenth century to achieve the proxy status often attributed to it for earlier periods. However, that is only part of the story, since prelection also flourished throughout and beyond the sixteenth century in new humanistic and domestic contexts (see chapter 5).

If we accept Brian Street's methodological guideline of allowing members of the culture we are studying "to be themselves active participants in ... model building" (1984: 69), we shall have to adjust our model of aurality to accommodate the evidence that, as far as they were concerned, medieval people read publicly because they benefited from and enjoyed the experience. While illiteracy and book-deprivation must certainly have influenced the development and persistence of this situation, these technological factors became deep background for what its practitioners perceived as an important cultural and social exercise.

A TYPOLOGY OF LATE MEDIEVAL ENGLISH LITERACIES

Having established, in chapter 1, that "literacy" is not a unitary, invariable entity, we now have the option of exploring some basic functional divisions among late medieval English literacies. ("Literacy" in this case is understood to include both aurality and dividuality.) A revised and expanded form of M. B. Parkes' schema of "professional," "cultivated," and "pragmatic" reading (1973: 555), the system comprises the following forms and subforms of literacy:

PRAGMATIC
- Public
- Private

RELIGIOUS
- Clerical
  - Public
  - Private
- Lay
  - Public
  - Private

PROFESSIONAL
- Scholarly
  - Public
  - Private
- Literary
  - Public
  - Private

RECREATIONAL
- Public
- Private

Whether reading alone or with others, readers in each category read different things, for a different reason, in a different way, and often in a different place. I will try to draw a brief profile of each mode, illustrating them with medieval miniatures when possible.[4]

Pragmatic reading – "the literacy of one who has to read or write in the course of transacting any kind of business" (Parkes 1973: 555) – would consist of utilitarian papers and documents (see figure 1). The reader would read such items to achieve discrete, pragmatic goals, such as to carry on a court case, implement an order, or obtain information. These readers would tend to be administrators, lawyers, merchants, and so on, but women (see figure 2), and men whose professions did not require literacy, e.g., military leaders, might also be pragmatic readers. The activity would most likely occur within a formal "business" setting – an office or a study (or, as in figure 1, a worksite). The goal of pragmatic reading is strictly to find out what the piece of parchment or paper says, and either public or private reading would serve – depending on the number of people who need and are qualified to know what the paper says, and the reader's or readers' literacy and preferences. Most likely, pragmatic goals tended to encourage private reading over time.

Religious reading would be the reading of the Bible, commentaries, books of hours, devotional treatises, saints' lives, and so on with the primary aim of promoting one's spiritual well-being (see figures 3–5). Clerical and lay, public and private forms of religious reading could intersect in a variety of ways. Religious reading could take the public forms of sermons and biblical passages read in church (clerical prelectors to clerical and/or lay auditors), and of mealtime and other domestic prelections within a religious order or academic college (clerical prelectors to clerical auditors) or of a secular household (clerical or lay prelectors to lay auditors). In all these instances, the primary intent would be to create and strengthen a sense of spiritual community, although status tended to accrue to the preacher in church prelections and to the head of household, as sponsor of the reading, in domestic prelections.

Commentators on medieval religious reading have distinguished two important subforms: *lectio* and *meditatio*. Parkes defines the monastic *lectio* as "a spiritual exercise which involved steady reading to oneself, interspersed by prayer, and pausing for rumination on the text as a basis for *meditatio*" (1976: 115). Mary Carruthers (1990: 162–74; see also Leclercq 1962: 23–26) explains *meditatio* as "a process of completely internalizing what one has read" (p. 163).

The setting for religious reading would vary from sanctified locations such as church, cloister, cell, hermitage, and prie-dieu to the more informal locations characteristic of recreational reading (see below).

Scholarly-professional reading would consist of abstruse or technical works on rhetoric, philosophy, religion, government, science, and so on (see figures 6–7). Scholars may have read in part for the pragmatic goal of professional advancement, but their reading would also, presumably, reflect a positive intellectual interest and pleasure; their reading material would have academic and moral dimensions lacking in business papers but would not be pursued with spiritual betterment as the primary goal.

Medieval higher education was premised to a considerable extent on aurality. The "ordinary" medieval lecture consisted of the prelection of a section of a text, followed by analysis and explication of its elements (Kenny and Pinborg 1982: 20), while "cursory" lecturers merely read the text aloud with little or no commentary. Public disputations provided the occasion for regent masters or students to demonstrate their grasp of the complicated texts and arguments they had absorbed (Cobban 1988: 166–67).

While the reliance on aurality is often explained today as a result of the scarcity or expense of books, medieval theorists emphasized the excitement of a shared, enacted, and high-context reading. The Parisian scholastic Radulphus Brito, for example, commented around 1300:

> I rightly contend that we learn more by being taught than we find through our own efforts, for one lesson heard is of more profit than ten lessons read privately. That is why Pliny says "the living voice affects the intellect much more than the reading of books." And he gives the following justification for his contention: the teacher's pronunciation, facial expressions, gestures, and whole behaviour make the pupil learn more and more effectively, and what you hear from another person is situated deeper in your mind than what you learn by yourself. (quoted in Kenny and Pinborg 1982: 16)

The scholastic *lectio*, according to Parkes, "was a process of study which involved a more ratiocinative scrutiny of the text and consultation for reference purposes" (1976: 115). Abelard explicates three possible meanings of this term: "There is the *lectio* of the master (I read the book to them), the *lectio* of the students (I read the book from him [i.e., I hear him read the book]), the private *lectio* (I read the book)" (cited in Chénu 1954: 67).

The importance that these scholars placed on such distinctions reflects the hierarchical structure of scholarly reading. In their lectures, the masters ideally relayed their privileged understanding of canonized texts to a subordinate, submissive audience. In illuminations (see, e.g., figure 6), the lecturer sits in his academic robes on a raised chair, often with a tester (the sounding-board roof that amplified the speaker's voice), and with a lectern to hold the text he is prelecting. Avicenna, in figure 6, is seconded by a beadle holding a mace. Usually, one of the lecturer's hands rests proprietarily on the book while the other points in the "speaking" gesture sometimes known as *declamatio*. Meanwhile, the students huddle on benches below him, some following in their own texts.

One would assume that scholars would be the sort of people most likely to indulge in the page-turning and passage-comparison so often cited as one of the great advantages offered by literacy and books. As Carruthers (1990) has shown, however, the systematic training of medieval scholars enabled many of them to carry and consult key texts in their memories. And even students who owned study texts, Kenny and Pinborg note, used them

> not as their only sources, but rather as abbreviations, reminders of what they had heard. They used written sources mainly as a source of useful arguments or distinctions, not as texts to be relied on for reconstructing the thoughts of others. The written records as we have them are only a limited reflection of a much richer oral culture. (1982: 17)

Nonetheless, we may assume that, outwith the lecture halls and disputations, most scholarly-professional readers would probably have read privately, whether in a library, a study, or (if they owned or had borrowed their own texts) anywhere they liked. For impecunious students such as Chaucer's Clerk, bed might have seemed the best because it was the warmest place to read. Those who read to grasp and possibly add onto complex theological, philosophical, or scientific arguments would probably need the text (and, possibly, its diagrams and illustrations) before their eyes and under their control.

Authors of recreational literature – what I am calling literary-professional readers – would bring to the reading of recreational material (see below) the specialist interest of fellow authors scanning their potential sources and analogues. They would thus combine recreational reading material with something of the attitude of the scholarly-professional reader (although, of course, they were "professional" by avocation only). Authors might read privately, to study or enjoy the subtleties of their fellow-writers, or as part of a search for matter or *sentence* to recast in their own works. Or they might choose to share in a public reading, to observe the audience's reaction or simply to join in the general pleasure. As prelectors of their own work, they would be seeking feedback from their fellow authors or else "publishing" their texts in approved medieval fashion (see Root 1913). All but one of the illuminations I found depicting the reading of recreational material show the author prelecting his text (see figures 8–9; the exception is reproduced as this work's frontispiece).

While "publication" prelections would take place in relatively formal settings such as an Oxford hall (e.g., Giraldus Cambrensis) or a lord's chamber (e.g., Jean Froissart), most literary-professional reading would take place anywhere convenient or comfortable, like recreational reading. In a way, then as now, there would effectively be no such thing for professional authors as strictly recreational reading, because everything they read – as for Chaucer, everything he read (or heard), from tail-rhyme romances to *The Consolation of Philosophy* – was likely to go into their writing in one way or another.

Finally, recreational reading – the reading of anyone outside of activities related to his or her actual vocation or literary avocation – would consist of "literature." Loosely, that category would comprise romances, poetry, chronicles, specula principis, etc., as well as "softer" versions or the less challenging of the professional readers' technical texts, and devotional texts such as saints' lives read in large part for entertainment. Recreational readers read (publicly or privately) to relax, for pleasure or enlightenment or both; and they would read wherever they liked.

Clearly, as in the modality chart offered in chapter 2 (chart 2.2), the categories within this reading typology overlap. Given the dominance of religious ideology within medieval society, in particular, it would be hard to effect a firm analytic separation between scholarly and religious reading of Augustine, for example, or between recreational and religious reading of a saint's life, or even of a popular text such as the *Roman de la rose*. Nonetheless, the various other aspects included in the profiles presented above – such as the setting and function of the reading – should make it possible to identify the dominant categorization of any reading event.

One useful point becomes clear when we distinguish kinds of *reading*, as opposed to kinds of *readers* – i.e., that a given individual reader could well indulge in two (or three) different forms of reading, and choose a different reading mode for each. A widow who has her maidens read romances to her might read her love letters in private; she would thus be a recreational public reader but a pragmatic private reader. A student who listens to a lecturer prelect philosophical texts in the classroom or reads to himself in a library might pass evenings at home reading a popular miscellany to his wife; he would thus be a scholarly-professional public and private reader and a recreational public reader. Chaucer himself qualified in at least two of these categories; as an administrator who needed to be literate to do his job he was a pragmatic reader, and as a professional man of letters he was a literary-professional reader.

The idea of "mixed-mode" reading further undermines the common evolutionist assumption that evidence of any sort of literacy is sufficient proof that the literate individuals would read literature privately. A scholar's ability to con over his texts, as a professional reader, or a merchant's ability to write and read business letters, as a pragmatic reader, cannot be considered evidence of how they would choose to read a romance or a saint's life. It is only the recreational private reader – the person who chooses to apply his or her literacy to the dividual reading of literature – whose habits provide evidence for any contentions about the way in which literature was read in the later Middle Ages.

PUBLIC READING AND THE PUBLIC SPHERE

Further undermining reductive assumptions about public reading is its role in a form of literature aimed particularly at the elite, educated audiences of late medieval England. Drawing on a concept Jürgen Habermas formulated to describe the impact of eighteenth-century periodicals, David Lawton claims that fifteenth-century English poets were engaged in "constructing a public sphere parallel to and connected with the structures of power" (1987: 793).

Terry Eagleton defines the eighteenth-century public sphere as

> a realm of social institutions – clubs, journals, coffee houses, periodicals – in which private individuals assemble for the free, equal interchange of reasonable discourse, thus welding themselves into a relatively cohesive body whose deliberations may assume the form of a powerful political force. (1984: 9)

Although notionally men of any class could contribute, the membership consisted mainly of "the bourgeois middle class and the titled gentry," Peter Hohendahl explains. Yet "status was suspended" in this environment, "so that a discussion among equals could take place" (1982: 53). This discussion addressed itself to the moral and civic issues raised in periodicals such as the *Tatler* and the *Spectator*, and it purported to base itself "not [on] power but reason. Truth, not authority, is its ground, and rationality, not domination, its daily currency" (Eagleton 1984: 17).

Public reading was obviously the quickest way to establish a focus for such public discussion and debate: "The Coffee House became a sort of small-scale Club," Alexandre Beljame notes, "where people read newspapers and pamphlets aloud, or where impromptu orators held forth for or against Whigs or Tories" (1948: 163). The orality of the coffee-house reading and debates encouraged the periodical essayists to adopt the pose of "a speaker from the general audience [who] formulates ideas that could be thought by anyone. His special task vis-à-vis the public is to conduct the general discussion" (Hohendahl 1982: 52). The proper tone for such a modest author was what Eagleton characterizes as "at once mannerly and pellucid" (1984: 22).

While there are differences, the profile these theorists draw for the eighteenth-century public sphere has some striking similarities to theories of late medieval English "public poetry" (Middleton 1978). Of course, the medieval writers worked within a more pervasive religious framework, wrote poetry rather than essays, and reached a much smaller audience. Yet they addressed many of the same issues, from the same point of view, to a similar readership, adopting the same modest poses and accessible style, and relying on a similar mechanism for the publicization of their sociopolitical agenda – public discussion, promoted especially by public reading.

The idea of Ricardian public poetry, notes Anne Middleton, is "to be a 'common voice' to serve the 'common good.'" It emphasizes "secular life, the civic virtues, and communal service ... its central pieties are worldly felicity and peaceful, harmonious communal existence." As the voice of "bourgeois moderation," it assigns "paramount value to peace." Gower, Langland, and Chaucer, she observes, "believe that poetry justifies itself within society, or ought to, as a moral force, in essentially public terms" (1978: 95, 96 n. 6, 104). Similarly, Robert F. Yeager notes that Gower saw poetry "as a powerful tool for moral and social reform" (1990: 66).

David Lawton's view of the fifteenth-century poets tallies closely with Middleton's analysis of the preceding period. He finds in the repeated self-proclaimed "dullness" of the writers he discusses a camouflage for their attempts to counsel the ruling classes. Their task was "to tell the truth, particularly to the great ... to know on behalf of, together with, and as well as any men living. It is to be any man living – a supreme commonplace" (1987: 770–71). This "public voice," as Lawton describes it, was engaged in "a ceaseless attempt to create continuity and unity where in the actual center of power there is instability and 'dyuisioun'" (p. 793).

The genre most allied to this sociopolitical agenda was the speculum principis, a broad category that may embrace any text that undertakes to advise a ruler on the principles of good government. While the ostensible addressee of these texts is usually the king or the heir apparent, the tone, as Middleton observes of the *Confessio Amantis*, "is not a matter of deferential politeness to a ruler, but of rising to sufficient largeness of mind and of reference for a public occasion, and a broad common appeal. The king is not the main imagined audience, but an occasion for gathering and formulating what is on the common mind" (1978: 107; see also Orme 1984: 88–89). Derek Pearsall describes Gower's tone as "that of a man speaking to other men and telling the truth: the simplicity, even transparency, of the English gives an impression of literal reality, of unimpeded communication" (1989: 16); one is reminded of Eagleton's characterization of the eighteenth-century periodical essay as "mannerly and pellucid" (1984: 22).

As Lawton notes, the scope of the fifteenth-century public sphere "reached across council and parliamentary factions, the party divide between court, administration and country, household and household, with a common culture and a uniform model of discourse" (1987: 793). This breadth of audience, which replicates the social mixture Hohendahl identifies as characteristic of the eighteenth-century public sphere, is reflected in the manuscript histories of some of the most popular medieval specula. Owners and readers of

Hoccleve's *Regement of Princes* are known to have included representatives of the "court, government, church, universities, and professions" (Seymour 1974: 257). The early ownership of Lydgate's *Fall of Princes* "greatly extends beyond the social range of Lydgate's initial patrons. It suggests that his audience encompassed the nobility, bourgeoisie, religious institutions and individual clerics – in fact a full spectrum of potential fifteenth-century readership" (Edwards 1983: 22).

The social mobility, the increasing bureaucratization of government, and the growing power of the middle classes were combining to create an articulate, interested audience for literature that expressed their social and political concerns. May N. Hallmundsson's research among Ricardian documents led her to envisage precisely such a society, "in which poetry was read aloud, manuscripts circulated, and political and philosophical conversations were carried on" (1970: 7).

The easy mingling of people and activities characteristic of the coffee houses and invoked by Hallmundsson is reflected in some of the reports we have of late medieval reading. A notice in the household book (the *Liber niger*) of Edward IV, written about 1471, notes that the king's esquires

> be acustumed, wynter and somer, in after nonys and in euenynges, to drawe to lordez chambrez within courte, there to kepe honest company aftyr theyre cunyng, in talkyng of cronycles of kinges and of other polycyez, or in pypyng, or harpyng, synging, other actez marciablez, to help ocupy the court and acompany straungers.[5] (ed. Myers, p. 129)

The squires, lords, and "straungers" who seem to congregate at every opportunity recall the coffee-house cliques, and their penchant for "talkyng of cronycles" seems to imply that for them prelection and discussion constituted one seamless, stimulating activity. The "polycyez" also discussed in these meetings might include specula such as Christine de Pizan's *Livre du corps de policie*, either in the original French or in the translation (*The Body of Polycye*, 3d qtr. 15th c.) that its editor attributes to Edward IV's stepson, Anthony Woodville, Earl Rivers (ed. Bernstein, pp. 31–36). Some such reception seems to be anticipated in the earl's epilogue, addressed to "knyhtis and noble men and all othre generally of what parte that euer they be of that heren or see this lytle wrytyng" (p. 193).

Read aloud to their royal patrons, these specula would give voice to the values championed by the upper echelons of those princes' subjects. Read aloud in the chambers of the nobility and the bourgeoisie, they would lead to joint consideration of the relationships among self-governance, power, and rulership. While readers must certainly have studied these texts in mute isolation at times, it seems their inherent interest and intent could be realized only when these readers went on to discuss what they had read with others, or shared in a group reading and discussion. Aurality, which is usually associated with deficiency or lack of sophistication, thus emerges as a key means of achieving very sophisticated sociopolitical goals.

THE AURAL-NARRATIVE CONSTELLATION

The various elements we have been reviewing as native to the transmission and reception of late medieval court-oriented literature fit together into a complex system of reception-phrases involving tradition, source, author, modality, and audience. Positioned between the unintellectualism of popular romances and the aggressive self-aggrandizement of the English Renaissance, authors within this system maintained a relatively exophoric stance as recreative purveyors of traditional "solace and sentence" to their audience of participatory listeners and readers. The typology offered above will enable us to disentangle important, and hitherto often occluded, distinctions between the literary-professional, usually private reading of the author and the recreational, usually public reading of the audience.

The idea of fitting these elements into a transmission-reception system emerged gradually from analysis of the reception-statements included in late medieval British literature. I call this system the "aural-narrative constellation" because its primary function is to frame the (usually) aural presentation of the (usually) brief, (usually) non-original narratives characteristic of the period. The system forms a "constellation" because all of its various constituents – i.e., its references to writing, reading, and hearing – are equally valuable but necessarily understood only in relation to each other. By contrast, a "complex," like the monopole "literacy complex" often imposed by critics on Chaucer's writing (see chapter 3), effects meaning by drawing all other phenomena into relation to one dominant, obsessive theme – "literacy." By selective quotation and emphasis, scholars may impose a "complex"-type, "literacy"-oriented interpretation on the constellation of interlinked professional and recreational, public and private reading that a less prejudiced approach may discover in medieval texts. That is what happens when scholars pick out Chaucer's references to private (professional) reading and ignore or downplay any references to public (usually recreational) reading – as though, looking at a pattern of dots, they connected only the ones that would make a straight line, refusing to "see" the dots left over.

The aural-narrative constellation is constituted and can be recognized by the use of certain recurrent verbs and phrases indicating transmission and reception. These stock elements are superficial markers that alert us to the system's operation and that reliably direct energies along the accustomed conceptual channels. They may be scattered indiscriminately through the text or packed closely together within a prologue or proem, while the text may or may not invoke actual reading events as well. I will outline the chief points here, based largely on the work of Chaucer. Chapter 7 will follow the course of this constellation through to its declination in the late fifteenth century.

This analysis will look mostly at the verbs "write," "read," and "hear" or "hearken." Given the limitations of time, I have not attempted to collect and analyze statements that use the verbs "say" or "tell" to carry a source-reference, or "endite" and "make" to describe composition (see Middleton 1980: 50–51 n. 13 *re* "endite," and 53 n. 14 *re* "make"). I have also refrained, on the same grounds, from investigating "see," "look," and "behold." While these sometimes refer obviously to private reading, they often seem to float around in a very loose semantic space, suggesting any form of experience from actual visual contact to understanding, experiencing, or interior visualization.

Invitations to "hear" or "hearken" what an author is about to "say" may also be no more than metaphorical or rhetorical. This is especially so with the aureate fashion for what may be called "afflatus imagery"; the author of the *Court of Sapience* (mid 15th c.), for example, implores Clio "that my mouthe maye blowe and encense oute / The redolent dulcour aromatyke / Of thy depured lusty rethoryck!" (lines 26–28). Such "oral" imagery obviously cannot be cited as evidence of the reception format the author was anticipating for his work. Yet, as D. H. Green points out, "to establish the possibility that *hoeren* and *sagen* [*hear* and *say*] can be used figuratively is not the same thing as demonstrating that they must always so be used" (1984: 296–97). In collecting the "hear" verbs assessed below and in chapters 5–7, I have tried to weed out any obviously figurative cases.

Sources "write"

There is no doubt about the textuality of the transmission end of the aural-narrative constellation. Chaucer speaks in many ways of sources that "write." These include specific or generic sources who provide commonplaces, as well as specific authorities mentioned generally or cited as the source of a particular tale. The idea of generic authority – tradition concatenated into anonymous "clerks," "philosophers," "men," or even impersonal constructions – seems, appropriately, most allied to the use of formulas. The Manciple, for example, uses a stock expression when he declares it foolish "To spille labour for to kepe wyves: / Thus writen olde clerkes in hir lyves" (CT 9: 153–54).

Another popular phrase is "as I/men written find"; e.g., the Second Nun's comment that Cecilia "nevere cessed, as I writen fynde, / Of hir preyere" (CT 8: 124–25). The "Melibee" has a penchant for the solemn "it is written"; Prudence, for example, announces: "For it is writen that 'he that moost curteisly comandeth, to hym men most obeyen'" (CT 7: 1857). Also contributing to the sense of traditional authority is Chaucer's frequent use of the word "old" to describe authors and books; at one point he even reads "a bok, was write with lettres olde" (PF: 19). These phrases and terms serve to reinforce – even within Chaucer's only obliquely didactic texts and despite his endophoric ironies and masks – his commitment to the idea of a massed, communalizing force of traditional wisdom lying behind any given writer's personal variations.

Chaucer's direct references to named authorities are less formulaic, consisting usually of some arrangement of some or all of the basic syntactic elements: author writes book about subject. The Clerk states simply, "Petrak writeth / This storie" (CT 4: 1147–48), while the Monk apostrophizes at length: "Lucan, to thee this storie I recomende, / And to Swetoun, and to Valerius also, / That of this storie writen word and ende" (CT 7: 2719–21).

The insistent invocation of written sources characteristic of Chaucer and other authors of court-oriented literature (that is, of the more ambitious vernacular literature) contrasts with the easy-going sourcelessness of the earlier and contemporary popular romances in

English. The authors of these were content to establish the provenance of their stories with vague phrases – "as it is told in tale" (e.g., *Emaré* [c. 1400], line 465), for example; or "as says the book" (e.g., *Ywain and Gawain* [1325–50], lines 9, 3209). If a romance cites a purportedly academic source, it is with considerable and un-ironic naïveté; *Le Bone Florence of Rome* (late 14th c.), for example, reaches heights of self-authentication with its:

> Pope Symonde thys story wrate
> In the Cronykyls of Rome ys the date
> Who sekyth there he may hyt fynde.
> (lines 2173–75)

Although, as noted, Chaucer seeks to build the sense of a large body of generic authority lying behind his and his characters' statements, authority for him does not reside in bookless tales or authorless books. His statements about sources generally specify either (or both) that they are written or that somebody wrote them. Instead of "as it is told in tale," he has, "as writen folk biforn" (CT 5: 551); instead of "as says the book," "as seyth myn autour" (T&C 3: 502). This balance between the exophoric communality of tradition and the endophoric authority of the individual is characteristic of the aural-narrative constellation.

Author "reads" sources

If there is no doubt that the source is written, there is equally little question that the author reads it privately. A standard phrase by which Chaucer introduces his source material is "as I read" (e.g., "In sondry wises shewed, as I rede, / The folk of Troie hire observaunces olde" [T&C 1: 159–60]); the words readily evoke a picture of the author working with his sources open before him. The common use of the phrase "as I read" in contemporary vernacular sermons adds to the connotation of serious consultative reading (see Owst 1961: e.g., pp. 150, 161, 168, 191, and esp. p. 179).

In four of his dream visions – the *Book of the Duchess*, the *House of Fame*, the *Parliament of Fowls*, and the prologue to the *Legend of Good Women* – Chaucer also depicts himself reading. As argued in chapter 6, while Chaucer usually introduces his bibliophilia casually, as though it were a purely recreational pastime, each poem eventually connects his reading to the creation of further poems (especially the one in which the reading is recounted). These dramatized reading-events thus align with the emphasis on the sources that the poet is recycling into his own, re-narrated tale; along with the "as I read" phrase borrowed from pulpit rhetoric, they promote a sense of the author as a professional reader conning over and creatively reinterpreting established sources.

Author "writes"

Having read, and probably with his books still open around him, the author writes. Chaucer does not have any regular formulas for this process, unless "I write" could be considered a formula. Nonetheless, he refers to his writing numerous times, either directly in his own voice or through that of the Man of Law and the God of Love. His awareness of writing as the process of creating physical texts comes through in a couplet rhyming carefully distinguished verbs: "And now my penne, allas, with which I write, / Quaketh for drede of that I moste endite" (T&C 4: 13–14). The issue of writing comes up several times as part of an *occupatio*; this becomes a poignant motif in the *Legend of Good Women*, where for the third time in the tale of Phyllis, for instance, Chaucer declines to carry on: "But al hire letter wryten I ne may / By order, for it were to me a charge" (LGW: 2513–14). Here "write," as an activity pursued under mounting difficulties, seems to verge on the reduced sense of "transcribe."

Chaucer's various uses of the verb "write" – in invocations, to comment on or condense the narrative – create a sense of the author actively engaging with his tradition, his sources, his own resources, and the innumerable professional issues of narrative content, procedure, and style to produce the text his audience is experiencing.

Audiences "hear" (or "read"), or "read and/or hear"

The author may envisage an actual audience, whose traits he will describe and whom he will address directly (sometimes in apparent jest, as in the common reference to irate female hearers). When he speaks of his audience receiving his text, the author may occasionally refer unambiguously to private reading (although Chaucer rarely does); far more often, however, he uses an apparently format-neutral "read" or else a "hear" or "now hearken." Chaucer's audience, for example, "may the double sorwes here / Of Troilus in lovynge of

Criseyde" (T&C 1: 54–55); or they are told, "Now herkeneth, as I have yow seyd, / What that I mette" (HF: 109–10).

Chaucer uses the verb "read" infrequently in referring to his audience's reception of his own work. The two clearest indications of a possibly private reading both occur in poems addressed to a particular friend: his advice to Bukton, "The Wyf of Bathe I pray yow that ye rede" ("Lenvoy a Bukton," line 29); and his plea to an unknown woman, "Shewe by word, that ye wolde ones rede / The compleynte of me" ("Complaynt d'amours," lines 67–68). It may be significant that he expected his own intimates to "read" but his larger, unknown audiences to "hear." By contrast, Chaucer uses "hear" verbs to refer to his audience's reception some forty-four times (see chapter 6). The association of authors with the reception-verb "read" and of audiences with "hear" is one of the strongest and most consistent aspects of the aural-narrative constellation.

The bread-and-butter work of keeping the narrative organized is often done with "hear" phrases. Chaucer's Cook, for example, "seyde his tale, as ye shul after heere" (CT 1: 4364), and when Pandarus goes to visit Criseyde Chaucer reminds us brusquely: "Ye han wel herd the fyn of his entente" (T&C 3: 553). Although "as ye shall hear" is also a common phrase in popular romances, Chaucer seems to use it fluently, with no suggestion that he is quoting from a minstrel phrase-book. The one unmistakable carry-over from such usages comes in the mock-minstrel tale "Sir Thopas," with the repeated "Listeth, lordes ..." (CT 7: 712, 833); this phrase occurs nowhere else in Chaucer. There are no standard reception-phrases along the lines of "as ye shall read" or "as ye have read above" (although Gower has a weakness for "as ye have heard above"; see below).

The reception-phrase most common in metatexts – prologues, epilogues, and rubrics – is "read and/or hear," which is very often used in excusing the "rudeness" of one's writing to one's future audience or in asking for their prayers. An example comes in the introduction to the *Treatise on the Astrolabe*:

> Now wol I preie mekely every discret persone that redith or herith this litel tretys to have my rude endityng for excusid ... (lines 41–44)

The modest authors of such formal and wordy excuses may be invoking two different reception channels out of a desire to list all possible reception formats – so that "read" means "read privately" and "hear," "read publicly" (a "hard" contrast).[6] Or "read or hear" may mean "whether you are reading the book aloud or hearing someone else read it" (a "soft" contrast). Or the entire phrase may be "format-neutral"; i.e., the author is content for the phrase to mean whatever the reader thinks it means. Often a series of "reads" or "hears" in a prologue or epilogue will be capped by a "read and/or hear" in a final "sweep" position that seems intended to embrace all possible preferences.

The general pattern of authors and source-consultation "reading" (or "seeing") and of audiences "hearing and/or reading" leads to the hypothesis that two different kinds of reading are being described. As a clerical or professional activity, "read" generally implies the sort of scholastic *lectio* that Malcolm Parkes describes as "a more ratiocinative scrutiny of the text and consultation for reference purposes" (1976: 115). Preachers, teachers, and writers read source texts in this manner, usually privately, in order to generate (re)interpreted texts. Chaucer explicitly connects the two processes, explaining his love of reading in the *Parliament of Fowls*:

> For out of olde feldes, as men seyth,
> Cometh al this newe corn from yer to yere,
> And out of olde bokes, in good feyth,
> Cometh al this newe science that men lere.
> (PF: 22–25)

Many medieval illustrations of authors writing show them surrounded by other books, open and closed (see figures 10–11). In one manuscript of the *Grands Chroniques de France* (Valenciennes, Bibl. mun. 637, f. 1; see figure 11), the following instructions for illustrating the author survive: "Docteur seant en une chere ... vestu en guise de moine et devant lui une table plaine de livres" ("Scholar sitting in a chair ... dressed as a monk and having before him a table full of books") (Mangeart 1860: 513).[7] The "table plaine de livres" is as much an attribute of authors as a lily was of Mary or a scallop shell of St. James.

Invitations to "read" sources function as covert assertions of authorial reading

The poet may refer to the general idea of sources existing and being read – a move that in Chaucer often introduces a morsel of folk or clerical wisdom: e.g., "We han no fre chois, as thise clerkes rede" (T&C 4: 980). Many other references in Chaucer build up a sense of authorities available for consultation by competent readers – "Eek Plato seith, whoso kan hym rede" (CT 1: 741), for example. The formulas "whoso can him read," "(as) men (may) read," "men read (that) ...," and the imperative "Read [a cited author]" occur in numerous variations.

Whether such a comment comes from Chaucer himself or from one of his in-frame narrators, it seems generally intended more to bolster the authority of the one making it than actually to encourage the listener to turn away from the narrator towards the written source. When the Merchant tells his auditors, "In Claudyan ye may the stories rede" (CT 4: 2232), he surely doesn't expect them to gallop off in search of the nearest monastery library; rather, he naturally hopes that they will listen, duly impressed, to his own retelling of Proserpine's capture. Chaucer himself maintains a rather shy but knowing relationship in his oblique source-references. Often a daunting list of authorities is combined with an *occupatio*, as in his summary of Aeneas' descent to Hell: "Which whoso willeth for to knowe, / He moste rede many a rowe / On Virgile or on Claudian, / Or Daunte, that hit telle kan" (HF: 447–50). One is reminded of a lawyer rattling off precedents from his casebooks in order to convince a client to trust his legal interpretations.

These source-references usually use the verb "read." As with the overt references to the author's reading (see above), this usage seems tied to the (in this case covert) professionalism of the reading. "Read" as attached to an authorial or author-like activity of consulting sources, that is, carries a sense of aggressive, interpretive, and recreative interaction – distinct from the more receptive stance of the recreational listener or reader. Even so, the interpretive act is not necessarily a dividual one. As described in a preceding section, academic, or scholarly-professional, reading had a strong aural component. Thus it is no surprise to read the Squire's learned allusion:

> They speken of Alocen, and Vitulon,
> And Aristotle, that writen in hir lyves
> Of queynte mirours and of perspectives,
> As knowen they that han hir bookes herd.
> (CT 5: 232–35)

Speaking directly as narrator, Chaucer remarks in another place, concerning Troilus' martial prowess: "His worthi dedes, whoso list him heere, / Rede Dares" (T&C 5: 1770–71).

In-frame narrators replicate the system

If a character within the text starts to tell a story, he or she is likely to refer to written sources and to move the narration along with a standard "as I read" or "as ye have heard devise." The Pardoner strikes the original clerical note, intoning "For whil that Adam fasted, as I rede, / He was in Paradys" (CT 6: 508–9). The Knight, in relating Arcite's death speech, introduces it with "Thanne seyde he thus, as ye shal after heere" (1: 2762); the Man of Law summarizes a bit of Custance's story with "As heer-biforn that ye han herd devyse" (2: 613). Chaucer's pilgrims are even more ready than he is to instruct their listeners to read various sources; even the loathly lady in the Wife of Bath's tale advises Gawain, "Reedeth Senek" (3: 1168). Such duplication of basic phrases (and modes) within embedded narratives seems to support the hypothesis that aural phrases are the basic building blocks of narrative structure, rather than evidence of any nostalgia-creating strategy or lame-duck minstrelisms.

Occasionally, in-frame narrators replicate the system too *much*

Due perhaps to this isomorphism of narrative phrases, authors presenting in-frame oral narrations sometimes mix their own voice inappropriately with that of their ostensible narrator. The most famous example is the Second Nun who, in introducing her tale to her fellow-pilgrims, beseeches the indulgence of "yow that reden that I write" (CT 8: 78). The Nun is not alone, however; the Knight, the Franklin, the Monk, and Chaucer the pilgrim himself also speak of themselves as "writing" their oral narrations.[8] It is usual to attribute the Knight's and the Nun's mistakes to Chaucer's carelessness in adapting these tales – known from references in the *Legend of Good Women* (G prol.: 408–9, 416) to have been written earlier – to their new framework (see, e.g., Pearsall 1992: 228). That the Franklin, the Monk, and Chaucer in the link to "Melibee" make the same mistake, however, despite the apparent contemporaneity of their tales' composition, suggests a more systemic problem.

Moreover, Chaucer is not alone. Lydgate, supposedly telling the tale of the *Siege of Thebes* to the pilgrims as they return from

Canterbury, not only repeats his master's error – claiming of Oedipus' marriage "I am wery mor therof to write" (line 823) – but trumps it with an aural back-reference – "And of his exile the soth he told also, / As ye han herde in the storye rad" (lines 1406–7). Gower shows a similar affinity for a different form of crossed wires; his Confessor has a habit of referring Amans to tales the latter has "heard above" (e.g., CA 4: 3274–75), a form of reference also found in Hoccleve (*Series*, lines 631–34, 657–58), and in a different form in Chaucer himself (the falcon in the Squire's Tale manages a back-reference with "as I have seyd above" [CT 5: 540]).

As psychologists and linguists know, it is often a speaker's "mistakes" that offer the most telling evidence of underlying structures. As a characteristic mistake within the aural-narrative constellation, the ascription of writing to oral narrators or of textualized experience to oral narratees suggests the fundamental aurality of the process. Creating a fictional situation involving a speaker narrating to listeners, that is, authors have trouble keeping it separate from the "real-world" event of a writer writing a book that will be read aloud to a listening audience. They are liable to think of the oral narrator as writing, and to describe the in-frame oral audience as "hearing read" or "hearing above."

Texts exist in manuscript

The aural-narrative constellation's overall mixture of private and public reception formats, ascribed to author and to audience, coexists easily with references to the present or future writtenness of the story being related – to, that is, its textuality. This text may be invoked in its most physical aspect, as recorded in a manuscript, on parchment, with ink, and as handled by its readers. The obvious example is Chaucer's "turne over the leef" passage (CT 1: 3177), whose aurality has often been ignored (see chapter 3).

Like Chaucer, Lydgate has no problem combining scribal mechanics with a listening audience. Recording Fortune's words to "Bochas," for example, he continues: "But as soone as she gan disapeere, / He took his penne & wrot as ye shal heere" (*Fall of Princes* 6: 986–87).

In summary, the aural-narrative constellation reflects a cultural matrix in which texts are derived from written sources by a literary-professional private reader who in turn is writing for a bimodal recreational audience of public or possibly private readers. Whether or not he will be the prelector, if there is one, this author maintains a strong sense both of his authority as professional reader/mediator of an authoritative tradition and of his actual or vicarious presence to his audience (as narrator or in the person of the prelector). This authority underlies an important cryptotypical distinction between the text's citational "reads" – designating a consultative, recreative activity proper to authors and to others imitating the authorial stance – and the receptive, format-neutral "reads" applied to the audience. The first almost always designates a dividual, the other an aural or bimodal form of engagement.

The author, and his characters, are strongly aware that stories become texts, which become physical books, which, most likely, become prelected words. Neither the presence in this system of a privately reading author, nor the ready acknowledgment that the recreated story is stored on the pages of a manuscript, excludes aurality as the medium for the audience's experience of the text. Oral narrations by characters within the fiction show the same profile of authority-claiming author mediating tradition to his or her audience – which in in-frame narrations, of course, obviously consists of listeners.

No given text is likely to have every aspect and phrase of the narrative constellation operating within it; but many have enough to be judged as participating in the reception-culture the constellation entails and enacts. While aspects of the constellation can be found in Mannyng, it seems to make its first strong appearance in Chaucer. It is not very present in his two greatest contemporaries – the *Gawain*-poet and Langland – but can be found flourishing in Gower's *Confessio Amantis*, written in 1390. Thereafter it appears in the works of many of Chaucer's successors – as a result either of direct imitation or, more likely, of operating within the same tradition and under the same literary-cultural conditions.

By giving equal time to the various participants in the literary communication-loop, the idea of the aural-narrative constellation allows us to model the reading behavior in Chaucer's texts more accurately than does a literacy-biased "transitional" model. Rather than conflating professional with recreational reading and focusing obsessively on evolution along the one narrow track from "oral" to "literate," it frees us to perceive subtle shifts of influence and weighting across a complex system of transmission and reception. Moreover, it allows us to resolve the apparent paradox by which aurality seems to disappear on the eve of the Renaissance while (as various records make clear) persisting long past that date. The explanation is that the end of the Middle Ages in England saw the passing not of aurality, nor of orality, but of the aural-narrative constellation as a way of conceiving and organizing the relationship among author, tradition, and audience.

CONCLUSION: PUBLIC READING ON THE MODALITY PLATEAU

The preceding sections unite along the one axis of public-ness, discovering in many aspects of late medieval English literature a consistent attraction to publicly mediated forms of experience. Medieval writers portray public reading not as a by-product of technological deficiencies but as an emotionally and intellectually engaging, multisensory, sociable, satisfying, and productive focus of human interaction. What strikes them as odd is private reading – or even simple privacy itself. Not only does Chaucer humorously associate private reading with the loss of physical or mental health (see chapter 6), but he portrays solitude as "most characteristically a tragic predicament, forced upon one ... Nobody seems to enjoy solitude or to seek it for pleasure's sake. It seems to be viewed as an unnatural condition to be remedied" (Goodall 1992: 4). With the isolated exception of the *Partonope* prologue, it is not until the early sixteenth century that writers begin to associate aurality with the factor that dominates modern scholars' explanations: illiteracy.

The literary, theoretical, and artistic testimony reviewed in this chapter – along with the detailed discussions in the following chapters – establish that a preference for public, shared experience encouraged medieval English readers to go on reading publicly long after technological improvements had removed the "deficiencies" with which modern scholars associate the practice. It had not occurred to them that they read that way only because of illiteracy and the shortage of books, and it did not occur to them to stop as these conditions changed.

5

Aural history

In amongst the battles, intrigues, and acts of ostentation that form the substance of their accounts, medieval chroniclers also preserved for us an occasional, often fascinating glimpse of contemporary reading habits. In this chapter I will quote and analyze historical descriptions of the recreational reading of secular vernacular texts, in England and Scotland, and in two regions – France and the duchy of Burgundy – with which England had close cultural ties. The Franco-Burgundian material is included both because there are more "field reports" to draw on from those regions, and because they make a highly instructive contrast to the British texts. I will also cite a few reports of the lay reading of devotional material in Britain,[1] again for the sake of contrast to recreational British reading.

This survey is not exhaustive, but within the items included I have applied an ethnographic methodology of bracketing the texts in time and place, reading them in their full context, and seeking to work outwards from the detail they provide. This cumulative procedure has revealed a complexity of reading behavior rarely if ever tapped in the usual quick paraphrase or isolated quotation.

Overall, the extracts that follow below reveal monarchs, nobles, lawyers, and theologians, from the mid fourteenth to the late fifteenth century, reading romances, lyrics, histories, and other works – by having them read aloud. These findings would not be vitiated by any reports of a monarch, noble, or other person choosing to do their recreational reading privately. More such reports may indeed exist than the few I note below. But the two formats[2] do not cancel each other out; as noted in chapter 4, nothing prevented the same individual from reading privately one time and publicly another. What matters, in this context, is not that people may have sometimes read privately, or even that some people only read privately, but that many people – and many important people – went on reading publicly at the same time. Although the evidence below chiefly concerns members of the upper classes, it would seem logical to assume that less notable readers would also tend to read publicly, both because they too preferred that format and, possibly, in imitation of the habits of their social superiors.

While the votes for public reading pile up over the coming pages, the texts will be able to make a further, more focused, and unique contribution, providing many fascinating details about the personnel, manner, time, and places involved in actual instances of public reading. They confirm, too, that public reading took as many and as complex forms as any other kind of reading; within genres and across them, and from one cultural area to the other, we will see a wide variety of motives and functions underlying the experience of public reading. Exploration of these various auralities should help to dispel the essentialist assumption that orality or aurality always entails a fixed set of cultural and literary traits.

The material will be reviewed in two sections, the first dealing with French and Burgundian reading, and the second with English and Scottish reading. The translations are mine unless otherwise noted; I have tried to follow the text as closely as possible.

FRANCE AND THE DUKEDOM OF BURGUNDY

I will begin with the reports from France and from the dukes of Burgundy. These regions and their courts are generally considered to have always been "ahead" of England in various ways, including in the sophistication and self-awareness of their writers and artists. If private reading is a symptom of a more sophisticated, "literate" audience, and if it is to be found anywhere in the Middle Ages, then we should surely find it in the courts of magnates such as Charles V and Philip the Good.

The reports of Franco-Burgundian reading behavior fall into three categories, by genre of text read: romance, love poetry, and histories (often grouped with philosophical and devotional works).

Romance

The evidence of Franco-Burgundian reading events includes a surprisingly small number of romances, although one of them is the single best-known and most often-cited instance of medieval public reading: Froissart's prelection of *Meliador* to Gaston de Foix.

We will begin, though, with Froissart's account of his own reading, from the supposedly autobiographical *Espinette amoureuse* (*c.* 1370). Froissart describes himself as an adolescent during a winter in which he "wanted only to read romances," especially "treatises of love" ("Ne vosisse que rommans lire ... les traitiers / D'amours"; lines 314–16). That he mentions his pleasure "in relating / And in hearing the deeds of love" ("au retraire / Les fais d'amours et al oïr"; lines 322–24) suggests that this reading was shared with friends.

His sentimental education complete, Froissart sallies out, come spring, in search of an appropriate love-object. He soon discovers "a damsel amusing herself / In reading a romance" ("S'esbatoit une damoiselle / Au lire .I. rommanc"; lines 697–98). Froissart approaches the young woman, learns that her book is the romance *Cleomadès*, and accepts her offer to read some of it to him. Then he reads a few folios to her. Later, she asks to borrow a book from him, into which he inserts a love poem – and the relationship is launched.

Ruth Crosby cites the lady's perusal of *Cleomadès* as "one of the few instances ... in the romances in which mention is made of anyone's reading to himself" (1936: 97 n. 4). Nonetheless, her innovative behavior easily gives way to shared reading, which reveals itself as a ready medium of flirtation. Froissart accepts the lady's offer to read the book with compliments about the beauty of her voice (lines 722–23), and fills some eleven lines of verse (lines 726–36) with praise of the "sweet movement" ("douls mouvement"; line 727) of her mouth as she reads him a humorous episode. As with the damsel in *Ywain and Gawain* and the "fair maid of Ribblesdale" (introduced in the previous chapter), prelection, particularly of romances, seems to have had an understood function as a means of self-display for attractive young people (generally women). By taking on the role of reader they invited the admiring gaze of their auditors, while the subject-matter was stimulating without being too serious or too personal.

It was presumably not contemplation of Froissart's beauty that inspired Gaston de Foix to sit through ten weeks of *Meliador*, however – although modern scholars have been puzzled for any better explanation (see, e.g., Tucoo-Chala 1981: 128–29). In his *Dit du florin* (1389), Froissart relates that the celebrated reading began six weeks before Christmas 1388 and lasted until four weeks after. Every night over that span, Froissart left his lodgings at midnight and traveled, often through rain and wind, to Gaston's castle.[3] There he found the count at supper, either in "hall" or "chamber" ("salle" or "chambre"; lines 358–59). In the brightly lit room, Froissart every night read seven pages of his text, as Gaston "listened willingly" ("ooit volentiers"). The reading lasted so long that the count "aloit couchier" (line 365) – either left to go to bed or was already in bed. After sending the poet the rest of his wine to drink, from a golden goblet, Gaston bid him good night.

Book 3 of Froissart's *Chroniques* (1390) adds a few details. As he read, Froissart notes complacently,

> [in Berners' translation] none durst speke any worde, bycause he wolde I shulde be well vnderstande, wherin he tooke great solace; and whan it came to any mater of questyon, than he wolde speke to me, nat in Gascoyne, but in good and fayre frenche. (Berners, II, 71)
>
> (nulluy n'osoit sonner mot, ne parler, car il vouloit que je fuisse bien entendu. Certes, aussi il prendoit grant soulas au bien entendre, et quant il chéoit aucune chose où il vouloit mettre argument, trop voulentiers en parloit à moy, non pas en son gascon, mais en bon et beau franchois.) (ed. de Lettenhove, XI, 85)

A listener so autocratic and sophisticated as Gaston would surely not have given away so much of his time if the readings produced no pleasure. One might suppose, therefore, that Froissart's prelections were the medieval equivalent of a soap opera, with every evening bringing the latest installment. They may have seemed an enjoyable way to pass time during the darkest, coldest months of the year. As the sponsor of this event, Gaston had the opportunity to exhibit his dominance over his courtiers, to exercise his connoisseurship by intelligent comments to the author, and, perhaps, to strengthen his links with Froissart's patron, Guy de Blois.

Romances seem, on this little evidence, to attract some private but mostly public reading; only in the one notable case of *Meliador* was the prelector the author. The single feature that seems to characterize these cases of romance-reading is an exploitation of the genre's episodic nature (see Taylor 1992). This is what allows Froissart and his demoiselle to dip into and out of the text as their flirtation develops, and what keeps Gaston de Foix and his court on the hook (if that's where they were) from night to night over ten winter weeks. Romance seems to go with an atmosphere of relaxation; it offered an

Figure 1: Pragmatic public reading: Vitruvius reading to masons (*c.* 1400–5; France; Vitruvius, *De architectura*; Bibl. Med. Laur., Plut. 30.10, f.1)

Figure 2: Pragmatic private reading: Criseyde reads a love letter privately
(3d qtr. 15th c.; W. France; *Roman de Troilus*; Bodl. Douce 331, f. 19v)

Figure 3: Clerical-religious public reading: Lector reads to monks at meal (mid 15th c.; Flanders; Suso, *Horloge de Sapience*; Bibl. Roy. IV.111, f. 20v)

Figure 4: Clerical-religious private reading: St. Catherine reading
(*c.* 1460; Loire region; book of hours; Pierpont Morgan M. 1067, f. 8)

Figure 5: Lay-religious public reading: Woman reading to Mary as she spins (*right*) (2d half 15th c.; Northern Low Countries; panel painting [detail], Musée d'Art Ancien, Brussels)

Figure 6: Scholarly-professional public reading: Avicenna portrayed as a medieval university lecturer
(bet. 1475–1500; France; Gerard of Cremona, *De medicina*; Hunterian 9 [S.1.9], f. 1)

Figure 7: Scholarly-professional private reading: Charles V of France reading an astronomical treatise
(*c.* 1364–73; Paris; St. John's Coll. Oxford MS. 164, f. 1)

Figure 8: Literary-professional public reading: Sappho reading to three men (early 15th c.; France; Boccaccio, *Des cleres et nobles femmes*; Brit. Lib. Royal 16 G.v, f. 57v)

Figure 9: Literary-professional public reading: Flavius Vegetius reading *De re militari* to an emperor and his knights
(early 15th c.; France; Flavius Vegetius, *De re militari*; Bodl. Laud lat. 56, f. 1)

Figure 10: Socrates writing (Xantippe about to dunk him)
(2d half 15th c.; Anglo-French; Gower, *Confessio Amantis*; Pierpont Morgan M. 126, f. 54v)

Figure 11: Author writing
(*c.* 1400; Paris; *Grandes Chroniques de France*; Bibl. Nat., fr. 73, f. 86v)

interesting narrative relieved of the intensity of the love poem or the truth-claims of history.

One other report, however, builds a more austere framework around the reading of romance. "Why should one praise a reading," Christine de Pizan demands, writing in 1401, "that wouldn't dare be read or delivered, in its original form, at the table of queens, of princesses, and other worthy women, who would have to cover their faces, red with shame? What good could one then gloss from it?" ("que fait a louer lecture qui n'osera estre leue ne ramenteue en propre forme a la table des roynes, des princesses et des vaillans presentes fames, a qui convendroit couvrir la face de honte rougie! Quel bien donques y puet on glosser?"; *Le Débat*, ed. Hicks, p. 56). Pierre Col defends the *Roman de la rose* by disparaging the listening ladies – not because they're not reading privately, but because their blushes suggest, he murmurs, a guilty conscience (p. 103).

Both sides of this famous *querrelle*, therefore, agree in accepting mealtime prelections as an ordinary feature of life for upper-class women. Christine's mention of glossing seems further to suggest that the reading was accompanied or followed by commentary, in which the listeners extracted good lessons from the text. If glossing was one goal of such prelections (rather than an idealization by Christine – who tends to be more prescriptive than descriptive), then the *Roman de la rose* probably qualified as potential reading material less in its character of romance than as a *livre de sapience*.

Love poetry

For the purposes of the present discussion, "love poetry" can be defined very generally as any form of verse dealing primarily with the personal experience of romantic love, in either an autobiographical or a theoretical vein. This genre includes short, occasional pieces, in the sense of poems (ostensibly) written for a particular lady. Other texts are of greater length and usually retrospective of a bygone love or of an alleged love-debate; these longer poems often serve among other things as the setting for many of the shorter, occasional verses.

In his famous *Art de dictier* (1392), a theoretical and practical guide to the short verse forms used primarily for love poetry, Eustache Deschamps cannot even conceive of such poetry as read silently or privately. Rather confusingly, he describes it as a "natural music," "because the *dits* and songs or metered books they [the poets] make are read with the mouth, and proffered by voice if not sung" ("pour ce que les diz et chançons par eulx [les poètes] faiz ou les livres metrifiez se lisent de bouche, et proferent par voix non pas chantable"; p. 271).

Deschamps notes that such recitation or prelection of poetry would sometimes be preferable to singing, "as between lords and ladies in secret and private retreat, ... or [one might] read a book of these pleasant things before a sick person" ("comme entre seigneurs et dames estans a leur privé et secretement, ... ou [on pourrait] lire aucun livre de ces choses plaisans devant un malade"; p. 272). The "seduction context" here invoked would naturally encourage a poet to recite or read his poem aloud himself. Even when recorded in "metered books," however, this poetry "is read with the mouth"; Deschamps, as a sophisticated French poet and contemporary of Chaucer's, writing a theoretical treatise on vernacular poetry, never considers any other format possible.

An example of the retrospective account of a love affair that records the composition and reception of such short pieces as Deschamps describes is Jean Froissart's *Espinette amoureuse*. As mentioned above, the young Froissart began his courtship of his demoiselle by sending her a book, with a poem tucked inside (and duly reproduced, like the others to follow, in the *Espinette*). The lady returns the book, the poem apparently undisturbed. Next, the aspiring lover has a confederate hand his lady a poem and ask her to read it; her response is to mutter it to herself, exclaiming only, "He's certainly asking a lot!" ("Ce qu'il demande, c'est grant cose!"; line 1296). At last, however, she allows him to read a poem to her, and soon is calling upon him to entertain her friends with his poems.

In this literary French courtship, public and private forms of reading flow gracefully together, demarcating not zones or eras of illiteracy and literacy, or of Old and New Readers, but the variable permeability of personal, sexual boundaries. When the lady finally allows Froissart to read his poetry to her, it means she has accepted his love. Thus the poet's struggle is, in a way, to give himself a voice, to create an audience, and thereby to achieve both literary and (at least partial) sexual viability.

The more impersonal love-debate seems to have been equally aural in orientation. The four noble authors of the *Cent Ballades* – Jean de Saint-Pierre, called le Seneschal; Jean le Maingre de Boucicaut;

Philippe d'Artois, count of Eu; and Jean de Crésecque – presented their divertissement to Charles VI, probably during his residence in Avignon in early November 1390. Thirteen of the nobles present then responded with ballades of their own (no doubt prepared in advance) to the pilgrims' *demande d'amour* (Raynaud 1905: xxxiv–lvi). The length of the text (200 printed pages, without the responses) suggests that the reading may have taken place over several days, consecutively or otherwise.

One final example of the reception of love poetry reveals an interesting variation on the patterns established so far. In one of his ballades, Deschamps recounts how he prelected some of the *Voir Dit*, his friend Guillaume de Machaut's supposedly autobiographical account of his love affair with a young noblewoman. Addressing Machaut, Deschamps relates that he presented the poem to Louis de Mâle, the count of Flanders, at Bruges:

> He made me read it, before many knights;
> I began by addressing myself to the place
> Where Fortune speaks so sternly,
> How she bestows her goods on one, and deprives another.
> Of this they spoke, but none left speaking
> Who said anything that wasn't praise of you.
>
> (Lire m'y fist, present maint chevalier;
> Si adresçay au lieu premierement
> Ou Fortune parler si durement,
> Comment l'un joint a sens biens, l'autre estrange.
> De ce parlent, mais nulz n'en va parlant,
> Qui en die fors qu'a vostre louenge.)
> (ballade 127, lines 19–24)

In the spring of 1375, when this reading probably took place, Louis de Mâle was playing host to Anglo-French treaty negotiations (see Vaughan 1962: 10–11). Deschamps, who was already a member of Charles V's household, had probably arrived with the French delegation (whose leader was Philip the Bold, duke of Burgundy). The English party (led by John of Gaunt) also included a poet, Oton de Granson (*Itinéraires*, p. 116). While a variety of contemporary records note the processions, tournaments, dances, feasts, and exchanges of gifts that attended the negotiations (see, e.g., Froissart, *Chroniques*, ed. Raynaud, VIII, 217–19; *Grands Chroniques*, II, 176; *Itinéraires*, pp. 115–16), only Deschamps mentions his prelection, and

Oton figures only in a list of guests at one of Philip's feasts. Poets, apparently, were so commonplace as to deserve no particular mention.

Nonetheless, Deschamps' choice of passage to prelect reveals him as a man of no little diplomacy himself. Rather than read any of the many love poems in the *Voir Dit*, or any of the lovers' highly self-conscious letters, Deschamps settled on the lines "Where Fortune speaks so sternly, / How she bestows her goods on one, and deprives another." No precise equivalent of these lines occurs in the *Voir Dit*. The reference must be to a long section in which Machaut describes a statue of Fortune; the closest analogue to the lines paraphrased by Deschamps seems to be the first motto attributed to the goddess:

> "I overflow and withdraw without restraint,
> Such is the game to which I give myself."
>
> ("J'afflue & me depars sans bonne [borne],
> Tels est li geus où je me donne.")
> (*Voir Dit*, lines 8257–58)

Machaut applies these words of Fortune to his progress in love, but Deschamps tones down the sexuality of Fortune's metaphors, changing the overflowing river and the "game" to a distribution of "goods." His rewording recalls Laurent de Premierfait's somewhat later translation of Boccaccio's *De casibus virorum illustrium*, where Fortune "gives and takes from men and women the good things of the world" ("donne et depart aux hommes et aux femmes les beneuretez mondaines"; BL Royal 14 E.v, f. 291). By invoking the favored commonplaces of medieval political science, Deschamps seems to be moving Machaut's text away from love poetry towards the speculum principis. He seems, thus, to have adapted his reading very cannily to his audience – present in Bruges, precisely, to decide which power would acquire or cede which goods of Fortune.

Deschamps' audience apparently responded with appreciation; they "spoke" ("parlent") and "went away speaking" ("[s]'en va parlant"; ballade 127, line 23) about the unreliability of Fortune, and praising Machaut. Between them, therefore, prelector and audience had turned a love poem into a philosophical treatise, adapted to an environment in which the fortunes of war took temporary precedence over those of love. Meanwhile Deschamps, perhaps exemplifying the function and ambitions of court poets such as himself and Oton de Granson, walked off having gained an important new patron in Philip of Burgundy (Doutrepont 1909: 371–72).

The reports cited above agree in describing public readings (or recitations) by the author (or an author-surrogate, in the case of Deschamps' prelection of Machaut's *Voir Dit*) to literate audiences – either the poet's lady or the members of royal or ducal courts. In either case, public reading (or recitation) seemed best adapted to serve the author's purpose. While a lady's dividual reading of a love poem might advance the poet's suit, surely he would prefer to recite or read it to her himself in some "private retreat," as envisioned by Deschamps. Yet one wonders if even this ideal reading environment would fulfill the poet's whole desire, since it is often hard to believe that the love endlessly announced and analyzed in such poetry was much more than the vehicle for the poet's attempts at linguistic virtuosity, or the ambitious man's entrée to the court's attention. Such certainly seems the case for the Froissart of *L'Espinette amoureuse*. And why else would Deschamps have written a how-to book for noblemen likely to be struck by *amour courtois* and needing a little advice on how to decant their passion into a virelay? As in the case of the *Cent Ballades*, having a poem to read entitled one to take center-stage before the court, dominating its attention and advertising one's skill or, more simply, one's existence. Thus beyond any amatory ambitions, the publicity entailed in the courtly mode of reading poems of courtly love was of itself a key inducement to take up the muse.

Histories (with philosophical and devotional writings)

"Histories," in this discussion, includes chronicles, memoirs, and biographies but excludes documentary records. It may seem odd to lump this relatively informal genre in with philosophical and devotional works, but that is what several of the readers do in the reports examined below – or at least, that is what their chroniclers undertook to ascribe to them.

One is spoiled for choice, in surveying these records of kings and dukes, for reports of aural reading. The *Songe du vergier* (1378) notes that Charles V "every day reads or has read before him from [Aristotle's] *Ethics* and the *Politics*, and the *Economics*, or other moral treatises" ("chascun jour lit ou fait lire devant luy de Ethyques, de

Pollitiques ou de Yconomiques, ou d'autres moralités"; ed. Schnerb-Lièvre, I, 222). Christine de Pizan incorporates this habit in her description (written 1404) of the king's exemplary life-style:

> In winter, especially, he often occupied himself in hearing read various fair histories, holy Scripture, or the *Fais des Romains*, or the *Moralités des philosophes* and other [works of] knowledge until the hour of supper, to which he sat down rather early and at which he ate only lightly; afterwards he amused himself for a while with his barons and knights, then retired and went to bed: and thus, by constant order, the wise and well-educated king conducted his life.
>
> (En yver, par especial se occupoit souvent à ouir lire de diverses belles hystoires de la Sainte Escripture, ou des *Fais des Romains*, ou *Moralités de philosophes* et d'autres sciences jusques à heure de soupper, auquel s'asseoit d'assez bonne heure et estoit legierement pris; après lequel une piece avec ses barons et chevaliers s'esbatoit, puis se retraioit et aloit reposer. Et ainsi par continuel ordre, le sage roy bien moriginé usoit le cours de sa vie.) (*Fais*, ed. Solente, I, 47–48)

Similar habits are regularly attributed to other magnates. Christine assumes that her biography of Charles (written for the king's brother, Philip the Bold of Burgundy) will similarly be read aloud; she ends the first book at a certain point, for example, "because an overlong narration often begins to weary the hearers and referendaries [official reporters]" ("Pour ce que trop longue narracion souventes foiz tourne aux oyans et refferendeurs à anuy"; ed. Solente, I, 103). Another royal brother, Jean de Berry, "dearly loves and gladly hears all subtly made and masterfully fair and polished works," among which Christine lists "books of moral teachings and worthy histories of Roman government, or other laudable teachings" ("moult aime, et voulentiers en ot, tous ouvrages soubtilment fais et par maistrie beaul et polis"; "livres des sciences morales et hystoires nottables des pollicies rommaines ou d'autres louables enseignemens"; ed. Solente, I, 142). Of Charles V's brother-in-law, Louis de Bourbon, Christine notes that "books of morality, of the holy Scriptures and of teaching please him greatly, and he willingly hears them" ("livres de mouralités, de la Sainte Escripture et d'enseignemens moult lui plaisent et voulentiers en ot"; ed. Solente, I, 159).

In 1409, the biographer of Jean le Maingre de Boucicaut noted that the *maréchal*

> takes great pleasure in hearing read fair books about God and the saints, the *Fais des Romains*, and true histories ... On Sundays and feast-days, he spends the time going afoot on pilgrimages, or in hearing read some fair books of the lives of saints, or histories of old heroes, of the Romans or others.
>
> (Moult lui plaist ouyr lire beaulx livres de Dieu et des sains, des *Fais des Romains* et histoires autentiques ... Aux jours des dimenches et des festes, il occuppe le temps a aler en pelerinages tout a pié, ou a ouyr lire d'aucuns beaulx livres de la vie des sains, ou des histoires des vaillans trespassez, des Rommains ou d'autres.) (ed. Lalande, pp. 416, 433)

Philip the Good of Burgundy was described in 1462 as "accustomed to have old histories read before him every day" ("accoutumé de journellement faire devant lui lire les anciennes histoires"; Aubert, *Chronique des empereurs*, quoted in Doutrepont 1909: 467). The anonymous author of the *Histoire de Charles Martel*, dedicated to Philip around 1463, offers a very typical didactic rationale for such reading. "The high, noble and virtuous deeds of the ancients," he notes, "should one willingly hear, read, and most diligently retain for the good and profit that one may acquire thereby" ("Les haulz, nobles et vertueux fais des anciens doit l'en volentiers oyr lire et très dilligamment retenir pour le bien et prouffit que l'en y poeult acquérir"; Brussels, Bibl. Roy. 6, f. 9r, quoted in Doutrepont 1909: 34).

An extraordinary piece of pictorial evidence gives us some idea of the setting for such courtly prelections. Guillaume Vrelant's frontispiece to volume II of the *Chroniques de Hainault* (Bibl. Roy. 9243, f. 1) shows Philip, his son Charles, and his court listening to a kneeling man read the chronicle to them (see frontispiece to this book). In painting this miniature – in 1468, a year after Philip's death at the age of 71 – Vrelant seems to have looked back to the period of the old duke's prime. The scene may represent the "trial reading" of the translation in 1447 (as suggested by the caption to Gaspar and Lyna 1944: 10, pl. 26), or the finished text's official "publication"; or it may simply give Vrelant's idea of how the duke, his son, and his court would have looked during their early interaction with the text.

As is common for audiences in illuminations showing prelection, the courtiers crowd into a tight group, suggesting the bonding effects of group listening. Most of the audience seem to be looking towards the reader, but in the second row of courtiers on the right, two men are evidently carrying on a private conversation – perhaps commenting on what they are hearing, perhaps talking about something unconnected. The award for least enthusiastic listener, however, would have to go to the man shown slipping out the door (left-center foreground) to join his friends outside for some hawking (is the saddled horse held by the squire further down the street waiting for him as well?).

The frontispiece to volume III of the *Chroniques* (Bibl. Roy. 9244, f. 3) shows Philip visiting Jean Wauquelin to commission the translation, while volume I (Bibl. Roy. 9242, f. 1) opens with a beautiful and frequently reproduced presentation scene showing Philip receiving the book from Wauquelin. Although the different volumes present the scenes out of chronological order, it seems clear that the sequence is dedicated to explicating the relationship between the duke as patron and the textual process he sponsored. The volume II frontispiece suggests that public reading is the capping event in this process.

Philip the Good's penchant for hearing books was carried on by his son, Charles the Bold. One chronicler noted that Charles "full willingly takes time to hear read in order to retain the deeds of the ancients" ("moult voulentiers preste temps à oyr lire pour retenir les fais des anciens"; *Anciennes Chroniques de Pise en Italie*, quoted in Doutrepont 1909: 468). Olivier de la Marche notes further that Charles

> never went to bed without having someone read before him for two hours, and there often read before him the lord of Humbercourt, who read and retained [remembered] very well; and he [Charles] used to have read in those days the high histories of Rome and took very great pleasure in the *Fais des Romains*.
>
> (Jamais ne se couchoit qu'il ne fist lire deux heures devant luy, et lisoit souvent devant luy le seigneur de Humbercourt, qui moult bien lisoit et retenoit; et faisoit lors lire les haultes histoires de Romme et prenoit moult grant plaisir ès faictz des Rommains.) (II, 334)

The primary texts provide an abundance of evidence concerning the Franco-Burgundian reading of histories. The hands-down winner in the genre is clearly the *Fais des Romains*, an anonymous history in French prose composed between 1211 and 1214 and concerned mostly with Julius Caesar. That its success, was, as Guenée claims, "immediate, general and lasting" (1976: 262–63) is confirmed by its popularity with Charles V, Boucicaut, and Charles the Bold. Besides the *Fais*, Charles V and the various nobles surveyed above favored histories of Roman, "ancient," or French worthies, which they seem to have heard interchangeably with the Bible, saints' lives, and books of morality and philosophy. This conjunction is justified by the emphasis on the didactic supertext of the historical narratives.

The prelectors

Unlike the love poetry, which was always prelected by the author or by an author-surrogate, the histories in these reports are prelected by someone who is *not* the author. Even in the illumination showing the *Chroniques de Hainault* being read aloud, the standard iconography of authorial prelection is ignored in favor of a "real-life" setting in Philip's throne room and a prelector who seems not to be the author.

The material surveyed above provides some precious details about the men employed to prelect these improving texts. According to Christine, Charles V's favorite prelector was his valet Gilles Malet (who also served as the first librarian in the Louvre palace). Among the "several capacities" ("plusieurs vertus") for which Charles favored Malet was "this, especially, above all others, [that he] read and 'pointed' magnificently well, and was an intelligent man" ("cellui, par especialment sur tous aultres, [qu'il] souverainement bien lisoit et bel [bien] pontoit, et entendens homs estoit"). Christine's word "pontoit" is a technical term of rhetoric; it means that Malet read with a dramatic emphasis that underlined the key emotional or intellectual points of the text. Even on the day his little son died in an accident, Christine comments approvingly, the broken-hearted Malet "was before the king reading for a long time, with an appearance and expression neither more nor less than he usually had" ("fu devant le roy, lisant longue piece autel semblant et chiere, ne plus ne moins comme acoustumé avoit"; ed. Solente, II, 63).

Charles the Bold's favorite reader, Guy de Brimeu, lord of Humbercourt, was not a valet-librarian but a nobleman and warrior. As count of Meghen, chamberlain to the dukes of Burgundy, captain of the castle of Remy, and so on, he accompanied Charles in his wars but was ultimately convicted of treason and beheaded after the duke's death (Prevost and D'Amat 1956: 323).

Although the backgrounds and status of these two men differ

markedly, the texts use almost the same vocabulary in describing their reading skills: Malet "read and 'pointed' magnificently well, and was an intelligent man," whereas Humbercourt "read and retained very well." The chronicler Philippe de Commines adds that Humbercourt was "one of the wisest and most intelligent knights that I ever knew" ("ung des plus saiges chevaliers et des plus entenduz que je congneü jamais"; ed. Calmette, I, 104). Thus both the bourgeois bookman and the noble warlord are singled out as intelligent men who read well. Malet has the extra talent of "pointing," while Humbercourt is noted for his memory – deployed, presumably, for comment and discussion on the text.

That this congruence occurs between texts written many decades apart in different regions suggests a well-understood contemporary idea of what makes a good prelector. As we do today, when listening to tapes or the radio, the medieval listener preferred a reader who could understand and effectively interpret a text when reading it aloud. Thus, rather than being a jury-rigged substitute for private reading, prelection seems to have been viewed as a serious encounter governed by a well-understood performance esthetic.

Private reading

Charles V, Philip the Good, and Charles the Bold are described as liking to "read or hear read" their books, which must mean that they sometimes chose to read privately. These, and the private reading of *Cleomadès* by Froissart's demoiselle, are the only references to dividual reading that I found in this material. Two more private readers may be gleaned by deduction. The author of the *Croniques et conquestes de Charlemaine* (1458) remarks flatteringly that Jean de Créquy, an official of Philip the Good, "by nature enjoys seeing, studying, and having books and chronicles about everything" ("de sa nature il est affecte a veoir, estudier et auoir livres et croniques sur toutes-riens"; ed. Guiette, I, 14). The passage conveys a sense of possession and manipulation that implies, although it does not specify, private reading. Another Jean – Jean d'Orléans, count of Angoulême – also seems to have read his books privately, since their margins are full of his comments (Doutrepont 1909: 466; see also Strohm 1971).

One factor often cited as evidence of private reading in this period – the libraries assembled by the kings and nobles of France and

Burgundy (cf., esp., Saenger 1982: 408) – has little predictive value after all, as this survey has shown. Charles V built a library that reached 900 volumes (Sherman 1969: 13) – and not only is he on record as having frequently preferred to hear these books prelected, but his favorite prelector was, precisely, his librarian. David Aubert praises Philip the Good's aurality and his library with equal fervor: this "most famous and most virtuous prince," he says,

> has since long ago been accustomed to have old histories read before him every day; and to be provided with a library beyond all others he has since his youth had in his employ several translators, great clerks, master orators, historians, and writers, and in various countries a great number diligently working; so much so that today he of all Christian princes, without a single exception, is the best provided with an authentic and rich library.
>
> (Très renommé et très vertueux prince ... a dès longtemps accoustumé de journellement faire devant lui lire les anciennes histoires; et pour estre garni d'une librairie non pareille à toutes autres il a dès son jeune eaige eu à ses geiges plusieurs translateurs, grans clers, experts orateurs, historiens et escripvains, et en diverses contrées en gros nombre diligemment labourans; tant que aujourd'hui c'est le prince de la chrestienté, sans réservation aulcune, qui est le mieux garni de autentique et riche librairie.) (quoted in Doutrepont 1909: 16–17)

Propaganda values

Although the authors and translators of all these bespoke chronicles and biographies always emphasize their virtue of offering "patterns of nobility and perfect chivalry" ("patrons de noblesse et parfaitte cheualerie"; Aubert, ed. Guiette, I, 13), one factor may have ensured not only that the patrons wanted to hear these texts themselves but that they wanted many other people to hear them: their propaganda value. It was surely no accident that these patterns of nobility were usually based on French or Burgundian heroes, and that the prologues usually underlined the patron's participation in that lineage. With such self-promotion in mind, and given the difficulties of mass-producing texts (and ensuring that they would be read if so produced), what better way to spread such propaganda than a public reading, such as the one Philip presides over in Vrelant's frontispiece?

Charles V's program of commissions seems to have incorporated an explicit attempt to defend the Valois monarchy against the persistent counter-claims of the English (Sherman 1971: 85–87). Even the *Cité de Dieu* translated by his *avocat* Raoul de Presles at his request (1375) reflects this effort. Raoul tells the story of Clovis' conversion, with God sending both the device of the three fleurs-de-lys and the baptismal oil, and of the oriflamme sent to Charlemagne (printed in de Laborde 1909, I, 63–67). The prelection of such texts among the upper classes would help to assert the legitimacy of the French line, while, as Jacques Krynen hypothesizes, the ideas developed by Charles' stable of intellectuals would achieve further general distribution via "pamphlets, ballads, and songs circulated by ... heralds, jongleurs, or preachers" (1981: 243–44). One wonders if this ideology even trickled down as far as Domremy, whence Jeanne d'Arc emerged with a ready-made belief in the rights of the Valois monarchy to secure the succession of Charles V's grandson, Charles VII.

We have a perfect illustration of the propagandistic use of historical texts in a detailed description from the reign of the intervening Charles, the sixth. Jean Cabaret d'Orville, the biographer of Louis de Bourbon, describes the dangerous situation following the assassination in November 1407 of the king's brother, Louis d'Orléans. Charles himself had fallen into one of his periodic fits of insanity, and his uncle – the 71-year-old Louis – undertook to fill the gap by holding open house for the hungry and possibly disaffected "noblemen and officers" ("nobles hommes et officiers") of the court:

> [The duke] willingly ate in the hall, in order to see this company. And in order that no one should listen to anything but that for which they sat at table ... he willed that no one should speak, and in order to see that silence was better kept while he was at table, he had ordered that no one, or hardly anyone, should stand before him, except for those who were ordered to serve him ... And so that no one should interrupt him when he was eating, at either end of his table were closed gates, so that no one could pass behind him to disturb his concentration; and to understand better the great affairs he had in the kingdom, as much as counsellor as in other things, which he knew well how to manage, and to renew his memory, he had read continually at his dinner the *gestes* of the most famous princes, the former kings of France, and of other men worthy of honor, ... And when dinner was over, and grace said to God, everyone left, and afterwards returned frequently. This dance went

on so long, that the duke of Bourbon found himself well in debt.

(voulentiers [le duc] mangeoit en tinel, pour veoir celle compaignie. Et pour ce que nul n'entendist se non à ce pour quoi séoit à table ... il vouloit que nul ne parlast, et affin que plus grande silence fust tenue, lui estant à table, avoit ordonné que devant lui ne fussent nulles gens, ou pou, se non ceulx qui estoient ordonnés à le servir ... Et pour ce que nul ne l'occupast en son mangier, aux deux bouts de sa table estoient barres closes, si que on ne peust passer au derrière de lui pour tourber son entendement; et pour estre plus ententif aux grans affaires que il avoit au royaume, tant en conseil comme ès autres choses, dont il savoit bien venir à fin, et pour avoir plus haulte mémoire, faisoit lire à son disner continuellement les gestes des très-renommés princes, jadis rois de France, et d'aultres dignes d'honneur, ... Et le disner estre fait, grâces dictes à Dieu, s'en partoit chascun, et après retournoient souvent. Si dura si longuement ceste dance, que le duc de Bourbon se trouva bien endebté.) (ed. Chazaud, pp. 272–73)

Jean frames his account with political events: Louis d'Orléans' assassination, the king's madness. While describing the meals, however, he emphasizes only the old duke's generosity and the didactic function of the reading. Bourbon supposedly uses it to improve himself, to understand and remember history. His guests, listening in enforced silence, presumably are meant to derive similar apolitical benefits. Yet politics seem to lurk throughout the scene; the elaborate seating arrangements that Bourbon demands, and that Jean attributes strictly to his desire to hear the reading without distraction, seem designed to prevent all but a few trusted people from approaching the duke. In opening his house to Charles VI's hangers-on in the wake of the murder of Louis d'Orléans, was Louis afraid that he'd let in a potential assassin? Did he enforce silence because he was afraid that conversation would become conspiracy – or, at least, be a vehicle for criticisms of the king and his regime? Into this charged situation, Louis chose to launch a public reading of "the *gestes* of the most famous princes, the former kings of France" – i.e., royal propaganda designed to induce continued loyalty to the line currently represented by the mad Charles. Perhaps Jean signals his awareness of the undercurrents and ironies in this chapter of his authorized biography by ending his respectful account with the surprisingly blasé comment: "This dance went on so long, that the duke of Bourbon found himself well in debt."

While, as exemplary narratives or as propaganda, histories raise the sort of issues that could potentially provoke public-sphere debate (see chapter 4), Franco-Burgundian readers seem not to have responded with such general discussion. Rather, the readings proceed in an atmosphere of strict if benign hierarchy, dominated by the high-ranking patrons who sponsor the event. Any *assistants* are expected to admire the patron's role as learned listener, and to submit meekly to the propaganda incorporated into the customized text they are hearing. As we shall see, British prelection of such material falls into a very different pattern.

Conclusion

The data collected and analyzed above have provided an embarrassment of riches. The implications are hard to summarize because the texts point in so many directions – but that is one of the most important facts about them. They clearly demonstrate that public reading in late medieval France and the Burgundian court was as complex in nature and function as any kind of reading, anywhere – rather than being trapped within essentialist categories of "additive rather than subordinative," "aggregative rather than analytic," and all the other traits ordained by the polarized Ongian approach (Ong 1982).

In the material above, we've seen texts read aloud by their authors (Froissart, the *Cent Ballades* authors), by author-surrogates (Deschamps for Machaut), by a professional bookman (Malet), by a professional warlord (Humbercourt), by anonymous court functionaries (the kneeling man in the *Hainault* frontispiece), by a young noblewoman (Froissart's demoiselle). The readings have provided their audiences (always, in these samples, courtly ones) with amusement, flirtation, edification, information, propaganda, self-aggrandizement, and role models. Audience members have kept still or interrupted (or happily contemplated the reader's beauty, or slipped out to go hunting); they've commented on the author's chutzpah or his philosophy; perhaps they've critiqued the text with the prelector. At least one listener (Jean de Berry) seems to have appreciated the same things we do in literature, i.e., the writer's subtlety and skill.

Each of the three genres involved (romance, love poetry, histories) has revealed a distinctive profile that, even so, displays intrageneric variation. The reading of romances, about which there was least evidence, seemed to suggest the one common trait of allowing for episodic reading, either in selected fragments or nightly installments. As the most personal form, love poetry was usually prelected by the poet himself. It combined intensity of feeling with great formalism of style and acute self-consciousness. Its focus on women alembicates it subtly with its society's manifold ambiguities about gender relations, so that in bemoaning, usually, the poet's utter helplessness before the power of love, it yet stands out as the most sophisticated, artificial, and virtuosic of genres. The discussions of romance and of love poetry each provided one case – Deschamps reading from the *Voir Dit* to diplomats, and Christine de Pizan rejecting the *Roman de la rose* as dinner-table reading for great ladies – in which prelection pulled in the direction of the didacticism of history-reading, the highest-status aurality. The formality imposed by Gaston de Foix during the prelection of *Meliador* also carries some hint of such reading.

Compared to the usual profile for romances and love poetry, the histories create a very formal environment around themselves. Often commissioned in this period by nobles eager to promote the knowledge of history and/or to control how it gets written, these texts were nonetheless not prelected (within our sample) by the author or translator. The prelectors were chosen for their skill in reading, and the sessions are universally regarded (by the writers of memoirs, chronicles, and biographies) as edifying and praiseworthy. What the contemporary historians may be discreetly eliding is the propagandistic value of such public readings before the court. Thus, while an author reading his love poetry before a lady or a court achieved a personal expression and aggrandizement, the public reading of histories served the far different goal of imparting information and influencing individuals towards a single approved understanding of history and the key social values it is presented as illustrating.

Evidence that extends from Charles V to Charles the Bold (from the 1360s to 1477), among the highest classes of France and Burgundy, thus shows that these commissioners of translations and builders of libraries spent considerable time hearing books read aloud – and that no one at the time thought this anything but admirable. Any distortion perpetrated by the artists recording these historical events would certainly err on the side of flattery. If public reading implied illiteracy, low caste, lack of education or sophistication, stupidity, poor taste, or even effeminacy, only an extraordinarily foolish writer or artist would think of attributing it to any of the "tres haults, tres puissants et tres redoubtés" dukes and monarchs whose reading habits we have glimpsed above. Thus to the medieval hearers, readers, or viewers, it cannot have seemed in any way uncouth to depict a literate nobleman or woman being read to.

That Jean d'Angoulême, one of the few private readers in this sample, spent over half his life in captivity in England may not be irrelevant to his habits of manuscript-annotation. A lord actively ruling his territory might not have had sufficient time or training to make a serious study of the weighty books he collected. In fact, one comes away from contemplating the evidence about Gilles Malet, Jean de Berry, Philip the Good, and so on with an attitude oddly inverted from the norm. Instead of looking down on prelection as an inadequate form of reading forced on people by illiteracy or the scarcity of manuscripts, one begins to pity the people who hadn't the wealth or position to retain a skilled prelector – someone with a good voice who could read the text to them, bringing out its meanings, "pointing" its key phrases, drawing on a trained and capacious memory to explicate any difficulties. Apart from professional scholars and writers, would most people have chosen to struggle with a text on their own, when the monarchs of France and the dukes of Burgundy were praised unstintingly for the willingness with which they listened to readings?

ENGLAND AND SCOTLAND

Across the Channel from France and the court of Burgundy, we find fewer sources and less of a culture of reading, in the sense of an officially sponsored and systematically invoked value attached to the (usually public) reading of certain texts. There was no equivalent propaganda machine; no British king subsidized the formulation of monarchist political theory and historiography in the manner of Charles V, and no British nobles sought to legitimize their own dynastic claims by commissioning official histories in the manner of the dukes of Burgundy.[4] Unlike the *Chroniques de Hainault* frontispiece, the famous frontispiece to the Corpus Christi manuscript (no. 61) of *Troilus and Criseyde*, its closest English counterpart, has no known official connections and therefore little or no value as a historical record per se. Although there were occasional commissioned works – such as the *Vita Henrici Quinti* that Tito Livio da Forli wrote at Duke Humphrey's request – it seems that most of the English histories that survive arose from some personal interest or ambition of the author (Kingsford 1913: 10).

Nor does there seem to have been the same competitive-display use of love poetry; there is no direct historical or semi-historical evidence of equivalent English poems being presented to ladies, courts, or other entities. French merchants had founded a *puy* in London for the presentation of such poetry, and Englishmen had certainly figured among its members. But this organization is not attested past 1320, the probable date at which its regulations were interpolated into the Guildhall's *Liber custumarum* (Fisher 1965: 78–79; see also *Liber custumarum* pt. 1, pp. xlviii–liv).

But though the English and Scottish records give a sparser picture of reading behavior, enough survives to reveal that British reading differed from French and Burgundian in various definite and consistent ways. Diverse as the two traditions are, however, they agree in that the readers surveyed are all literate and upper class, and that their reading is almost all prelected, from the late fourteenth to the late fifteenth century.

One important way in which the British patterns differ from the Franco-Burgundian is in the generic distributions. While the latter read romance, love poetry, and histories (along with philosophical and devotional texts) each in a different way, the British pattern seems basically to divide reading material into the secular and the devotional. Chronicles, romances, poetry, and "miracles of the world" (see below) tended to be read in a cheerfully relaxed atmosphere that might include some awareness of their improving effect,[5] while even laypeople read the Scriptures, saints' lives, homiletic treatises, and so on in a much more hierarchical context and with sedulous earnestness. In two cases, however – both associated with Henry VI – Scripture and chronicles were read together, as improving texts more on the French model. The following survey will thus combine the evidence of the reading of secular material into one section (including the two mixed cases), with a few instances of lay devotional reading presented afterwards as an instructive contrast.

I exclude below several cases that are often invoked in discussions of medieval English reading. One is the ordinance for Edward IV's son, instructing that at meals there should "be reade before him, such noble storyes as behoveth to a prynce to understande" ("Ordinances," p. *28). The value of this passage as evidence of royal reading habits is undercut by the fact that in 1474, when it was written, Prince Edward was only four years old. I also omit any reference to the letter-writing Pastons, Celys, Stonors, and Plumptons, since, I regret to say, not one of them offers any report about time spent reading, either publicly or privately. Certainly, the Paston letters witness to a lively circulation of books among family and friends, including the commissioning of exemplars from a scribe, William Ebesham. Although book-ownership is obviously a contributing factor to reading behavior, however, in and of itself it provides no information about how the readers actually read their books.

Finally, although my focus is on English behavior I include here one Scottish instance, James I's evening reading, because it is such a useful report (and James, of course, spent his youth in England). When my analyses are meant to include James, I will speak of "British" reading; when not, of "English."

Secular texts

Secular reading by the kings and in the courts of Britain usually carries a sense of spontaneity foreign to the auralities of their French and Burgundian counterparts. This atmosphere is well invoked in a passage from the *Liber niger*, an ordinance book describing the duties and perquisites of the household of Edward IV. Written *c.* 1471, the text is partly based upon a lost ordinance book of Edward III (R. F. Green 1980: 84).

After explaining how "the statutes of noble Edward the iij" organized the distribution of leftovers from feasts, the *Liber* goes on to note, pleasantly:

> Thes esquiers of houshold of old be acustumed, wynter and somer, in after nonys and in euenynges, to drawe to lordez chambrez within courte, there to kepe honest company aftyr theyre cunyng, in talkyng of cronycles of kinges and of other polycyez [specula principis], or in pypyng, or harpyng, synging, other actez marciablez, to help ocupy the court and acompany straungers, tyll the tym require of departing. (ed. Myers, pp. 128–29)

The dating of this practice to "of old," and the preceding reference to Edward III, suggest that these companionable occasions were typical of that Edward's reign, in the mid-fourteenth century (a hypothesis backed by R. F. Green 1980: 84). But were royal esquires, lords, and "straungers" still mingling prelection with a variety of other enjoyable pastimes in the reign of Edward IV, in the late fifteenth century –

or was the author of the *Liber* merely indulging in a little of the aural nostalgia so often attributed to Chaucer?

The *Liber*'s editor suggests not. "The book is conservative enough to include terms and rules which had not been definitely abrogated," notes Myers, "but it is not safe to suppose that it is so antiquarian as to repeat rules which have become plainly inoperative" (pp. 19–20). When the old rule has been modified, moreover, the *Liber* notes how: e.g., "In the noble Edwardes houshold there were xij messagers, wich were minnisshed by the avoydance of priue seale from houshold" (p. 133). In the description of the companionable readers, as of the preceding business about distributing the leftovers, no such modification is noted, indicating, by the protocol practiced throughout the text, that the descriptions represent a venerable and *ongoing* feature of court life.

Having bracketed our period with this image of happy public readers, we may readily expect to find more of the same during the interim span; and we do. According to a contemporary account, James I of Scotland spent the night before his assassination in 1437

> yn his chambur, talkyng and playng with the lordes, knyghtis and squyers that were abowte hyme ... So both afore soper and long aftire ynto quarter of the nyght [9 pm], ... wher thay wer occupied att the playing of the chesse, att the tables, yn redying of Romans, yn syngyng and pypyng, in harpyng, and in other honest solaces of grete pleasance and disport. (Shirley, "Dethe," ed. Stevenson, pp. 53–54)

This description echoes that from the *Liber* remarkably. Both feature a similar set of personnel (lords, knights, and esquires), a similar location (the king's or lord's chamber), a similar program of entertainment (chess, backgammon, singing, piping, and the prelection of installments or favorite bits of secular works [cf. Taylor 1992: 61]), and a similarly positive assessment of the whole event (they constitute "honest company" or "honest solaces"). This congruence between two wholly independent historical records suggests that the phenomenon is being accurately reported.

Chamber-reading

Before pursuing the further implications of this style of reading, we should take special note of its location. Certainly as late as 1437, when

James and his attendants were hearing romances read in his chamber, and very likely as late as 1471, when Edward IV's courtiers were "talkyng of chronicles" and "polycyez" in lords' chambers, private chambers and public reading were happily coexisting. This suggests a flaw in the common interpretation of another, often-cited reference to kingly reading: Richard II's reaction to the collected works presented to him by Jean Froissart in 1395:

> [in Berners' translation] he sawe it [the book] in his chambre, for I had layde it there redy on his bedde ... Than the kyng demaunded me wherof it treated, and I shewed hym how it treated maters of loue; wherof the kynge was gladde and loked in it, and reed yt in many places, for he coulde speke and rede French very well; and he tooke yt to a knyght of hys chambre, named syr Rycharde Creadon, to beare it into hys secrete chambre. (2: 619)

> (Si le vey en sa chambre, car tout pourveu je l'avoie, et luy mis sur son lit ... Adont me demanda le roy de quoy il traittoit. Je luy dis: "D'Amours." De ceste response fut-il tous resjouys, et regarda dedens le livre en plusieurs lieux et y lisy, car moult bien parloit et lisoit le franchois, et puis le fist prendre par ung sien chevallier qui se nommoit messire Richard Credon et porter en sa chambre de retraite.) (*Chroniques*, ed. de Lettenhove, XV, 167)

The "secrete chambre" invoked here, and the book's consignment thereto, is often cited as proof that the king – and contemporary courtly readers in general – read privately. Noting that he cannot imagine Chaucer among the companionable esquires of the *Liber niger*, for example, Paul Strohm declares that the passage would "probably have been anachronistic in the court of Richard II" (1989: 22). As evidence he cites Richard's "chambre de retraite" (p. 196 n. 73). Yet not only was Chaucer's presence among the *Liber*'s esquires highly likely – since the poet had been a "resident esquire" in Edward III's service (Pearsall 1992: 48) – but the *Liber* explicitly places those aural sessions in "lordez chambrez within courte," just as the "Dethe of the Kynge of Scotis" places James' reading within his "chambur." Froissart himself says nothing about how Richard read his book in his *chambre de retraite* – although, in linking Richard's skim-reading to his fluency in spoken French, he suggests that the king read the book aloud in his bedchamber. The historical movement from hall to chamber did not extinguish aurality; it simply made it a little cosier.

Public sphere

The non-hierarchical and congenial atmosphere characteristic of the British readings discussed above has a resonance beyond the merely agreeable, however. Such assemblies would have offered the ideal setting for public-sphere discussions (or gossip) about issues of current importance, brought into focus by shared readings of chronicles and specula principis. That the *Liber niger*'s esquires and lords are said to be "talkyng of" rather than "reading" their chronicles and "polycyez" combines the idea of the spoken-aloud text with the idea of the conversation and commentary that probably attended the prelection.

The English material provides an example suggestive of such a setting. This is the "Moral balade," a mini-speculum principis written by Henry Scogan sometime between 1400 and 1407 for his tutees, the four sons of Henry IV. When John Shirley copied this poem out some forty or fifty years after the event (Watson 1984: 5), he introduced it with a short note of its original performance:

> Here foloweth next a Moral Balade, to my lord the Prince [later, Henry V], to my lord of Clarence, to my lord of Bedford, and to my lord of Gloucestre,[6] by Henry Scogan; at a souper of feorthe [?worthy] merchande in the Vyntre in London, at the hous of Lowys Johan. (ed. Skeat, p. 237)

The poem is a very serious exhortation, over twenty-four stanzas, to virtuous living, and would presumably have fit into the earlier, more sober part of the evening. Its opening lines support the idea that it is a public admonition addressed to Scogan's royal tutees, whether it was prelected by Scogan himself or someone else:

> My noble sones, and eek my lordes dere,
> I, your fader called, unworthily,
> Sende un-to you this litel tretys here
> Writen with myn owne hand full rudely;
> Although it be that I not reverently
> Have writen to your estats, yet I you praye,
> Myn unconning taketh benignely
> For goddes sake, and herken what I seye.
> (lines 1–8)

Although discussion of Scogan's poem tends to be dismissive, a closer analysis suggests some surprising depths. The ballade begins with comfortably familiar moral reflections such as:

> ... tyme y-lost in youthe folily
> Greveth a wight goostly and bodily.
> (lines 36–37)

Later in the poem, however, Scogan begins to venture a little beyond the commonplace or safe, in his warnings – all put in Chaucer's mouth – that nobility is a quality of soul, not of birth. "My mayster Chaucer," he begins,

> god his soule have!
> That in his langage was so curious,
> He sayde, the fader whiche is deed and grave,
> Biquath nothing his vertue with his hous
> Unto his sone ...
> (lines 65–69)

After quoting all three stanzas of Chaucer's "Gentilesse" – with its refrain claiming gentility comes not to the virtueless, "Al were he mytre, croune, or diademe" (lines 111, 118, 125) – Scogan rises to a more impassioned tone:

> And if your youth no vertue have provyded,
> Al men wol saye, fy on your vassalage!
> Thus hath your slouth fro worship you devyded.
> (lines 147–49)

By the end of his seemingly conventional and derivative poem, therefore, Scogan has raised some perhaps touchy issues to the sons of Henry IV, who had only recently usurped the crown of England. Smuggled in with the function of reassurance, thus, is the "impassioned direct address" and the "secular and civic piety" Anne Middleton considers characteristic of the "public poetry" of the Ricardian era (1978: 94–95). Scogan has transformed the conventionality of his opening remarks and the derivativeness of his quotations from Chaucer into a common voice defending a communal concern. In so doing he may well have expressed to the young princes the opinions of the upper-middle-class men who were hosting this banquet, and even, perhaps, provided those hosts an opening for some discreet political discussion with their guests. The publicness of the poem's delivery reflects the publicness of the issues and of the voice the poet assumes in raising them.

Henry VI

There is one interesting exception to this convivial pattern of British secular reading. According to his confessor, John Blacman, Henry VI spent his time working "or in reading of the scriptures or of authors and chronicles," not in "sloth or vanities, not in banquetings or drunkenness, not in vain talk or in other mischievous speech or chatter" (trans. James: 37) ("aut in scriptuarum lectionibus, vel in scriptis aut cronicis legendis ... non in ocio aut vanitatibus, non in commessationibus aut ebrietatibus, non in vaniloquiis aut ceteris nocuiis dictis aut loquelis"; p. 15). Henry seems to have divorced the reading of chronicles from the easy assemblies recorded in the *Liber niger*, combining them rather with Scripture, like his French and Burgundian counterparts.

The austere feeling of this description suggests that Henry read his Bible and chronicles privately. Blacman tells one story, however, that suggests otherwise. He was alone with the king in the latter's chamber,

> employed together with him upon his holy books, and giving ear to his wholesome advice and the sighs of his most deep devotion. There came all at once a knock at the king's door from a certain mighty duke of the realm, and the king said, "They do so interrupt me that by day or night I can hardly snatch a moment to be refreshed by reading of any holy teaching without disturbance." (trans. James: 37–38)
>
> (in sanctis suis libris com eo laborans, ejus salubribus monitis & profundissimae devotionis suspiriis intendens: dato pro tunc interim sono super hostio regio a quondam potentissimo regni duce, rex ait: *Sic inquietant me, ut vix raptim per dies et noctes valeam sine strepitu aliquorum sacrorum dogmatum lectione refici.*) (ed. James, p. 15)

This account seems to imply some sort of shared reading, mingled with commentary and meditation.

As austere as Henry himself might have been, however, there is evidence that the rest of his court carried on in the spirit of the *Liber niger*. Speaking of the Inns of Court, Henry's adherent, Sir John Fortescue, reports proudly (bet. 1468–71):

> In these greater inns, indeed, and also in the lesser, there is, beside a school of law, a kind of academy of all the manners that the nobles

learn. There they learn to sing and to exercise themselves in every kind of harmonics. They are also taught there to practise dancing and all games proper for nobles, as those brought up in the king's household are accustomed to practise. In the vacations most of them apply themselves to the study of legal science, and at festivals to the reading, after the divine services, of Holy Scripture and of chronicles. This is indeed a cultivation of virtues and a banishment of all vice. (*De laudibus*, trans. Chrimes: 119)

(maius aliis consimilis status hominibus ipsi nobilitatem curant et conservacionem honoris et fame sue. In hiis vero hospiciis maioribus eciam et minoribus, ultra studium legum est quasi gignasium omnium morum qui nobiles docent. Ibi cantare ipsi addiscunt, similiter et se exercent in omni genere armonie. Ibi eciam tripudiare ac iocos singulos nobilibus convenientes exercere, qualiter in domo regia exercere solent enutriti. In ferialibus diebus eorum pars maior legalis discipline studio, et in festivalibus sacre scripture et cronicorum leccioni post divina obsequia se confert. Ibi quippe disciplina virtutum est et viciorum omnium relegacio.) (p. 118)

This "academy of manners" that Fortescue describes seems designed to equip these ambitious young men for just the sort of activities described in the *Liber*: singing (and dancing), games, and public reading.

Recreational readings at Oxford and Cambridge

Finally, one report gives us a glimpse of secular public reading used as part of a carefully regulated form of communal life. The statutes drawn up by William of Wykeham for New College, Oxford (1379), ordain that

when in reverence to God and his mother or any other saint a fire is lit in winter in the hall for the Fellows; then the scholars and Fellows, after the time of dinner or supper, will be permitted to linger in the hall for the sake of recreation in singing and other honest solaces, and seriously to study poems, chronicles of kings, and wonders of this world, or other things which suit the clerical state. (trans. in *Statutes*, I, New College, pp. 40–42)

(quando ob Die reverentiam, ac suae matris, vel alterius Sancti cujuscunque, tempore hyemali ignis in aula Sociis ministratur; tunc scholaribus et Sociis, post tempus prandii aut coenae, liceat gratia recreationis in aula in cantilenis et aliis solatiis honestis moram

> facere condecentem, et poemata, regnorum chronicas, et mundi hujus mirabilia, ac caetera quae statum clericalem condecorant, seriosius pertractare.) (*Statutes*, I, New College, pp. 40–42)

Given the setting, the poetry spoken of would presumably be religious or philosophical verses. The "wonders of this world" probably means informative texts such as Bartholomaeus Anglicus' *De proprietatibus rerum*, although Mandeville would fit the description as well.

The idea of this recreational hall-reading seems to have originated with Wykeham (see Rashdall and Rait 1901: 24–25; Cobban 1988: 187–88 for discussion of the influences behind Wykeham's statutes), and certain Oxford and Cambridge foundations for over a century after reproduced his instructions nearly verbatim. Almost the same words occur, for example, in Henry VI's 1443 statutes for King's College, Cambridge (in Myers 1969: 896–97), and in Bishop Fox's 1517 statutes for Corpus Christi, Oxford (Ward 1843: 163–64). Presumably, the hall-readings survived not out of carelessness or antiquarianism – odd indulgences for someone about to make a costly and prestigious benefaction – but because the founders still felt it was a legitimate and useful pastime for scholars.

Wykeham proposes these prelections as one way of discouraging the "scurrilities, evil speaking and, what is worse, insults and squabbles" ("scurrilitates, turpiloquia et, quod pejus est, detractiones et jurgia"; *Statutes*, I, New College, p. 40) likely to follow on a good meal. This fear was well founded, given the youth and past performance of the typical Oxbridge undergraduate in the Middle Ages. In this context, public reading (of a wide variety of genres) functions as a form of social control that substitutes an approved, centralized, and supervised source of group interest for the potentially disruptive misbehaviors of individuals.

With the exception of Blacman's comments on Henry VI, all these reports of secular British reading seem, in one way or another, to emphasize the communality and enjoyability of the experience. Unlike Franco-Burgundian reading, and the lay readings of devotional material analyzed below, they are not dominated by one clear social superior (with the minor exception of Richard's reading, which was only a moment's skim). The most powerful members of the Vintry audience, the four sons of Henry IV, are put in the position of docile listeners to Scogan's advice. The description of reading in James I's chamber fixes him merely as one of the happy participants, and the crowd in the lords' chambers, as per the *Liber niger*, apparently mingles in easy disregard of relative status. There is no stipulation that a senior member of the group deliver or monitor the New College hall-readings. The general impulse is to assemble, to pool resources (and "cunyng") to entertain each other, and in such a context private reading would obviously be out of place. This *gemütlich* feeling is characteristic of British reports of reading, and will reappear when we look at literary texts in the next two chapters.

The function of such reading is neither to indoctrinate courtiers with official propaganda nor to show off and compete with love poetry, but, mostly, to sit around fires, laugh, sing, and listen to interesting stories. Recreational prelection universally attracts glowingly positive descriptions; it is equated with "honest solaces of grete pleasance and disport" (James I), "honest company" (the Edwardian esquires), and "a cultivation of virtues and a banishment of all vice" (Inns of Court). Richard II was "tous resjouys" with Froissart's book on love. Even the leisure readings at New College are described as "honest solaces" ("solatiis honestis") – precisely the term used of James I's romances!

Devotional texts

Along with the Scripture reading of Henry VI and the students at the Inns of Court (see above), we can review two further reports of the lay reading of devotional texts. The first is a screed titled by William Pantin "Instructions for a devout and literate layman," which seems to have been written in the first half of the fifteenth century, by a confessor or spiritual director for a married layman (pp. 400–3).

Among its other advice, the screed recommends public reading at the family meals:

> And lest the tongue speak vain or hurtful things, let there be reading, now by one, now by another, and by your children as soon as they can read; and think of the wicked Dives, tormented in hell in his tongue more than in any other members.
>
> Let the family be silent at table, and always, as far as is possible.
>
> Expound something in the vernacular which may edify your wife and others . . .
>
> . . . and let all be done as above at dinner. (trans. Pantin: 399–400)

> (Et ne lingua proferat vana seu nociva, legatur nunc ab uno, nunc ab alio, et a filiis statim cum sciant legere, et cogitetis de divite nebulone cruciato apud inferos in lingua magis quam in aliis membris.
> Sileat familia in mensa et semper, quatenus est possibile.
> Aliquando exponatis in vulgari quod edificet uxorem et alios ...
> ... et fiat ut supra [in prandio].) (pp. 421–22)

Another and more famous lay patron of devout prelection was Cecily Nevill, duchess of York, the mother of Edward IV and Richard III. The "Orders and rules" of her household, written around 1485, record that at dinner the duchess

> hath a lecture of holy matter, ether Hilton of contemplative and active life, Bonaventure de infancia, Salvatoris legenda aurea, St. Maude, St. Katherine of Sonys, or the Revelacions of St. Bridgett ... and in the tyme of supper she recyteth the lecture that was had at dynner to those that be in her presence. ("Orders and rules," p. *37)

Cecily's reading list (see Armstrong 1942) combines works of practical advice with popular religion and models of female devotion.

On this little showing, devotional material seems to have suited either private or public reading. Henry VI may have read privately; on the other hand, he certainly sometimes read his texts together with John Blacman, combining study, discussion, and meditation; and the students of the Inns of Court, along with the devout layman and Cecily, were all read to. In most of these cases, the public reading was mixed with or succeeded by more discussion and explication, with the chief listener in each case taking the role of teacher. Interpretation thus seems to go hand in hand with devotional reading, whether private or public.

Apart from the anticipated spiritual benefits, there seem to be two primary social functions of the reading of devotional material. First, it tended to place one individual in an exalted role as mediator of a body of highly valued texts – a function that obviously depended on the reading being a public one. The person who dominated these devotional reading events was not the most learned but the most powerful individual in the room. Although John Blacman was a priest, a former fellow of Merton, and currently a fellow of Eton (ed. James, p. xv), he meekly let Henry explain the Bible to him. Similarly, although Cecily no doubt had one or more priests in her retinue, it was she who reviewed the previous meal's reading to her tablemates. The devout and literate layman expounded in English to his more ignorant dependents, and enforced silence on the children with the terrifying image of Dives tortured in his tongue. In this way the hierarchy embedded in the religious world view seems to have transferred some of its authority to the lay sponsor of the reading event.

The second, and corollary, social function of devotional reading was to control the audience. This function also depended on the reading being public. The prelector dominates Cecily's table at supper, and she dominates at dinner with a repetition of what she'd heard at supper. The devout layman's family was to be "silent at table, ... as far as is possible"; the prelection is intended explicitly to prevent any tongues speaking "vain or hurtful things." All other forms of interaction or conversation are suppressed, in favor of the one heavily valorized flow of formulated text.

If any characteristic could be said to dominate among the texts surveyed above, it would be the idea of a "rulebook" outlining in detail the conduct of various forms of group life, whether courtly (the two kings and the prince), collegiate (the Oxbridge colleges, plus Fortescue's account of the Inns of Court), or domestic (the devout layman's "instructions" and Cecily). Some are prescriptive and others more descriptive, but all are alike in generating an idealized vision of the physically and spiritually prosperous society, structured along a spine of rigid social hierarchy.

CONCLUSION: MAPPING AURALITIES

Our examination of Franco-Burgundian and of British reading has enabled us to identify a variety of auralities within each system. At the same time, as the analysis below will demonstrate, the overall reading patterns of the two cultural areas also differ in consistent ways, constituting two higher-order auralities.

Franco-Burgundian versus British aurality: genres

The British "reading map" is, above all, far less organized and centralized than the one found across the Channel. Without an official patronage system subsidizing the production of chronicles and histories, for example, there were fewer such texts, and their authors had less motivation to include exemplary scenes of kings or lords listening (and exposing their courts) to improving (and propagandistic) texts. Although British chronicles and histories certainly were written, their authors rarely invoke the ideas that explicitly or implicitly inform French historiography: that history provides its readers with patterns of nobility and chivalry; that these models, as well as the dynastic propaganda encoded within them, can be effectively publicized by reading the texts aloud; or that they as authors can augment their genre's importance by emphasizing its appeal to and consumption by high-status readers. In general, British historians seem to have paid little attention to reading behavior, and consequently such works make only a small showing among those cited in this section.

Of the three British texts included above that could fit into the category of history, one, Froissart's chronicle, is obviously a French text[7] that includes an English episode. Both of the others are associated with Henry VI: one is Blacman's memoir, written to memorialize the king after his usurpation by Edward IV (Lovatt 1981: 431–33); the other is Fortescue's treatise on English law, which he wrote while with Henry's family in exile in France (ed. Chrimes, p. lxxiv). Both these texts do service as a form of propaganda, promulgating a theory and practice of monarchy, and both include exemplary forms or acts of reading. Neither Blacman nor Fortescue carries the idea further, however, for instance with a dedication suggesting their own books as suitable for public reading. This may partly be because, owing to the timing of their composition, both texts exist at an oblique angle to official culture and its conventions.

In most of the British reading events surveyed above, it is not even clear what language the text was in. Except when the text itself is the evidence, as with Froissart's book and Scogan's ballade, we are left to guess whether our readers read in English (or Scots), French, or Latin. This linguistic uncertainty contrasts with the systematic Franco-Burgundian program of commissions and translations designed to provide a full selection of worthwhile reading material in the vernacular. Such material found its way into English in a much more haphazard way, reflecting both the relative inefficiency of the patronage system and the relatively lower status of the language.

Franco-Burgundian versus British aurality: functions

Where French (and Burgundian) reading was, in a word, official, British reading, in a second word, was communal. This difference may explain the dominance of histories among the French and Burgundian sources drawn on here, and of "rulebooks" among the English sources. French reading, as reported in the histories, was isolated as an event and carried on with a certain self-consciousness and intensity. It featured the ruler in his official capacity as patron, supporter, and exemplar of officially approved values, and channeled attention towards texts designed specifically to augment the prestige of the political establishment. As such, aural readings deserved and received notice in official histories.

Unlike his French and Burgundian counterparts, the British king or other magnate as reader was not an official person; his reading was not a public, official act – nor had he thought of commissioning histories that would enshrine his official self, including his reading. In this way the most "French-style" English reader, Henry VI, was entirely un-French; his reading – though combining genres on the French model – was completely anti-"public," in the sense that it took him away from his public duties, with ultimately catastrophic effect. The records that preserve the secular reading behavior of James I and Richard II attribute no great moral or political virtue to their activity, beyond the simple pleasure it brought them. Although, no doubt, due respect was observed, the king or lord as reader is generally subsumed into the background, part of the happy group.

Unlike France and the Burgundian court, therefore, where the social superior clearly dominated the reading situation, British reading almost invokes a sense of festival, of ritual inversion and status relaxation. It is hard to imagine a favored prelector of either Richard II or James I feeling duty-bound, like Gilles Malet, to turn up for an evening's prelection on the day his son had died. None-theless, these carefree British assemblies tended to turn shared reading into occasions of public-sphere debate as naturally as the starchy Franco-Burgundian system tended to turn literature into propaganda. While differing in character, both political functions depended equally on the publicness of aural reading.

In contrast to the status-suspension characteristic of British secular reading, the few cases of lay devotional reading included above seem to replicate and reinforce the social hierarchy. In this way these readings seem more to resemble the Franco-Burgundian reading of historical, philosophical, and devotional material. But the equation is not total, because in the reading of the devout layman and of Cecily we still see a more communal event. The prelection tends to bond the listeners as a social unit – a family or a household – within an atmosphere of reassuring spiritual and social authority. By comparison, the francophone texts focus on the principal listener alone.

Apart from its overt role of promoting mutual enjoyment or spiritual welfare, lay devotional reading in Britain – and perhaps to some extent secular public reading as well – also functioned as a means of basic social control, a way to suppress any possible "scurrilities, evil speaking and ... insults and squabbles." This is a role never suggested among the texts of the better-behaved French and Burgundians – although the prelections at Louis de Bourbon's dinners were possibly intended to stifle disloyal gossip.

The communalism of British reading may also explain why the material we have examined above never singles out one person as a particularly skilled prelector, along the lines of Gilles Malet or the lord of Humbercourt. Except for Froissart's remark that Richard II spoke and read French very well, we get no insight into the artistry of British prelectors. Nor do we get any idea whether British kings and lords in this period regularly employed household functionaries as prelectors. One thing that does emerge from all these reports, however, is the distinct lack of minstrel prelectors. It is possible that one or two lurk, unidentified, in James I's chamber or among Edward IV's "honest company." But from what we know or can surmise about the prelectors in the material surveyed above, minstrels were no more evident as aural readers in and after Chaucer's time than they were before (see chapter 4).

The evidence presented here may serve to set another favorite myth to rest, the one about private chambers evolving as the natural setting for private reading. The data we have reviewed suggest strongly that the increasing tendency of the high-born to seek the privacy of their own chambers did not affect the publicness of the reading undertaken there.

The British texts reviewed above should also provide a conclusive refutation of the "deficiency theory" (see chapter 3) that associates aurality with illiteracy and lack of books. The people we have seen sharing in public readings include kings, princes, lords and ladies, esquires, merchants, priests, the upper- and upper-middle-class students of New and other colleges and the Inns of Court, and authors. The literacy of none of these listeners could be in doubt, and their access to books must have been as good as that of any other readers in their period. Nor do their reading practices follow the smooth evolutionary path from "orality" to "literacy" customarily assigned to their time. Rather, the "modality plateau" discussed in chapter 4 prevails, with aural reading retaining its popularity despite rising literacy rates and book-production, from at least the 1370s (the end of Edward III's reign) to the 1470s (Fortescue's treatise and the *Liber niger*).

Post-medieval public reading

As suggested in chapter 1, moreover, this elite aurality did not vanish in the glow of Renaissance literacy. Rather, humanism, as it took root in Britain and other countries, tended to replace the old exophoric (socially bonding, communalizing) aurality of the Middle Ages with a relatively more endophoric (individualizing, self-asserting) aurality. I will not consider here the forms that dividuality took under these influences, but it will be of use to survey briefly some of the forms of Renaissance, and post-Renaissance, British aurality.

While undoubtedly literate themselves, Renaissance scholar-princes often employed their humanist protégés to read and interpret classical texts to them, in the original language or in specially commissioned translations. This model – exemplified by, for example, Cosimo de' Medici; Federico da Montefeltro, duke of Urbino; and François I (Vespasiano da Bisticci, p. 234; Grudin 1991: 670; Bourrilly 1905; Doucet 1920) – makes its appearance in England at least by the reign of Elizabeth. The queen's former tutor, Roger Ascham, records that after a dinner party in 1563 she invited him into her privy chamber: "We read then together in the Greek tongue, as I well understand, that noble oration of Demosthenes against Aeschines" (*Schoolmaster*, p. 7). Sir John Stanhope and Elizabeth's physician, Dr. James, both later acted as court prelectors, the former mentioning in a letter to a friend that "my eyes be worn with reading." Stanhope proposed Sir John Harrington to be "reader to her majesty" in 1601 (Nelson 1976/77: 114–15).

Other Elizabethans emulated the queen; Ascham also reports reading to the English ambassador in Augsburg, in 1551, "whole Herodotus, five tragedies, three orations of Isocrates and seventeen orations of Demosthenes" (quoted in Nelson 1976/77: 114). A scholar in the employ of the earl of Leicester, Gabriel Harvey, records in a marginal note: "The courtier Philip Sidney and I had privately discussed these three books of Livy, scrutinizing them so far as we could from all points of view, applying a political analysis, just before his embassy to the emperor Rudolf II" (quoted in Jardine and Grafton 1990: 36).

The sort of public-sphere responses generated in medieval readings of specula principis or chronicles here merge with scholarly aurality to promote a more focused "political aurality" among the actual agents – or opponents – of government. The "purytane skoller" Henry Cuffe was hanged in 1601 for his part in the Essex rising, which consisted of being "sente by my lo: of Essex to reade to my lo: of Southampton in Paris where hee redd Aristotles polyticks to hym with sutch exposytions as, I doubt, did hym but lyttle good" (quoted on p. 34). Jardine and Grafton hypothesize that noble Elizabethan households regularly employed scholars to read and provide "interpretations of textual material on pragmatic political themes, ... acting less as advisers in the modern sense than as facilitators easing the difficult negotiations between modern needs and ancient texts" (pp. 34–35). Among other features they note that such reading "was normally carried out in the company of a colleague or student; and was a public performance, rather than a private meditation, in its aims and character" (p. 31).

Ordinary citizens were also invited to hear readings of classical or otherwise improving texts. Such aural sessions may have been considered especially suitable for women, partly as a means of discipline and partly because they spent more time doing sedentary handwork. Thomas Salter, in his *Mirhor Mete for All Mothers, Matrones, and Maidens* (1579), opines that "our wise matrone shall reade, or cause her maidens to reade, the examples and liues of godly and vertuous ladies" (quoted in Wright 1931: 674). Sidney's *New Arcadia* (1581–84) presents a romanticized scene of recreational reading: Argalus is found "sitting in a parlour with the fair Parthenia; he reading in a book the stories of Hercules, she by him, as to hear him read" (but more absorbed in gazing at him) (p. 371). The fair Parthenia later reads a letter to herself (p. 372), proving that her aurality was not dictated by illiteracy.

Of course, and finally, aurality did also emerge in the role to which it is generally supposed to have been confined after the time of Chaucer: as the modality of necessity for those masses now perceived, against an increasing emphasis on literacy, as illiterate (see Cressy 1980: 1–3). The spread of literacy drove aurality downmarket, in this subform, not because all the middle and upper classes had begun to read dividually but because there were now more lower-class literates. This meant that there was someone to prelect to members of the lower classes and, accordingly, a literature intended to be read aloud to such audiences. As the word "read" was slowly drifting, over the fifteenth and sixteenth centuries, towards the sense of "read privately," so aurality was beginning, through this one manifestation, to acquire the association with poverty and illiteracy that it usually carries today.

That it would be a long time before this association, and the practice of dividuality, achieved dominance may be illustrated by a quick review of post-Renaissance reports of reading. Alexander Hume's denunciation of the goings-on among the upper-class youth of 1599 suggests that Presbyterianism had not removed every trace of James I's Scotland. Hume fulminates:

> In Princes courts, in the houses of greate men, and at the assemblies of yong gentilmen and yong damesels, the cheife pastime is, to sing prophane sonnets, and vaine ballats of loue, or to rehearse some fabulos faits of Palmerine, Amadis, or other such like raueries. (p. xiv)

Aurality was equally serviceable among the devout, however. The Puritan Lady Margaret Hoby, for example, mingled her private devotions with much aural religiosity. A typical diary entry, for January 21, 1599, notes: "after [dinner], I wroughte, hearinge Mr Rhodes Read of a booke against some newe spronge vp herisies" (ed. Meads, p. 98). In her diary, Lady Anne Clifford records reading and hearing a wide variety of books, including literature, history, political science, and devotional texts. On November 9, 1616, for example, "I sat at my work and heard *Rivers* and *Marsh* read Montaigne's Essays which book they have read almost this fortnight" (p. 41). The breadth of Clifford's reading suggests the educational aspirations of Protestant England interacting with the easy availability of books to produce a sort of intellectual consumerism.[8]

As literacy moved down the social scale, scenes like those Clifford records were reproduced in such petty bourgeois households as that of Thomas Turner, an eighteenth-century Sussex shopkeeper. A typical entry from his diary reads:

> *Weds. 15 Oct. [1755].* At home all day. Paid for milk 1/2 *d.* Nothing more of moment; only posted part of my day book. My wife read

> part of *Clarissa Harlowe* to me in the even as I sat a-posting my book. (p. 16)

As reflected in the accounts of Anne Clifford's and Thomas Turner's reading, the inner-directedness and the individualism traditionally supposed to have been fostered by the new genres of essay and novel seem not to have interfered with the practice of aurality.

The popularity of public reading as a domestic amusement on into the Victorian age is well evidenced. A particularly impressive cast of aural readers appears in a letter of Mary James to her son Henry; writing in 1871, she notes that "[Oliver] Wendell Holmes ... has read Browning aloud to us most charmingly – and I hear him now in the next room reading to Will [William James]" (quoted in Strouse 1981: 143). It might fittingly wind up this section to quote another American source, Nathaniel Hawthorne's *Blithedale Romance* (1852). The narrator finds himself wondering why public lectures had recently "come strongly into vogue, when the natural tendency of things would seem to be, to substitute lettered for oral methods of addressing the public" (p. 196). Although this comment concerns lectures rather than prelections, it seems to encapsulate both the ineradicable human affinity for the oral/aural and the progressivist's equally unquenchable impatience to pronounce its demise. Both tendencies, it would seem, have survived intact into the present day.

6

An "ethnography of reading" in Chaucer

The survey that follows assembles the internal evidence from Chaucer's work for my thesis that he expected his texts to be read aloud, perhaps by himself to his immediate, first audience but as well by other prelectors[1] to later audiences. For many medievalists, Chaucer's address to his "litel bok" at the close of *Troilus and Criseyde* (5: 1786–98) proves that he was consciously directing his work not only to posterity, but to a posterity inhabited by private readers. Yet the only foundation for this common assumption is the technological determinism of standard orality/literacy theory.

If technology *were* the only force governing reading behavior, then we could justifiably assume that an author who composed in writing for an elite, educated audience would expect that audience to read his work privately. But this premise, as the previous chapters have demonstrated, is both untenable as theory and inaccurate as history. Literate elites had enjoyed having books read to them for centuries before Chaucer, and literate elites went on having books read to them for a century and more after Chaucer. Thus it should not be in the least surprising to discover in Chaucer's texts evidence that he expected both his contemporary and future audiences to hear his books.

To substantiate the contention that Chaucer anticipated a posterity of literate listeners, this chapter will look closely at his references to hearing and reading, with minimal attention to the secondary literature. Rather than selecting a few examples that seem to support my case – as is the general practice in discussions of Chaucer's aurality or "literacy" – I will adopt the "ethnographic" methodology described in chapter 4. The first phase of that effort was to collect all the references to or instances of public and private reading in Chaucer; the next phase was to look for the patterns these data seemed to make. Two generalizations that emerged from this analysis – namely, the typology of late medieval literacies and the aural-narrative constellation – were presented in chapter 4, because they seemed to suggest viable frameworks in which to read other medieval authors as well. I will refer here to these ideas without repeating the detailed exposition.

There is still much to say in the present chapter, however, about Chaucer's particular viewpoint on modalities. This material will be discussed in ascending order of realization: first, Chaucer's references to the reception of his own work; then his explicit references to the reception of other people's work; and finally his dramatized depictions of reception.

This analysis will assume that Chaucer's references to reception channel can be taken at face value. I am setting aside for the time any arguments about "oral" traits as survivals of minstrel practice or as Chaucer's nostalgic evocation of a superseded reception format. As the discussion of "fictive orality" in chapter 3 suggests, these theories derive their force from the fallacious assumption that "orality" becomes superfluous upon the appearance of its evolutionary successor, "literacy." The history reviewed in the previous chapter suggests that Chaucer's "hears" address a pertinent, contemporary reality; at the very least, they deserve a hearing.

Finally, I will not be considering here the stylistic traits cited by Ruth Crosby (1938) and by Bertrand Bronson (1940) as proof of Chaucer's aurality. More note needs to be taken of the varieties of orality, aurality, and dividuality before firm equations should be made between modality and style. One might say, however, that I am extending the sort of survey Crosby conducted of Chaucer's style to his invocations of reception channels. Surprisingly, no one to date has systematically surveyed these descriptions in an effort to discover how Chaucer presents private and public reading and what sorts of material he associates with each. Yet, as will appear below, such a survey produces some interesting results.

REFERENCES TO THE RECEPTION OF CHAUCER'S OWN WORK

A survey of Chaucer's references to, respectively, the hearing and the reading of his own texts (excluding prose works except the two prose Canterbury tales) reveals forty-four passages in which Chaucer, speaking directly to his audience, assumes they will "hear," "hearken," or, in one case, "listen" (see chart 6.1, section A). Of these forty-four, nineteen are versions of "as ye shall hear" and ten of "as ye have

Chart 6.1: *Hearing and reading in Chaucer*

A. Chaucer's references to the hearing of his own work:

As ye shall (may) (after) hear: HF: 512; A&A: 357; PF: 658; T&C 1: 30; T&C 4: 1085; T&C 5: 637, 854, 952, 1316, 1589; LGW, F: 281 [G: 184]; LGW: 1085, 1927, 2627; CT 1: 858, 4364; CT 2: 98; CT 7: 452, 3462.

As ye have heard (me say) (devise) (before): T&C 2: 966, 1547; T&C 3: 553; T&C 4: 807; T&C 5: 629; LGW, G: 106; LGW: 2139, 2459; CT 1: 849; "Complaint unto Pity": 51.

(Now) hearken/hark/listen: HF: 109, 509, 511, 1549; T&C 1: 52; T&C 2: 31; LGW: 665, 1276; CT 10: 1081.

Hear: HF: 83; T&C 1: 54, 398; T&C 3: 495; LGW: 2402; CT 1: 3176.

B. Chaucer's references to the reading of his own work: T&C 5: 270, 1797; LGW: 2139; CT 10: 1081; "Lenvoy a Bukton": 29; "Complaynt d'amours": 67; (anomalous case) CT 8: 78.

C. Chaucer's references to the reading of source-texts:

(This list does not include: "reads" that describe a character reading; "read" used in the sense of "speak, tell about, give account of"; and readings of inscriptions, dreams, stars, paintings, expressions, etc.)

1. Chaucer as narrator, from identified sources: HF: 377, 477, 1352; T&C 1: 147; T&C 5: 1771; LGW: 1367, 1457; CT 1: 741.
2. Chaucer as narrator, from unidentified and/or proverbial sources: BD: 55; HF: 385, 590; T&C 1: 241; T&C 3: 1063; T&C 5: 19, 1753; LGW: 1263, 1557.
3. Fictional narrators, from identified sources: CT 2: 84; CT 3: 183, 981, 1168 (two uses); CT 4: 1154, 1362, 2232; CT 6: 586, 742; CT 7: 2319, 2460, 2579, 2580, 3121, 3130, 3312, 3329; CT 9: 207, 344, 345 (two uses).
4. Fictional narrators, from unidentified and/or proverbial sources: T&C 3: 289, 1429; T&C 4: 980, 1644; LGW, G: 286; CT 2: 894; CT 5: 211, 1429; CT 7: 2974, 2984, 3137, 3263; CT 8: 35; CT 9: 112.
5. "(As) I read":

a. Chaucer: PF: 12; T&C 1: 133, 159, 495; LGW: 1825, 2239; "Complaint of Mars": 78.

b. Fictional narrators: CT 2: 1095; CT 3: 862; CT 6: 508; CT 7: 3110; CT 10: 434.

D. Chaucer's references to the hearing of source-texts:

1. Chaucer as narrator: T&C 3: 498; T&C 5: 1770.
2. Fictional narrators: LGW, G: 308; CT 3: 981; CT 5: 235; CT 7: 2459, 3264.

E. Chaucer's references to the transmission of stories:

1. Chaucer as narrator: HF: 1515 ("hear"); T&C 4: 799 ("read or song").
2. Fictional narrators: HF: 347–48 ("read and song ... on every tongue"), 721–22 ("what so cometh from any tonge, / Be hyt rouned, red, or songe"); T&C 5: 1061 ("rolled shal I ben on many a tonge"); LGW, F: 572 ("read and hear"); CT 7: 956 ("heard"), 2633 ("heard").

heard," basic formulas useful in moving a story along or tying it together. The first often introduces a pilgrim's tale or otherwise signals a transition in the narrative; e.g.,

> And to Criseyde, his owen lady deere,
> He wrot right thus, and seyde as ye may here ...
> (T&C 5: 1315–16)

The second formula does duty as a mini-*occupatio*, saving Chaucer the trouble of recapping things the audience should remember while giving their memory a quick boost; e.g., in the prologue to the *Legend of Good Women*:

> Me mette how I was in the medewe tho,
> And that I romede in that same gyse,
> To sen that flour, as ye han herd devyse.
> (LGW, G: 104–6)

In addition, Chaucer uses "hearken" eight times, "hear" six times, and "listen" once: e.g., the *House of Fame*'s "Now herkeneth, as I have yow seyd, / What that I mette" (HF: 109–10) and, summarizing his way through Troilus and Criseyde's courtship, "I trowe it were a long thyng for to here" (T&C 3: 495).

As Ruth Crosby noted in 1938, the Canterbury pilgrims use these same narrative formulas and verbs of hearing many times in their storytelling (p. 415). The very workadayness of these formulas, their unobtrusiveness and usefulness, seem to offset the assumption that they figure in some elaborate Chaucerian strategy to recreate a departed performance situation for his nostalgic private readers (Mehl 1974). Nor need we suppose they represent residue from the time of minstrel performance (Burrow 1971) or, more vaguely, of the "oral mind" (McKenna 1988). "As ye shall hear" is a perfectly sensible way to address either a fictional listener to a Canterbury tale or a real person listening to a book being read aloud. In either case, such phrases are contemporary and functional.

This survey also helps to refute another popular misconception, i.e., that Chaucer evolved away from aurality over the course of his writing career (see, e.g., Strohm 1989: 56). Dividing the number of lines by the number of references to hearing, chart 6.2 shows a rise-and-fall pattern that nonetheless clearly has Chaucer using proportionately more hearing references in his later works than in his earlier.

Chart 6.2: *Chronological distribution of Chaucer's references to hearing**

Early poems	8 refs.	3,214 lines (total)	0.249%
Troilus	17 refs.	8,239 lines	0.206%
Legend	10 refs.	2,723 lines	0.367%
Canterbury Tales	8 refs.	2,251 lines (GP and links)	0.355%

* These figures count only the General Prologue and the links of the *Canterbury Tales*; they exclude the Wife of Bath's Prologue and one reference that occurs in a short poem whose date is uncertain.

While Chaucer assumes hearing as the reception channel of his work forty-four times, he makes only six references to people reading his work (see chart 6.1, section B). One case – "As ye han in this covenaunt herd me rede" (LGW: 2139) – clearly preserves an "aural read." Two are variations on the "hear and/or read" phrase: "herkne ... or rede" and "red ... or elles songe" (CT 10: 1081; T&C 5: 1797). As noted in chapter 4, these may preserve either a hard or a soft contrast – "read or hear" meaning either "read privately or listen to a public reading," or "read publicly or listen to a public reading." Given this uncertainty, these "reads" might be classified as format-neutral.

The address to "Thow, redere" in *Troilus and Criseyde* (5: 270) is often noted as a clear reference to private reading (e.g., Fichte 1988: 122); and the use of the second-person singular seems to support this idea. Finally, the last two examples of "read" – "The Wyf of Bathe I pray yow that ye rede" ("Lenvoy a Bukton," line 29) and "Shewe by word, that ye wolde ones rede / The compleynte of me" ("Complaynt d'amours," lines 67–68) – seem to incline toward private reading, since each is urging a particular reading task on a personal acquaintance.

Thus, of the six times that Chaucer anticipates readers for his text as opposed to hearers, one refers in fact to hearers, two are ambiguous, or format-neutral, and three probably refer to private readers. This results in an overall tally of forty-five clear references to hearers, two format-neutral references to readers, and three probable references to private readers (two in short poems addressed to Chaucer's intimates).

REFERENCES TO THE RECEPTION OF SOURCES

While Chaucer overwhelmingly addresses his own audience as hearers, "read" predominates over "hear" when he or one of his fictional narrators refers to other written works. The reason is that the first set of reception-verbs refer to audience reception, the second to authorial source-consultation. The books "read" in the latter case are the material from which the narrators have mined the stories or maxims they rework into their new tales, or with which they seek to bolster their authority.

These citational "reads," therefore, invoke the specialized form of reading characteristic of authors or of scholars, typologized in chapter 4 as literary- and scholarly-professional reading. Literary authors, in Chaucer, are always presented as processing "olde bokes" into "newe science" (PF: 24–25). The reason that there are so many "reads" in section C of chart 6.1 and so few in section B, thus, is that authors, usually, read while audiences, usually, hear – the two modalities existing not in rigid opposition or in an uncomfortable state of transition, but as naturally "mixed" complements in what I have labeled the "aural-narrative constellation."

This impression is further confirmed by section E, which collects reception-verbs used to describe the transmission of stories. Not coincidentally, hearing plays a large role in these passages. The sounds that arrive at the House of Fame, for instance, derive in part from the reading of books, while fallen women such as Dido and Criseyde lament that the writing of stories about them will lead to their names being rolled on many a tongue.

It is true that many of section C's "reads" take the form of syllabus recommendations to the audience; e.g., "The same wordes writeth Ptholomee; / Rede in his Almageste, and take it there" (CT 3: 182–83). Such suggestions, however, are surely intended more to impress than to educate the audience. Yet the situation is even more complicated, because there are two sorts of narrators in these tales. One, Chaucer, was a genuine literary-professional private reader, and his "reads" can be supposed to reflect, more or less reliably, his recreative efforts. In the mouths of his fictional narrators, on the other hand, these "reads" pose a variety of problems. Even if the Wife of Bath didn't "really" expect the Pardoner to go off and read the *Almagest*, had she "really" read it herself? If so, how? The vast majority of texts invoked by the pilgrim narrators were in Latin, French, and Italian. Even if they could have obtained the books and could have read them, how many of them knew these languages?

Such speculations, of course, soon dissolve into absurdity. The person who really could and did read the sources cited by his fictional characters was Chaucer; and in accepting this we accept the citations as instances of literary-professional private reading. Inasmuch as they can be read in character for the fictional narrators, they represent attempts to borrow the prestige of author or scholar – whom these oral performers seem far more eager to imitate than they are to play at minstrels, as many scholars assume. Their pretensions, of course, become part of the comedy: it is hard to credit source-citations delivered from astride a horse somewhere in the middle of Kent. If we are to suppose these narrators "really" knew their texts, we would probably have to suppose that knowledge, in most cases, to have been obtained aurally. Any acquaintance that laypeople would have with the Bible, the text cited most frequently, would probably come from aural readings and explications by clerics; and Alison of Bath, of course, could only have picked up her erudition second-hand, via Jankyn's aural readings or explications.

A detailed look at the passages listed in section C gives some idea of the complexities of Chaucer's citational "reads." Seven out of Chaucer's eight references to identified sources employ the same formula, "whoso [wants to know]/[can], read ..."; e.g., "Which whoso willeth for to knowe, / He moste rede many a rowe ..." (HF: 447–48). His fictional narrators, in their references to identified sources, are much more aggressive. Half the twenty-two passages use the simple, peremptory formula, "Read ..."; e.g., the Nun's Priest's "Redeth Ecclesiaste of flaterye" (CT 7: 3329). Along with the implicit second-person voice of the imperative, five further quotes use the pronoun "ye"; e.g., the Clerk's "As seith Seint Jame, if ye his pistel rede" (CT 4: 1154).

Thus Chaucer, in his own narrative voice, adopts a stance at once more self-effacing and more self-assured; should someone want to catch up with his reading, he suggests with a politely indirect third-person "whoso" and "he," that person might have some work to do. The second-person formulas of the fictional oral narrators, on the other hand, seem to mix ostentation with insecurity: if you think I'm wrong, they might be saying, go and read the book yourself – if you can. Chaucer's sole excursions into the second-person come, interestingly, with the impatient tone of the two quotes from *The Legend of Good Women*: "Ye may as wel it sen as ye may rede" and "Ye gete namore of me, but ye wole rede / Th'origynal" (lines 1263, 1557–58). The effect, perhaps, is to emphasize the unlikelihood of his female audience being able to read the Latin original – a rare ungracious gesture from an author eager to move on to more important projects.

Finally, the formula "(as) I read" shows us the author/narrator in the very moment of recreative composition: e.g., "But now to purpos; in the story I rede ..." (LGW: 1825). It is the natural complement, as noted in chapter 4, to the reception-phrase "as ye shall hear," coordinating the professional reading of source-texts with the recreational listening to the new texts that reading produces.

While their use in different contexts carries different shades of meaning, Chaucer's citational "reads" also serve the trans-narrative strategy of constituting a sort of "fictive literacy." These professional and pseudo-professional "reads" proliferate in order to bolster the sense of an aggregated written tradition standing behind the vernacular storytelling event. The effect is reinforced by the background buzz of "as men read" and "rede auctour" phrases, referring to unidentified or proverbial sources, and by the replication in the fictional narration of the phrases Chaucer uses when speaking *in propria persona*.

For all the forms of authorial literacy flourished in his texts, however, Chaucer gives no hint that he wishes his audience would read him in a similarly dividual fashion. He provides no passage along the lines of Boccaccio's famous exhortation to "those who would appreciate poetry": "You must read, you must persevere, you must sit up nights ..." (in Hardison et al. 1974: 208). The only person in Chaucer who sits up "A-nyght ful ofte [his] hed to ake" (HF: 632) is Chaucer himself, working away among his books in his study to provide texts destined to arrive, translated into sound waves, at the House of Fame.

RECEPTION DRAMATIZED

Having surveyed Chaucer's reception-phrases, I will next take the "ethnography of reading" approach deeper into the texts, to examine the "reading events" that Chaucer depicts within the frame of his fictions. This analysis will be structured around the typology of medieval reading offered in chapter 4. Along with the categories of pragmatic, scholarly-professional, literary-professional, religious, and recreational reading developed there, two further subcategories will be added. The first takes account of the many instances in which texts are read not only privately but "privily," that is, secretly. The second includes those "hypothetical" cases where a reading event is invoked not as a "real" occurrence but as something imagined by or for a character. The instances of "hypothetical religious private readers" are striking enough to merit a separate discussion.

The guideline for selecting a text as an instance of "dramatized reception" was that the character is actually shown reading or talks directly about how he or she read something, or that at a minimum there is strong circumstantial evidence about the character's reading style. Thus the Man of Law's impressive knowledge of the works of Chaucer and Gower doesn't qualify – any more than does Chaunticleer's reading of Macrobius or the Nun's Priest's nonstop citation of authorities – because these readers give no clue as to how they read their texts (if they did read them). Similarly, although we might assume that the Merchant read his business papers privately, Chaucer never shows him doing so or has him describe such events, so that his presumptive habits do not count as evidence for a particular mode of reading. And while many of his characters write and read letters, Chaucer less often specifies whether the recipients read their letters to themselves or (as was a not uncommon habit) had someone else read them aloud. Finally, for now I will list the four cases in which Chaucer shows himself reading within his fiction simply as "Chaucer reading"; their possible interpretations will be discussed at some length below.

Chaucer, his texts, and his age are often associated with – and explicated in terms of – the rise of an English middle class and the literacy its members acquired as they went about their increasingly complex business. In view of the importance of this phenomenon and its clear impact on Chaucer – as reflected, for example, in the social composition of the Canterbury pilgrims – it seems odd that he presents only two instances of classic (i.e., commercial) pragmatic reading.

Among the traits of the Man of Law, Chaucer mentions:

> In termes hadde he caas and doomes alle
> That from the tyme of kyng William were falle.
> Therto he koude endite and make a thyng,
> Ther koude no wight pynche at his writyng;
> And every statut koude he pleyn by rote.
> (CT 1: 323–27)

Literacy is clearly integral to the Man of Law's profession, and one would surely be justified in assuming that he often read his "termes" (legal yearbooks), documents, and statutes privately. While he keeps his precedents in books, however, the Man of Law has internalized his key texts, the basic laws of the country. These he would have learned, presumably, both by private study and by attending legal lectures such as those described by Paul Brand, which combined a reading of the statute with commentary (1987: 148). Although the claim that the Man of Law knew "every statut ... pleyn by rote" may be exaggerated, it reflects the persistent interaction of modalities even in a pragmatic setting: written texts that are transmuted through prelection and private reading into memorized texts presented orally.

While the Man of Law's reading styles must be conjectured, Chaucer provides an explicit example of pragmatic private reading for business purposes. In this case, however, the reading is not only pragmatic and private; it is secret. Chaucer particularly notes the care the Shipman's merchant takes, when he goes to read over his books and count his money, to shut himself in:

> His bookes and his bagges many oon
> He leith biforn hym on his countyng-bord.
> Ful riche was his tresor and his hord,
> For which ful faste his countour-dore he shette;
> And eek he nolde that no man sholde hym lette
> Of his acountes, for the meene tyme;
> And thus he sit til it was passed pryme.
> (CT 7: 82–88)

But in shutting himself in, the merchant is also shutting himself out: while he is putting his commercial affairs in order, his withdrawal from social life leaves the way clear for Don John to seduce his wife. As clear an advance as pragmatic reading may seem to the social historian, in fabliau terms it functions merely as an adjunct to cuckoldom.

There are several other instances of secret-pragmatic reading, however, all focused on the one genre one would suppose most suited for such reading: namely, love letters. As with the Shipman's merchant, Chaucer emphasizes the "privy"-ness of this correspondence, suggesting the asocial nature of such undertakings. The classic illustration of the secret love letter involves an unavoidable pun: May's "privy" reading of Damian's first epistle:

> She feyned hire as that she moste gon
> Ther as ye woot that every wight moot neede;
> And whan she of this bille hath taken heede,

> She rente it al to cloutes atte laste,
> And in the pryvee softely it caste.
> (CT 4: 1950–54)

May writes a letter back to Damian and takes an opportunity to stick it under his pillow (4: 1995–2008), "rede it if hym leste" (line 2004). Damian is thus another secret-pragmatic reader. The two lovers carry on their courtship "by writyng to and fro / And privee signes" (lines 2104–5).

When Criseyde receives Troilus' first love letter, she takes to her chamber to read it "pryvely":

> And streght into hire chambre gan she gon;
> But of hire besynesses this was on –
> Amonges othere thynges, out of drede –
> Ful pryvely this lettre for to rede.
> (T&C 2: 1173–76)

An illumination from a copy of one of Chaucer's sources, the *Roman de Troilus* (see figure 2), reflects the perceived oddness, and peril, of a reader allowing herself to be thus cut off from the mainstream of society. The crowd pressing against the left-hand wall of the right panel seems to emphasize the isolation of Criseyde in the left panel, as she holds her letter up to the light to read.

Once the correspondence is under way, it seems to proceed in the same conditions of privacy (T&C 2: 1318–30; 3: 488, 501–3). After Criseyde leaves Troy, Troilus finds solace in more private reading:

> The lettres ek that she of olde tyme
> Hadde hym ysent, he wolde allone rede
> An hondred sithe atwixen noon and prime,
> Refiguryng hire shap, hire wommanhede,
> Withinne his herte, and every word or dede
> That passed was . . .
> (T&C 5: 470–75)

This description is a tribute to the ability of the written word to preserve and imaginatively recreate a departed time or person. The final set of letters Troilus and Criseyde exchange relay his requests that she return and her increasingly futile promises to do so.

Although Paul Christianson has cited these private letter-readings as proof of the importance of literariness in Chaucer's work (1976/77: 113), they are clearly framed as functional. Indeed, how else would one read love letters? Since, for her leisure reading, Criseyde chooses to have one of her maidens prelect the *Siege of Thebes* (see below), her reading habits reflect not a triumph of "literacy" but the sophisticated coexistence of a variety of situation-sensitive literacies.

When Chaucer mentions the mode of reading for non-love letters, it seems to be a public reading. In *Troilus and Criseyde*, Helen and Deiphebus read their "business" letter from Hector together – "this ilke thing they redden hem bitwene" (T&C 2: 1706) – as they ponder the correct response. No reception modality is specified in the *Legend of Good Women*, where Dido, Hypsipyle, Medea, and Phyllis each writes a letter to her seducer. Phyllis' letter to Demophon closes, however, with lines that suggest it was intended to publish his iniquity to the world at large:

> And whan this letter was forth sent anon,
> And knew how brotel and how fals he was, ...
> (LGW: 2555–56)

One might classify such a text as an open letter – a genre that R. F. Green notes "was in fact often employed for propaganda purposes" (1980: 185).

Most of the scholarly-professional readers presented by Chaucer belong to the sensationalistic category of secret-private readers; they are educated men dipping into proprietary texts with the aim of gaining arcane powers. The "yonge clerkes" known to Aurelius' brother in the Franklin's Tale, for example, strayed off the standard curriculum in pursuit of heterodox, magical skills:

> ... hym fil in remembraunce,
> That whiles he was at Orliens in Fraunce –
> As yonge clerkes that been lykerous
> To reden artes that been curious
> Seken in every halke and every herne [every nook and cranny]
> Particuler sciences for to lerne –
> He hym remembred that, upon a day,
> At Orliens in studie [in a study hall] a book he say
> Of magyk natureel, which his felawe,
> That was that tyme a bacheler of lawe,
> Al were he ther to lerne another craft,
> Hadde prively upon his desk ylaft ...
> (CT 5: 1117–28)

The word "prively" clues us to the asocial implications of such reading, which is confirmed when the magic of the "subtil clerk" (CT 5: 1261) whom Aurelius recruits almost forces the faithful Dorigen into adultery.

The would-be alchemists envisaged by the Canon's Yeoman study as eagerly as the clerks of Orléans, but to less purpose:

> "Ascaunce [Do you think] that craft is so light to leere?
> Nay, nay, God woot, al be he monk or frere,
> Preest or chanoun, or any oother wyght,
> Though he sitte at his book bothe day and nyght
> In lernyng of this elvysshe nyce loore,
> Al is in veyn, and parde, muchel moore."
> (CT 8: 838–43)

We do not see Nicholas reading in the Miller's Tale, but the Miller does describe the clerk's books as part of his astrological gear:

> His Almageste, and bookes grete and smale,
> His astrelabie, longynge for his art,
> His augrym stones layen faire apart,
> On shelves couched at his beddes heed.
> (CT 1: 3208–11)

The Miller has earlier noted that Nicholas "hadde lerned art [the university arts curriculum], but al his fantasye / Was turned for to lerne astrologye" (1: 3191–92). Since Nicholas lives in his chamber "allone, withouten any compaignye" (line 3204), he presumably reads his books alone as well. Nicholas' solitary, extracurricular study of astrology, plus his locking himself in his room for supposed astrological study into "Goddes pryvetee" (line 3558), seem to place his form of reading within the category of secret-professional.

While secret-pragmatic reading seems to lead in a roundabout way to socially harmful results – cuckoldom for the Shipman's merchant and for January, and a doomed love affair for Criseyde and Troilus – the secret reading of professional scholars equips them to afflict others quite directly. Their arcane learning enables the magician to deceive and, almost, destroy Dorigen; the alchemist-canon to bilk the ignorant; and Nicholas to cuckold his host. In each case the individual benefits at the expense of the greater community. Despite the phenomenon's importance in the social history of fourteenth-century England, Chaucer thus tends to associate the privatizing of both pragmatic and scholarly-professional reading with a secrecy harmful to social relationships.

This point is underlined by an examination of the non-secret scholarly-professional and religious readers, of whom there are two well-known examples: respectively, the Clerk and the Parson. It makes sense to combine these two cases here, because they seem to be constructed as deliberate parallels. The Clerk is a professional scholar who shares Chaucer's passion for books. His reading consists of specialized texts "of Aristotle and his philosophie" (CT 1: 295). Like most university students, he would presumably have both heard these books read in lectures and read them privately on his own. His integrity and the sincerity of his pursuit of wisdom is emphasized in the famous line: "And gladly wolde he lerne and gladly teche" (CT 1: 308).

The Parson is the only other disinterested reader in Chaucer's fiction, a similarly idealized figure whose learning is acquired for the religious goal of preaching, presumably through a similar mix of hearing and private reading:

> He was also a lerned man, a clerk,
> That Cristes gospel trewely wolde preche;
> His parisshens devoutly wolde he teche.
> (CT 1: 480–82)

Pragmatic or professional secret readers, who hoard their knowledge to themselves, disrupt society; by contrast, scholarly-professional and clerical readers who gladly pass their knowledge on to others benefit society, communicating not only information but also the integrity and humility their studies encourage. Their reading exists in a dialectic with their society and their audience, serving the common profit and creating benefit for themselves and others.

That such reading also had the potential of creating harm, however, is illustrated by another clerical reader and preacher, the Pardoner. Chaucer emphasizes his public reading and singing abilities when introducing the character in the General Prologue:

> Wel koude he rede a lessoun or a storie,
> But alderbest he song an offertorie;
> For wel he wiste, whan that song was songe,
> He moste preche and wel affile his tonge
> To wynne silver . . .
> (CT 1: 709–13)

The Pardoner does not seem to be much of a scholar; beyond a superficial acquaintance with a few exempla and the odd Latin tag, his reading seems to have been as shallow as his preaching and teaching. Thus he has escaped, or been deprived of, the Parson's exalted poverty. The Pardoner's "half-made" condition underscores the lesson that, for Chaucer, scholarly/clerical learning properly transforms the individual; the reader does not merely acquire knowledge or rhetorical skill but becomes a different and better person.

Among the cases of hypothesized reading, three widely scattered instances stand out for their surprising congruence as forms of what could be called "hypothetical religious private reading." Criseyde resorts figuratively to such reading when Pandarus teases her with an invitation to go dancing:

> "I! God forbede!" quod she. "Be ye mad?
> Is that a widewes lif, so God yow save?
> By God, ye maken me ryght soore adrad!
> Ye ben so wylde, it semeth as ye rave.
> It satte me wel bet ay in a cave
> To bidde and rede on holy seyntes lyves;
> Lat maydens gon to daunce, and yonge wyves."
> (T&C 2: 113–19)

Criseyde's vision of private reading conjures up not the enfranchised literate so often imagined by scholars today but a mute anchoress – a female version of the "dazed hermit" that in the *House of Fame* the Eagle is afraid Geoffrey will turn into if he continues his eccentric habits:

> "For when thy labour doon al ys,
> And hast mad alle thy rekenynges,
> In stede of reste and newe thynges
> Thou goost hom to thy hous anoon,
> And, also domb as any stoon,
> Thou sittest at another book
> Tyl fully daswed ys thy look;
> And lyvest thus as an heremyte,
> Although thyn abstynence ys lyte."
> (HF: 652–60)

Few of the scholars who gleefully cite this passage as evidence of private reading have noted the humorously negative associations with which Chaucer surrounds it. (Equally few have noted that the description does not straightforwardly concern reading; see below.)

Finally, Chaucer offers one interesting negative case, of a character who might or should read privately but who prefers to hunt. "What sholde he studie and make hymselven wood," Chaucer says of the Monk of the *Canterbury Tales*,

> Upon a book in cloystre alwey to poure,
> Or swynken with his handes, and laboure,
> As Austyn bit?[2]
> (CT 1: 184–87)

Chaucer thus humorously suggests the potential hazards of private reading three times, in three widely separate contexts that echo each other remarkably. Each associates private reading with the contemplative religious life: Criseyde would become an anchoress, Chaucer (as hypothesized by the Eagle) lives like a hermit, the Monk could be *behaving* like a monk. Each emphasizes the reader's isolation: Criseyde in a cave, Chaucer alone in his study, the Monk in the cloister. The reading matter is implicitly unappetizing: Criseyde piously plowing through saints' lives, Chaucer sitting at another book (the Eagle's tone is surely disparaging), and the Monk poring over tracts. Each case is strongly associated with poor health and even madness: Chaucer refuses "reste and newe thynges," sits "domb as any stoon," and reads until he looks "fully daswed"; and the Monk is spared by his love of hunting from making himself "wood" with study. Although Criseyde does not picture herself becoming ill or crazy from her cave-reading, the context seems to attract such associations. Because Pandarus has suggested she go dancing with him she calls him "mad" and tells him, "Ye ben so wylde, it semeth as ye rave" (T&C 2: 116). (In a cognate instance in the Miller's Tale, Nicholas locks himself in his room and pretends to read the stars, until John concludes he must have fallen, "with his astromye, / In some woodnesse or in som agonye" [CT 1: 3451–52].)

Finally, in each case private reading is opposed not to public reading but to a public, social activity – although the opposition emerges within a different context for each. Criseyde retreats to her imagined cave in comic horror at being invited to go dancing; Chaucer really does read, and suffers the deficits involved, instead of getting out and talking to his neighbors; and the Monk could and perhaps should read but prefers to hunt.

In eschewing communal leisure activities, these hypothetical private readers are making a renunciation; they are turning their back on the world. Hence those who would make such a choice are appropriately likened to religious recluses. Unlike the Clerk and the Parson, ascetics neither teach nor preach. As Chaucer depicts them, they return nothing to society; their learning is arid, their reading merely a form of self-denial. Society loses the individual, and the individual, in painful isolation, risks losing both health and sanity.

Two Chaucerian "set pieces" of recreational public reading are very well known: Criseyde and her maidens being read to in the "paved parlour" (T&C 2: 78–84) and Jankyn reading to Alison of Bath by their hearthside (CT 3: 669–793). It's worth quoting the Criseyde scene at greater length than it is usually allowed:

> Whan he [Pandarus] was come unto his neces place,
> "Wher is my lady?" to hire folk quod he;
> And they hym tolde, and he forth in gan pace,
> And fond two othere ladys sete and she,
> Withinne a paved parlour, and they thre
> Herden a mayden reden hem the geste
> Of the siege of Thebes, while hem leste.
> ....
> [Pandarus:] "But I am sory that I have yow let
> To herken of youre book ye preysen thus.
> For Goddes love, what seith it? telle it us!
> Is it of love? O, som good ye me leere!"
> "Uncle," quod she, "youre maistresse is nat here."
>
> With that thei gonnen laughe, and tho she seyde,
> "This romaunce is of Thebes that we rede;
> And we han herd how that kyng Layus deyde
> Thorugh Edippus his sone, and al that dede;
> And here we stynten at thise lettres rede –
> How the bisshop, as the book kan telle,
> Amphiorax, fil thorugh the ground to helle."
> (T&C 2: 78–84, 94–105)

We know that Criseyde is literate, because she can read Troilus' love letters privately, and here she points out the rubric to Pandarus and reads it to him. The passage shows no trace of the supposedly innate contradiction between a hearing audience and a written book that allows modern scholars to interpret the mention of a book with turnable pages as marking a key transition point into private reading. Nor do any of the standard "deficiency" motives seem to be present. The listeners (at least the chief one) are literate; nor is there any sense that they are having to make the best of things by maximizing everyone's access to a unique copy of a desirable text. Criseyde at least seems to know the story very well; one gets the feeling that she (and thus probably her maidens) has heard it before.

Rather than reflecting any contradictions or deficiencies, the entire scene breathes elegance and refinement; this is a court (a small one) *being* a court – sharing a pleasurable activity in a way that unites the members while it entertains them. Even though Criseyde is obviously the dominant member of this group, their camaraderie comes through clearly in her three uses of the pronoun "we" to describe their joint activity: "This romaunce is of Thebes that we rede"; "we han herd how that kyng Layus deyde"; and "we stynten at thise lettres rede" (T&C 2: 100, 101, 103). In this literary example of courtly recreational reading, as in the historical British examples reviewed in the previous chapter, shared public reading tends to suppress status distinctions.

The courtly reading of the *Siege of Thebes* at first glance seems to do no more than make a pretty picture in a paved parlor. Yet it stands in a crucial position for Criseyde. It is the scene Pandarus and we see as he enters to begin his and Troilus' campaign for her favors. Reading with her women, Criseyde is engaged in a communal yet chaste activity, over which she has control and in which she is free and safe. Later, as a private reader of Troilus' love letters, she is in a way coming too much under the author's power, moving towards erotic merger and a consequent loss of chastity and control. Ultimately, because she has been Troilus' lover, her acceptance of Diomede destroys her reputation to posterity – a posterity that will experience her infamy through "bokes" whose texts will be "rolled ... on many a tonge" (T&C 5: 1060–61).

Chaucer matches his depiction of courtly leisure reading with another famous set-piece of domestic reading among the petty bourgeoisie: Jankyn's prelection of his book of wicked wives to his wife, Alison of Bath:

> Upon a nyght Jankyn, that was oure sire,
> Redde on his book, as he sat by the fire,
> Of Eva first, that for hir wikkednesse

> Was al mankynde broght to wrecchednesse ...
> Tho redde he me how Sampson loste his heres;
> Slepynge, his lemman kitte it with hir sheres ...
> (CT 3: 13–16, 21–22)

As noted in chapter 3, in reading aloud to his wife, the ex-"clerk of Oxenford" (CT 3: 527) Jankyn seems to be trying to adopt the same privileged stance towards her that an academic lecturer enjoyed towards his students. Rather than the relatively non-hierarchical reading, the "we rede" and "we han herd" of Criseyde and her maidens, we have the Wife's reiterated "Tho redde he me," "Tho redde he me," "He tolde me," "Of Lyvia tolde he me," "Thanne tolde he me" (CT 3: 721, 724, 740, 747, 757). Each unidirectional phrase introduces another instance of female perfidy. But Jankyn's attempt to impose these stories on his wife transgressed the rules of British recreational reading, in which the hearers expected to participate in the choice of text and the manner of its reading. There can be no bonding as a group when the text being shared grossly insults half the prospective group. Thus, as the students at a lecture could never do, Alison asserted her right not to hear a book she didn't like – the result being a rather messily conducted but nonetheless successful reorganization of the couple's relationship. Like Criseyde's reading with her maidens, *mutatis mutandis*, public reading seems to impel Jankyn and Alison toward consensus and security.

After these famous and perhaps archetypal illustrations of upper- and middle-class prelection, there are two other possible examples to cite. The first is the Franklin's short introductory reference to "thise olde gentil Britouns" who

> Of diverse aventures maden layes,
> Rymeyed in hir firste Briton tonge,
> Whiche layes with hir instrumentz they songe
> Or elles redden hem for hir plesaunce.
> (CT 5: 709–13)

This reading was presumably aloud; the description invokes a pleasant scene of public amusement, reminiscent of the historical descriptions of British prelection in chapter 5.

The second instance is an implied case of prelection. That devoted scholarly private reader, the Clerk, seems to suggest that he heard Petrarch's *De obedientia ac fide uxoria mythologia* – his source for the tale of Griselda – from Petrarch's own mouth. "I wol yow telle a tale," he says,

> which that I
> Lerned at Padowe of a worthy clerk,
> As preved by his wordes and his werk.
> (CT 4: 26–28)

Later he adds:

> But forth to tellen of this worthy man
> That taughte me this tale, as I bigan,
> I seye that first with heigh stile he enditeth,
> Er he the body of his tale writeth,
> A prohemye, . . .
> (CT 4: 39–43)

The Clerk fully acknowledges that Petrarch's text exists in writing, and one might even accept as metaphorical his imagery of learning the tale as taught him by Petrarch. By claiming this lesson took place at Padua, however, where Petrarch actually lived and where he himself might well have studied (Ginsberg 1988: 879, note to line 27), the Clerk conceivably expects his audience to understand that he learned this written text from hearing its author recite it or read it aloud. Petrarch was, in fact, in the habit of doing just this: not only was he fond of reciting Boccaccio's Italian version of Griselda, but he records inviting two different friends to prelect his own Latin translation (see Robinson and Rolfe 1898: 192–96). It thus seems quite possible that the fictional Clerk (or, as some editors like to speculate [e.g., Johnson 1923: 261], the real Chaucer) could have been audience to some such Petrarchan performance of the story he is about to retell.

Finally, under the rubric of dramatized episodes of reading aloud one might also cite two portraits of Chaucer. In the first, the famous *Troilus and Criseyde* frontispiece (Corpus Christi MS. 61, f. 1v), Chaucer is not reading but, apparently, reciting; he stands at a pulpit without a book, while below him sits an elegant group that is probably meant to represent the court of Richard II. Derek Pearsall (1977) and Elizabeth Salter (1978) have made an excellent argument that the illumination's iconography draws on preaching pictures, but it is hard to know how to interpret that fact. Whatever subtleties the illustrator meant to suggest, however, the picture does offer support for the sense that Chaucer's poetry existed in a matrix involving face-to-face interaction with the audience.

A similar impression might be derived from the altogether less elaborate and less famous Lansdowne portrait of Chaucer (BL Lansdowne 851, f. 2). Although M. H. Spielmann dismissed it as "hardly worth serious consideration" and endorsed Furnivall's allusion to it as a "stupid peasant thing" (Spielmann 1900: 11), there is a poignancy and expressivity in the picture. It shows Chaucer standing with an open book held somewhat tipped forward in his hands; both the book and his eyes are directed at an angle of about forty-five degrees from the page – reminiscent of the saints in books of hours who are shown holding an open Bible at a similar angle. This stance may combine the suggestion of an offer to communicate the book's contents – perhaps by reading it aloud – with the authority conveyed by possession of the book itself. The peasant-grade Lansdowne portrait, therefore, shares with the top-drawer *Troilus* frontispiece not only an idiosyncratic reliance on religious iconography in the depiction of a secular author but also a concept of Chaucer as an author who seeks urgently to reach his audience. Like other illustrations that show authors presenting or prelecting books, these pictures invite us into a community of readers and hearers.

If courtly widows, misogynistic clerks, ancient Bretons, and international literary figures read their recreational texts aloud, who reads such texts privately? Chaucer presents only two such dividual readers, one somewhat equivocal, and the other extremely equivocal: namely, Pandarus and Chaucer. In neither case is it entirely clear what the reader is doing, or what we are expected to understand about what he is doing. I will discuss Pandarus in this section and Chaucer in the following one.

Pandarus may be the only completely fictional recreational private reader in Chaucer. Or he may not. The issue arises when, after bringing Troilus to Criseyde's bedside, he makes a discreet withdrawal:

> And with that word he drow hym to the feere,
> And took a light, and fond his contenaunce
> As for to looke upon an old romaunce.
> (T&C 3: 978–80)

There is no telling if in "looking upon" an old romance Pandarus is supposedly reading it or just looking at the pictures. In any case he is evidently only pretending to do whatever it is he seems to be doing – a point emphasized in the three *Troilus* exemplars that give "feigning his contenaunce" for "and fond his contenaunce" (Jennings 1986: 126).

This scene makes one recall Paul Strohm's comment that "like characters in postmodern fictions, the protagonists of *Troilus and Criseyde* seem constantly on the brink of discovery that they are characters in a book" (1989: 61). Here Pandarus, who has "authored" the entire relationship of the two lovers, pretends to scan a written romance while behind him, in "real life," his puppets speak the classic lines of romance lovers. Yet in fairness one has to take the slippery Pandarus enough at face value to admit that his fireside perusal of the old book offers some evidence for the private reading of romances.

CHAUCER READING

After all the happy public readers we have met to date, the fictionalized Chaucer, reading quietly alone in his bed or study, may seem a forlorn figure. To many modern scholars, however, his solitude marks, as D. S. Brewer puts it, "a landmark in the development of the internalization of literary communication" (1982: 21). As I have suggested above, however, the distinctness of that landmark somewhat depends on how we classify the fictional Chaucer's status as a reader. The system constituted by the aural-narrative constellation accepts without problem that authors read privately while audiences read publicly. So, is the fictional Chaucer an author or an audience? Is he reading for fun or looking for copy? Before attempting to answer these questions, I will review the four texts in which Chaucer does his reading.

In the *Book of the Duchess* Chaucer puts himself to sleep reading Ovid's *Metamorphoses*. In the *House of Fame* the Eagle accuses him of reading (and writing; see below) all day instead of talking with his neighbors (HF: 652–60). In the *Parliament of Fowls* Chaucer confides that "Of usage – what for lust and what for lore – / On bokes rede I ofte" (PF: 15–16). "A certeyn thing to lerne," he passes "the longe day ful faste" reading Cicero's *Somnium Scipionis* (PF: 20–21). After his vision of the avian parliament

> I wok, and othere bokes tok me to,
> To reede upon, and yit I rede alwey.

> I hope, ywis, to rede so som day
> That I shal mete some thyng for to fare
> The bet, and thus to rede I nyl nat spare.
> (PF: 695–99)

In the *Legend of Good Women* his bibliomania is equally apparent:

> And as for me, though that I konne but lyte,
> On bokes for to rede I me delyte,
> And to hem yive I feyth and ful credence,
> And in myn herte have hem in reverence
> So hertely, that ther is game noon
> That fro my bokes maketh me to goon,
> But yt be seldom on the holyday . . .
> (LGW, F: 29–35)

These passages clearly establish Chaucer-the-character, in all four of the dream-visions, as a private reader. And certainly the first impression one might get of this reader, in all but the *House of Fame*, is of a friendly, naïve bibliophile, nattering on enthusiastically about books and literature. We may find ourselves relaxing into an identification with this fictional reader; we, who have just opened his book to read it, find him inside the text drawing us in by imitating our action, offering us his eyes to read the story he is now going to derive from the text he has before him. In this hall-of-mirrors effect, we perceive him as a simulacrum of ourselves, a recreational reader sitting down to another book; we somehow accept his experience of his text as passive: he merely reads it, as we merely read his. One of the most recent and eloquent scholarly exponents of this view, Jill Mann, states unequivocally that "Chaucer's role as reader of others' work is a covert surrogate for our own role as readers of his own" (1991: 2).

I think that this particular illusion, however charming, represents that ultimate in unlikelihood, the impossible improbable. It is impossible because even within the fictional framework the author/reader is not a passive but a very active reader, the maker of fictions, including the fiction in which he pretends (we think) to be passive. As I will show, in each of the works in which he shows himself reading, Chaucer ultimately connects that process of reading to the process of writing that follows; he thus retroactively identifies himself as a literary-professional reader. As A. C. Spearing comments in his book on medieval dream-poetry, "The treatment of the dreamer as a real person, based on the poet himself, inevitably implies that the dreamer shares the poet's profession as a writer of poems" (1976: 45–46). And, as noted in chapter 4's description of literary-professional reading, literary authors cannot *not* read professionally; whatever they read is a potential source for or influence on their own work. It seems disingenuous to equate, as Mann does, a recreative reading of texts that results in a new, written text with a receptive one that involves only some fairly transient mental activity – i.e., to equate the reading of sources with the reading of books.

It is furthermore improbable that a fourteenth-century person would accept the privately reading dreamer/poet as a simulacrum of him- or herself, because most audiences of that time would have perceived this devotion to reading as a clear indication of the reader's professional status. It would stand out because it was *unlike* their experience, not delude them because it was so like it.[3] This latter argument could be considered circular, since it relies on my general argument that most late fourteenth-century audiences consisted of hearers. But the point gains weight from a closer reading of Chaucer's texts themselves.

The pleasure Chaucer associates so persistently with his reading conceivably reflects not a book-lover's happy obsession but the delight of the knowledgeable fellow-practitioner. It recalls the Clerk's passion for Aristotle or Petrarch more than the genteel amusement of Criseyde and her maidens, or the "plesaunce" of the Franklin's ancient Bretons. If this seems unlike the often waspish assessments we are used to more recent authors bestowing on their colleagues' writing, we should note that, even when he speaks directly as his "real" self, Chaucer's comments on other authors are always positive. Any doubts he felt about the authority of tradition were expressed obliquely, through the juggling of variant sources or in-jokes at an unnamed Gower. Commentators on Chaucer himself, from Deschamps through to Henryson, competed to pile up his praises. The critical mentality considered synonymous with "literacy" waited until long past Chaucer's time to replace the exophoric valorization of a communalized tradition.

But is the fictional Chaucer a poet? The answer develops differently in each of the texts in which he makes an appearance, but the answer is always, ultimately, yes. To begin with, all four works under consideration are dream-visions, in which well-established genre, as Spearing indicates, the dreamer is always the poet and the poem is always his dream. Moreover, in Chaucer the dream is always related in some way to the reading of books. And, for Chaucer, the reading of books is always related to the writing of more books.

This relationship is perhaps clearest in the prologue to the *Legend of Good Women*. The poem's opening lines reflect – along with the narrator's "delyte" in books (F: 30) – a clear, if tongue-in-cheek, preoccupation with such literary-professional issues as the nature and reliability of authority. And long before he encounters the angry God of Love, Chaucer's persona reveals himself to be a poet. "Allas, that I ne had Englyssh, ryme or prose, / Suffisant this flour to preyse aryght!" (F: 66–67) he exclaims, contemplating his daisy. He continues with an appeal to other poets, lamenting that they had "herbiforn / Of makyng ropen, and lad awey the corn" (F: 73–74).

Once into the dream, of course, Chaucer encounters the angry Cupid and the benign Alceste spouting his own bibliography back at him, eliminating any uncertainty about his professional status. It is at this point that the relationship of these two hitherto separate functions, reading and writing, comes into focus, through the medium (in the G version) of Love's reproach:

> "... in alle thy bokes ne coudest thow nat fynde
> Som story of wemen that were goode and trewe?
> Yis, God wot, sixty bokes olde and new
> Hast thow thyself, alle ful of storyes grete."
> (LGW, G: 271–74)

Here books – the writer's reading – form the quarry from which he is expected to select the matter for his own narration. Alceste takes up Chaucer's defense by first emphasizing his role as a translator, who "rekketh noght of what matere he take" (F: 365) or who haplessly follows the orders of a superior. Chaucer-the-character tries a similar argument when he protests that, "what so myn auctour mente" (F: 470), he intended in his *Criseyde* and his *Romance of the Rose* to "forthren trouthe in love" (F: 472). Finally, the prologue ends, in the F version, with the couplet:

> And with that word my bokes gan I take,
> And ryght thus on my Legende gan I make.
> (LGW, F: 578–79)

Thus, what initially looked like the recreation of a book-loving but nonprofessional reader – for whom "ther is game noon / That fro my bokes maketh me to goon" (LGW, F: 33–34) – seems slowly to have involved itself in a very professional set of problems. Reading as the exposing of oneself to potential sources involves the question of choosing stories to retell, of telling them well, of relaying the original *sentence* or another one of your own devising. These issues, though surely faced by Chaucer-the-poet, are articulated as the ones confronting Chaucer-the-character, who has emerged unambiguously as himself a poet. By the end of the prologue he is diving eagerly into the heart of this relationship – taking (someone else's books) in order to make (his own books).

The reading/writing pattern that emerges so clearly in the *Legend of Good Women* is also not far to seek in the other three poems containing a reading Chaucer. The *Book of the Duchess* and the *Parliament of Fowls*, in particular, combine the same initial coyness or indirectness about his poetic persona with eventual, sometimes almost incidental, references to the character's identity as a poet. The Chaucer of the *Book of the Duchess* may seem at first too innocuous to be a poet. He is obsessed with his insomnia, and with the lovesickness that may underlie it. His reading seems a palliative, a fit occupation for someone too physically or emotionally weak to do anything less passive. Yet well into retelling the story of Ceyx and Alcyone, Chaucer describes himself as "I, that made this book" (BD: 96). With this passing reference, Chaucer-the-character identifies himself as a poet. The book he has described himself reading, moreover, has obviously now become a source for a retelling, which the character implicitly admits was his. Thus he is not just any reader but a poet who draws on his reading to write another poem. Chaucer falls asleep with his head in his book; he wakes to be a poet:

> Thoghte I, "Thys ys so queynt a sweven
> That I wol, be processe of tyme,
> Fonde to put this sweven in ryme."
> (BD: 1330–32)

The poet in the character is equally implicit and discoverable in the *Parliament of Fowls*. He reads for lust and for lore both (PF: 15) – and by now we know that the acquisition of lore, for Chaucer, is a step towards the creation of rhyme. It is the new corn coming from the old fields, the new science from old books (lines 22–25). Pausing before beginning to narrate his dream, he invokes Cytherea's help "my sweven for to write, / So yif me myght to ryme, and endyte!"

(lines 118–19). Later, Scipio leads him through Venus' gate, encouraging him:

> "And if thow haddest connyng for t'endite,
> I shal the shewe mater of to wryte."
> (PF: 167–68)

In both the *Book of the Duchess* and the *Parliament of Fowls*, then, Chaucer-the-character ultimately gets around to identifying himself as a poet, whose reading feeds into his writing. There is no sense of deliberate plotting about this, no revelation like the "She ys ded!" of the *Book of the Duchess* (line 1309) (no "I'm a poet!"). Rather, it feels as if Chaucer expected people to know he was a poet, that beyond the jokes about his dullness as a lover he fully acknowledged his persona as a fictionalized doer of what he himself did – forever tracing a Möbius curve on which reading turns into writing which turns into more reading.

There is a quirk in Chaucer's depiction of himself reading in the *House of Fame*, however, which is that he doesn't depict himself reading. His persona does not omit to identify himself as a poet, with now-familiar casualness, well before the Eagle takes up the issue. "Nere it to long to endyte," he says of Dido's death, "Be God, I wolde hyt here write" (HF: 381–82). In the proem to Book II he asks that the Muses "me to endite and ryme / Helpeth" (lines 520–21). Thus it is no surprise when the Eagle starts listing the "bookys, songes, dytees, / In ryme or elles in cadence" (lines 622–23) that Chaucer-the-character has made "in reverence / Of Love and of hys servantes eke" (lines 624–25). He describes how Chaucer

> "wold make
> A-nyght ful ofte thyn hed to ake
> In thy studye, so thou writest,
> And ever mo of love enditest."
> (HF: 631–34)

Moreover, the Eagle continues, Chaucer gets no tidings from either far or near, because "In stede of reste and newe thynges" after work, he goes home and "sittest at another book" (HF: 654, 657). The latter phrase is almost always taken to describe Chaucer – and Chaucer-the-*poet* at that – reading privately. Yet the word "read" occurs nowhere in the entire extended passage (HF: 620–60). When, in lines 655–58,

Chaucer is sitting dumbly and dazedly at another book in his house, is it not likely that we are returning to the scene already described in lines 631–34, in which Chaucer makes his head ache with late-night enditing in his study? The Eagle seems to be making one sustained argument: Jupiter has taken pity on Chaucer, who serves Cupid and Venus by incessantly writing songs and books in their praise; yet Chaucer has no direct tidings of the process of Love in the world precisely because of this habit – because he is always in his study sitting at – i.e., writing – another book. This would seem to be the most likely, text-based interpretation.

Not that there need be any doubt that this process of writing included reading; if that point hasn't been driven home by the phenomenology of writing noted in Chaucer's other texts, it seems to be the very heart of the *House of Fame* itself. The fact that modern scholars have picked up on the reading only may reflect their delight in finding a text that, they think, describes Chaucer as a silent reader, echoing Augustine's description of Ambrose and heralding simultaneously the much-anticipated Age of Literacy.

Thus it seems that, within the frame of his fictions, Chaucer always depicts himself as a literary-professional reader. As much as he enjoys dissimulating this identity at first, he never relinquishes it. It is his version, perhaps, of the "supreme commonplace" stance assumed by writers addressing the "public sphere" (Lawton 1987: 771; see chapter 4). A modern analogue might be the "On the Town" section of the *New Yorker* magazine. In these short pieces, a thinly veiled but elusive authorial self relates, with Chaucerian modesty, various adventures whose point usually comes around to some issue of public responsibility. One enjoys the author's genial pose of average man-about-town at the same time as one realizes, and he subtly communicates, that he is in fact a professional writer, being published in a prestigious magazine.

Chaucer-the-character's book-dazedness makes an odd sort of paradigm for potential private recreational readers: relatively few members of his audience would be likely to cast themselves as copycat Chaucers, if that meant turning their private reading into new books full of cleverly written verse. Robert Henryson tried it (see chapter 7), but Henryson was a professional author, using as his Chaucerian "seed-book" a volume of Chaucer himself. To understand the true nature of Chaucer's reading, modern readers have to strain against both the seductiveness of Chaucer's fictional persona and the historical developments that have left his specialist behavior seeming normative.

The kind of reading with which Chaucer-the-character should properly be aligned is not recreational but scholarly-professional and religious. As the Clerk's reading turns into teaching and the Parson's into preaching, so does Chaucer's turn into writing – and hence, most likely, into prelection. In each case, the individual's love of books reaches fruition in some form of validating social communication. The privacy into which these readers must withdraw is not noxious because it is not solipsistic; they leave society not to impoverish but to enrich it upon their return.

This sense of social responsibility emerges in the paradigmatic nature of the reading that Chaucer's persona undertakes in the *Book of the Duchess*, the *Parliament of Fowls*, and the prologue to the *Legend of Good Women*. In each of these works, Chaucer's statements about reading invoke a different standard medieval doctrine about the usefulness of books. The congruities of the literary function cited in each case with the poem that follows are striking.

Chaucer-the-insomniac reads in the *Book of the Duchess* in order to "drive the night away" (line 49), a hygienic use of literature related by Glending Olson to the *Tacuinum sanitatis*' discussion of the dangers and cures of sleeplessness (1982: 85–89). "For thus moche dar I saye wel," he says:

> I had be dolven everydel
> And ded, ryght thurgh defaute of slep,
> Yif I ne had red and take kep
> Of this tale next before.
> (BD: 221–25)

This reference stressing the hygienic uses of literature prefaces a text intended to help cure the Black Knight's grief for the death of his wife. In fact, the text is full of cure: Chaucer is cured of insomnia, Ceyx of intolerable anxiety, and the Knight of despair.

In the *Parliament of Fowls* Chaucer emphasizes the didactic usefulness of literature. He reads "for lust" but also "for lore" (PF: 15); he resorts to the *Somnium Scipionis* "a certeyn thing to lerne" (line 20). After awaking from his vision, he decides to "rede alwey" in hopes of meeting "some thyng for to fare / The bet" (lines 696, 698–99). These references establishing the teaching function of literature frame a debate whose format mingles not only those of a parliament and a court of love but also, with its emphasis on "resoun" and "replicacioun" (lines 534, 436), an academic disputation. Finally, in the prologue to the *Legend of Good Women* Chaucer prefaces his expressions of delight in reading with another medieval commonplace about books, that they offer "of remembraunce the keye" (LGW, F: 26). This reference, extolling literature for preserving the past, prepares the way for nine capsule history lessons.

In all of these references, Chaucer grounds his love of reading in typical medieval views on the uses of literature. Not only that: he prefaces each narrative with a paradigmatic piece of reading that illustrates the specific benefits the audience can derive from the poem to follow. In this subtle way, Chaucer-the-character's private lust for reading is transmuted through dream and imagination into material of broad social benefit – hygienic, educational, and historical.

CONCLUSION

It is surely the vividness with which Chaucer-the-poet presents his persona's bibliophilia that leaves most modern critics convinced of the proto-modernity of the reading environment within which the poet supposedly wrote. Chaucer certainly evinces a passion for and a breadth of reading that justify his reputation as a private reader committed to the inscribed word. But, as we have seen over the course of this book, the concept of "private reader" is not as transparent as is generally assumed. Whereas nowadays almost all reading, of any kind by any sort of person for any purpose, is private and silent, in the fourteenth and fifteenth centuries people read in different ways, privately or publicly, depending on context and role.

By distinguishing among pragmatic, professional, and recreational readers, it becomes possible to see clearly that Chaucer, inside and outside his fictions, read as a literary-professional reader, and would have been perceived as so doing. His contemporary audience would have had no illusions about the specialist nature of his reading because they would have recognized his passion for reading as an attribute proper to that professional status, just as illuminators considered a table full of books the fitting pictorial attribute of a writer (see chapter 4). To one of his contemporaries, I believe, the most conclusive evidence of the fictional Chaucer's professionalism would have been precisely his taste for reading in that most poignant of

Chaucerian conditions, "allone, withouten any compaignye" (e.g., CT 1: 2779).

The complement of that resonant solitude, however, was the aurality of the resulting text. Throughout his writings, Chaucer accepts without concern their probable oral delivery; he invokes such events in his reception-phrases and he depicts them in his fictions. To return into and in some ways to constitute and enlighten such a community is the rationale, at a deep level, for the entire enterprise of fiction. In this light, it may be interesting to consider a variation of the paradigmatic character of reading in the *Book of the Duchess*, the *Parliament of Fowls*, and the prologue to the *Legend of Good Women*. In the *House of Fame* the fictional Chaucer reads in order to write – seeking a good, literary creation, that is not as clearly utilitarian as health, education, or remembrance. It is important enough to Jupiter, however, that he arranges a voyage for Chaucer which, among other things, brings him among embodied sources: the great poet-pillars in the House of Fame, the babbling crowd of gossipers in the House of Rumor. Yet the poem does not present us with an instantiation of the function invoked by Chaucer's initial reading, as in the other three dream-visions. That is, reading in order to write does not result, in the text, in a new, perhaps improved literary creation – unless the unfinished *House of Fame* itself is that creation. Perhaps, even, that poem is as incomplete, chaotic, brilliant, and elusive as it is because Chaucer could not achieve coherence when talking about a kind of reading and thinking that is so self-directed, conceived in reference to himself and his internal creative processes only, without a clear link to the standard channels of general social benefit.

For all Chaucer's proto-modernity, or proto-postmodernity, then, a close reading or "ethnography" of his views on reading sends us firmly back to the medieval sense of literature's embeddedness within a community, and a community of hearers. If it's not true that the "lettre sleeth, so as we clerkes seyn" (CT 3: 1794), the letter encountered in solitude clearly has the potential to disrupt or harm that community; just as the poet who becomes too involved with his own involvement with letters ends up with a text too open-ended to be comprehensible.

7

An "ethnography of reading" in non-Chaucerian English literature

The preceding two chapters have scoured the pages of both history and the Chaucer canon to see how late medieval people read. Chapter 5 found that, in almost every case surveyed, where evidence chanced to survive about reading behavior in France and the duchy of Burgundy, and in England and Scotland, the readers were members of the upper classes, they were indisputably literate, and they were reading publicly, until at least late in the fifteenth century. This was so even though reading took place in different contexts and served different functions on either side of the Channel. Chapter 6's in-depth look at Chaucer's writings found that at many levels he embraced public reading as normative and beneficial. Private reading emerged as dangerous unless practiced by a reliable professional who would ultimately return his reading to a social context by preaching, teaching, or rewriting it.

The present chapter completes this three-pronged attack by turning to non-Chaucerian literary sources. It further weakens the "fictive orality" arguments of Mehl and Burrow (see chapter 3) by showing that, like Chaucer, many fourteenth- and fifteenth-century court-oriented poets addressed listeners and referred regularly to the hearing of books. Of course, most of these poets had read Chaucer, so one could conceivably argue that they were all imitating his fictive orality. It might be multiplying entities beyond reason, however, to maintain that a consistent assumption of aurality (or bimodality)[1] by a variety of writers in a variety of genres over a hundred and fifty years before, during, and after Chaucer derives from the somehow universal desire to give private readers the thrill of pretending to be hearers. Similarly, it seems a long time for a "survival" to persist, with no reinforcement from reality. It would also seem rather strained special pleading to claim that the "new," private reader flashed into existence during the lifetime and career of that one genius Geoffrey

Chauce r, then quick-dissolved into the nothingness of the "re-medievalized" poets who came limping along after him. Surely the most economical explanation of the persistent references to the hearing of literature would simply be that people *were* hearing: that literacy added an option rather than imposing obsolescence; that "read," when applied to audience reception, remained undifferentiated – neutral as to anticipated format – throughout the late fourteenth and much of the fifteenth century.

The present chapter will focus on the reading formats attributed to audiences by the authors of what can loosely be described as court literature, from the mid fourteenth through the late fifteenth century. "Court literature" for these purposes will describe works written by people known to be associated with the court and/or dealing with issues of national interest. The genres include dream-visions, specula principis, and the more ambitious narrative poetry and romances. The emphasis on "high-end" literary production is meant to ensure that the authors of these works would be addressing upper-middle- to upper-class readers, whom these authors would almost certainly expect to be literate.

The survey of non-Chaucerian literature will be divided into three chronological sections: 1350–1400, 1400–50, and 1450–91, with a brief concluding glance forward as far as 1525. These time-breaks are pegged to the convenient death-dates of three major figures: Chaucer's in 1400, Lydgate's *c.* 1450, and Caxton's in 1491. Thus we have the "age of Chaucer," the age of his immediate followers, and the dawn of the age of printing.

For the research presented below I reviewed all of the major and many of the more obscure surviving works of secular (non-religious and non-devotional) literature in English. I excluded the drama and most romances, histories, non-recreative translations, and scholarly works of science or philosophy. I read selectively among the Scots poets of this period; and finally, being only human, I restricted my reading of Lydgate to certain representative texts.

AUTHORS CONTEMPORARY WITH CHAUCER (1350–1400)

None of Chaucer's contemporaries mentions books and reading as often as he does. When they do address such topics, however, they show the same awareness of variant forms of professional and recreational reading, coupled with the same general assumption that audiences will be hearing their own or other people's books.

Reading events

John Gower's *Confessio Amantis* (1st rec., 1390) provides two instances of scholarly-professional private reading. Socrates' wife, hauling in a bucket of water on a cold winter day, is provoked to see

> how that hire seli spouse
> Was sett and loked on a bok
> Nyh to the fyr . . .
> (CA 3: 658–60)

When the aggrieved Xantippe dumps the water over her spouse, he remarks mildly that she has but "mad me bothe wynd and rein / After the Sesoun of the yer" (3: 692–93) (see figure 10).[2]

Socrates' happily single colleague, Diogenes, chooses a modest dwelling where he can

> studie in his Philosophie,
> As he which wolde so defie
> The worldes pompe on every syde.
> (7: 2245–47)

By contrast, his former fellow-student Aristippus "his bok aside / Hath leid, and to the court he wente" (7: 2248–49). But Diogenes, Gower repeats,

> duelte stille
> At home and loked on his bok:
> He soghte noght the worldes crok
> For vein honour ne for richesse . . .
> (7: 2266–69)

Gower also presents one case that recalls Chaucer's pejorative view of secret-private professional reading. Nectanebus, an Egyptian clerk, uses his proprietary skill as a scholarly-professional reader of astrology and magic to persuade Queen Olimpias that the god Amos wants to sleep with her. After showing her his astrolabe, he reads and expounds an astrological tome:

> the hevenely figures
> Wroght in a bok ful of peintures
> He tok this ladi forto schewe,

> And tolde of ech of hem be rewe
> The cours and the condicion.
> And sche with gret affeccion
> Sat stille and herde what he wolde.
> (6: 1893–99)

Olimpias duly impressed and compliant, Nectanebus proceeds to do his worst with his magic books: "His chambre he himselve tok, / And overtorneth many a bok" (lines 1955–56), looking up equations, constellations, conjunctions, and receptions as he fashions a wax image of the hapless queen. The propitious time selected, he turns up himself in Amos' stead and with Olimpias conceives a son who will grow up to be Alexander the Great.

Gower's attitude to scholarly-professional reading differs significantly from Chaucer's. He agrees in finding secret reading (even, in a category he introduces, secret-public reading) of proprietary texts dangerous. But he doesn't seem to care if his private professional readers complete the feedback loop. He is interested in how Socrates' and Diogenes' reading shapes them as individuals, functioning in an untrustworthy world, but he shows no concern about whether they return their learning to that world in the form of teaching or writing. Rather, he seems to idealize their withdrawal from the world.

William Langland includes two dramatized scenes of reading in *Piers Plowman* (B rec., 1379). However, both are so heavily allegorized that they offer little useful insight into probable real-life reading. In the first scene, Conscience accuses Lady Mede of misreading Solomon, comparing her to a lady who read "omnia probate" at the bottom of a page, without turning it to see the sentence's conclusion: "quod bonum est tenete" (3: 338–43). Conscience imagines Mede, "sittynge in [her] studie" (line 345), making a similar mistake.

The second scene is the famous tearing of the pardon, in which a priest "construes" the Latin text into English for Piers (7: 106). It seems credible enough that a plowman would need such assistance, yet Langland complicates the issue improbably by having Piers then give out a string of biblical quotations, in Latin. When the astonished priest exclaims: "Peter! as me thynketh, / Thow art lettred a litel – who lerned thee on boke?", Piers replies: "Abstynence the Abbesse ... myn a.b.c. me taughte, / And Conscience cam afterward and kenned me muche moore" (lines 131–34).

A Latinate plowman, educated by allegorical personifications, seems only somewhat less unlikely than two ladies (Mede and her hypothetical counterpart) in studies searching the Latin Bible for texts that could justify their dissolute lives. Langland, for all his many other virtues, thus proves fairly useless as an "ethnographic informant"!

The first example of recreational reading from this period occurs in the *Parlement of the Thre Ages*, a debate among Youth, Middle Age, and Age written between 1353 and 1370. Youth informs Middle Age that he likes to go falcon-hunting,

> And than kayre to the courte that I come fro,
> With ladys full louely to lappyn in myn armes,
> And clyp thaym and kysse thaym and comforthe myn hert;
> And than with damesels dere to daunsen in thaire chambirs;
> Riche Romance to rede and rekken the sothe
> Of kempes [warriors] and of conquerours, of kynges full noblee,
> How thay wirchipe and welthe wanne in thaire lyues;
> With renkes in ryotte [merry-making] to reuelle in haulle,
> With coundythes [conducts, part-songs] and carolles and
> compaynyes sere,
> And chese me to the chesse that chefe es of gamnes;
> And this es life for to lede while I schalle lyfe here.
> (lines 246–56)

The "riche Romance" passage stands syntactically isolated between Youth's dancing with damsels in chamber and his rioting with renkes in hall, so that it's not clear with whom or where he read; technically, it isn't even definite that he read with anyone else. Given the overwhelmingly social context of all his activities, however, we are surely justified in assuming that his reading was equally social; and given further his preference for tales of military conquest, we may assume he more probably shared the experience with his male friends.

Gower's *Confessio Amantis* provides a companion account to that of the *Parlement*. Amans explains eagerly to his Confessor that he is not guilty of Somnolence, because he is ready to wait on his lady at any time. He is there if she "list on nyhtes wake / In chambre as to carole and daunce" (4: 2778–79), as well as

> whanne it falleth othergate,
> So that hire like noght to daunce,
> Bot on the Dees to caste chaunce
> Or axe of love som demande,

Or elles that hir list comaunde
To rede and here of Troilus.
(4: 2790–95)

The authors of these two descriptions of audiences and romances have placed these remarkably similar contextualizations of prelected literature in surprisingly congruent literary contexts. Both are spoken by a character as a form of self-indicting *confessio*; both characters, and the lifestyles they pursue, are implicitly critiqued as senselessly frivolous. Both characters will learn better: Youth as he inevitably evolves into Middle Age, Amans when he is forced to confront his senescence. The pattern also fits Accidia's confession, in *Piers Plowman*, that he is ignorant of Scripture but "I kan rymes of Robyn Hood and Randolf Erl of Chestre" (B 5: 396), which he apparently has learned and performs memorially. All three confessions relate to the genre and ideology of the vices: Amans is seeking to defend himself against a charge of Somnolence (which is a subset of Sloth, or Accidia) while implicitly condemning himself for precisely that; Accidia, of course, is Sloth personified; and Youth's predilections mingle Sloth and Lechery as the sins appropriate to his age.

Despite the atmosphere of authorial disapproval, however, the courtly scenes invoked in Gower and the *Parlement* also strongly recall the real-life evenings in the courts of James I of Scotland and Edwards III and IV. Like those historical records, both literary scenes mix the prelection of romances with singing and with games. But both also add further, mixed-sex activities: dancing and, in the case of Amans, love-demands. The historical records of prelection do not mention women as present, but it seems that, when such entertainments are dramatized in literature, women are a necessary addition – not so much as potential listeners, but as potential love-partners. Here the author of the *Parlement* and Gower may be working a literary one-two: distorting the nature of recreational prelection to include an obligatory sex-interest, but placing the whole in a context of mature disapproval that fosters their self-image as wise counselors. It may be their aspirations to that role that led Gower, Langland, and the author of the *Parlement* – all writing in English – to be so ready to condemn works of English literature as potential accessories to Lechery or Sloth.

These dramatized incidents of reading behavior support the hypothesis that public reading during Chaucer's lifetime was associated with recreational contexts, and private reading with professional-scholarly or religious ones. There is also a basis for deriving author-specific "reading-maps," in the suggestion that Gower patterned his reading events differently from Chaucer.

One further matter for speculation is the persistently disturbing relationship of women, in these texts, to the reading of books. Amans' lady and Youth's paramours are associated with recreational reading, as part of a seductive environment dangerous to men; Olimpias is doubly the dupe of a lecherous clerk's professional reading (beguiled, first, by his display of erudition and, second, by the shape-shifting his books teach him); Xantippe is condemned for her stupid indifference to books, and Mede and the hypothetical lady for their stupid attempt to read them. By contrast, Chaucer's two most realized scenes of public reading both feature women in a non-sexualized and sympathetic manner: Criseyde and her maidens reading a vernacular romance are the image of self-sufficient femininity; whereas the Wife of Bath, in her more explosive behavior as listener, nonetheless wins admiration for her defense of her sex against the misogyny of clerks. Chaucer's less stereotyped, more sympathetic attitude towards women as readers is further evidence of what Arlyn Diamond calls his "painfully honest effort, this unwillingness to be satisfied with the formulas of his age ... [which shows that he] means to be women's friend, insofar as he can be" (1977: 83).

Reading channels

The aural-narrative constellation discernible in Chaucer's canon can be found also in the works of his contemporaries. I will take a close look at its operation in the work of the other chief storyteller of his period, Gower, before reviewing more cursorily the other texts in this section.

The prologue to Gower's *Confessio Amantis* takes up the issue of transmission right away:

> Of hem that writen ous tofore
> The bokes duelle, and we therfore
> Ben tawht of that was write tho:
> Forthi good is that we also
> In oure tyme among ous hiere
> Do wryte of newe som matiere,
> Essampled of these olde wyse

So that it myhte in such a wyse,
Whan we ben dede and elleswhere,
Beleve [Be left] to the worldes eere
In tyme comende after this.
(CA prol.: 1–11)

In this concise statement Gower covers most of the basic features of the aural-narrative constellation: written sources (lines 1–3), a writing author (lines 4–6) picking up the exempla (line 7) of his sources and presenting them in new form, to an audience conceived of as "the worldes eere" (line 10) – a striking phrase that vividly asserts the perceived perpetuity of aurality. Gower caps his argument by nominating his work "a bok for Engelondes [alt.: king Richardes] sake" (line 24), effectively ascribing to himself the status of national counselor (see chapter 4). Thus his public voice addresses, through the prelector's mediation, the public sphere he envisages as "the worldes eere."

The elements condensed in this prologue recur throughout the text. In his prologue, at the beginning of book 1, and in his epilogue Gower speaks directly to his audience, using standard aural phrases to describe their reception. In introducing his dream of Amans and the Confessor, Gower says he will write (prol.: 74) for hearers (line 66) who will read him (line 77). We note the familiar aural phrases "as ye shall hear" (prol.: 589; 8: 3055), "as ye have heard devise" (prol.: 822; 1: 96), and "Now herkne, who that wol it hiere" (1: 96).[3]

Like Chaucer, Gower connects the transmission of stories with aurality. He is rich in references to the basic equipment of such performance: ears, mouths, and tongues. Speaking of Moses and other lawgivers, for example, the Confessor declares:

For evere, whil there is a tunge,
Here name schal be rad and sunge
And holde in the Cronique write.
(7: 3047–49; see also 6: 1223–26, 1395–96; 2: 3030–32, 3038–40)

Of considerable interest is the closing Latin verse of the *Confessio*:

Here ends this book, let it pass on free, I beg,
That without envy it may flourish in the reader's mouth.

(Explicit iste liber, qui transeat, obsecro liber
Vt sine liuore vigeat lectoris in ore.)
(CA 8: following line 3172)

The fact that the lines are in Latin adds weight to the reference to prelection, since Gower used his Latin commentary to imbue his vernacular love-stories with a more ambitious and didactic *sentence*. He would be unlikely to foster a trivializing fiction about his text in these glosses; rather, he used them to *reveal* devices, such as "the author feigning himself to be Amans" ("fingens se auctor esse Amantem"; gloss to CA prol.: 60).

As Chaucer's pilgrims reproduced his narrative phrases, so does Gower's Confessor when relating his exemplary tales to Amans: e.g., "if thou wolt hiere" (2: 288), "as thou schalt hiere" (3: 277), and "as thou hast herd devise" (4: 3689). He often introduces or carries a tale with an "as I read": e.g., in telling of Ariadne, "And after this, so as I rede, / Fedra, the which hir Soster is ..." (5: 5480–81). He also falls into the same mistake as Chaucer's Second Nun, conflating writtenness and hearing when he reminds Amans that he has "heard" a story "above" – e.g.,

> "That riht as it with tho men stod
> Of infortune of worldes good,
> As thou hast herd me telle above,
> Riht so fulofte it stant be love."
> (5: 2445–48; see also 4: 3274–75, 3642–44; 5: 2643–44)

It seems odd to speak of someone listening to an oral narration as "hearing it above," and it certainly would be odd to speak of someone reading a written narrative privately as doing so; but the description makes a kind of sense for someone hearing someone else read a narrative aloud from a written text.

Despite the Latinity and superliterate *ordinatio* with which he surrounds his poem for England's sake, Gower seems to share with Chaucer the basic sense that writers transmit their rewritten sources to the ears of their audience. He refers many times and unambiguously to the hearing of his own and other texts. In moving beyond the standard phrases to such idiosyncratic ones as his address to "the worldes eere," he signifies that such invocations are not merely conventional but part of an ongoing reality.

Chaucer's two greatest contemporaries are sparser sources for references to reading behavior. Langland shows little interest in the general uses or reception formats of literature. He employs the classic introductory phrase one time, describing the field of folk:

> Barons an burgeises and bondemen als
> I seigh in this assemblee, as ye shul here after.
> (B prol.: 217–18)

A few other times he uses a format-unspecific "read," as in his advice to beggars: "Lat usage be youre solas of seintes lyves redyng" (B 7: 85). As in the case of the Latinate ladies and the Bible-quoting Piers cited above, however, Langland is unreliable as an "ethnographic informant": how many beggars did he think would be able to read, let alone have any books to read from?

The *Gawain*-poet, on the other hand, addresses the issue of transmission and reception several times, most notably in the second stanza of *Sir Gawain and the Green Knight*:

> Bot of alle that here bult of Bretaygne kynges
> Ay was Arthur the hendest, as I haf herde telle.
> Forthi an aunter in erde I attle to schawe,
> That a selly in sight summe men hit holden,
> And an outtrage awenture of Arthures wonderes.
> If ye wyl lysten this laye bot on littel quile,
> I schal telle hit astit, as I in toun herde,
> with tonge;
> As hit is stad and stoken
> In stori stif and stronge,
> With lel letteres loken,
> In londe so has ben longe.
> (*Gawain*, lines 25–36)

Here the author seems to say he has heard stories of Arthur in general, and specifically has heard this story about Gawain "in toun" (meaning, according to Tolkien and Gordon, "among men, in company" [p. 72]), "with tonge." Further, he seems to say that he expects his audience to hear his version of it now, since he asks them to "lysten this laye bot on littel quile." Finally, he links the tradition's durability to the alliterative form it is presented in.

Since *Gawain and the Green Knight* is one of the great poems of the Middle Ages, there has been some tendency to depreciate these apparent declarations of aurality, drawing on the standard strategies and confusions discussed in chapter 3. Larry D. Benson (1965), for example, gets lost within very hazily conceived ideas of "oral" and "written," persistently passing lines 31–32 off as a writing author's "debt" or even "compliment" to an older (therefore, presumably, superseded) oral tradition. He glimmeringly acknowledges a possible middle ground, noting that the poet's "insistence on oral transmission – 'with tonge' – seems to reflect at least a transitional stage of the sort A. C. Baugh discovered in the metrical romances, the stage of literary composition and oral transmission." But he immediately temporizes: "That tradition must have been very weak by the Gawain-poet's time" (pp. 119–20). Benson is tripped up, for one thing, by his difficulty in relating oral performance to anything but minstrel delivery, as reflected in his final pronouncement: "for though there is no doubt that an oral tradition existed, it is equally obvious that there was a sudden literary revival and that the poets who participated in it had more sophisticated goals than merely reducing to paper what once existed in song" (p. 121).

Polarization, conflation, and evolutionism combine in Benson to efface recognition of the "transitional stage" of aural reading in favor of a maximally literate, writing, sophisticated poet. In the context of widespread contemporary acceptance of the hearing of books, and in the context of this present book, however, we may find it easy enough to envisage a literate poet hearing various stories read aloud and then writing his own in the anticipation that it would be read aloud in turn. In writing under these conditions he might well include formulas or other features conditioned by his knowledge that the poem might be prelected or recited, some of which might well derive from the memorial or peroral history of the alliterative tradition he was writing in. The poet could do all this without himself being a minstrel *and* without having to write down to any presumed audience of unsophisticated illiterates.

The *Gawain*-poet addresses reception in only a few other places. In *Cleanness* he ascribes both private and public reading behavior to himself, noting

> Bot I have herkned and herde of mony hyghe clerkes,
> And als in resounes of ryght [true writings] red hit myselven,
> That that ilk proper prynce that Paradys weldes
> Is displesed at uch a poynt that plyes to scathe [applies to sin];
> Bot never yet in no boke breved I herde,[4]
> That ever he wrek so wytherly on werk that he made, [as on uncleanness].
> (*Cleanness*, lines 193–98)

If he both hears read and reads privately when it comes to religious writing, he seems more likely to hear recreational material read, as in the description of Gawain's wanderings:

> Mony wylsum way he rode,
> The bok as I herde say.
> (*Gawain*, lines 689–90)

The *Gawain*-poet also uses the standard aural phrase just once. When the Green Knight picks up his severed head he "meled thus much with his muthe, as ye may now here" (*Gawain*, line 447). Direct address and invocations of hearing audiences occur more frequently, e.g.:

> Wyl ye tary a lyttel tyne and tent me a whyle,
> I schal wysse yow therwyth as Holy Wryt telles.
> (*Patience*, lines 59–60)

The same sense of immediacy comes through in the late fourteenth-century Anglo-Norman biography of the Black Prince, Chandos Herald's *La Vie du Prince Noir*. The author, an Hainaulter who served as herald to Sir John Chandos and later became English king of arms, was obviously well acquainted with English court culture. His account of Richard II's father readily attributes aurality to his audience: he will begin his tale, e.g.,

> Thus as you will be able to hear
> If you but listen with a good heart.
>
> (Ensi come vous oier purrez
> Mais qe de bon coer l'escoutez.)
> (lines 53–54)

Perhaps the least notable, as well as the least likable, writer among those consulted for this period is Thomas Usk, who wrote his weighty *Testament of Love* (1387) in a vain attempt to win pardon from the Merciless Parliament after being convicted of treason. We may assume that Usk would hardly have offered his work for the "profit of the reders, [and] amendement of maners of the herers" (p. 106) if such a phrase might have offended the merciless MPs with an implication of illiteracy or backwardness.

Surprisingly, Usk provides some of the most thoughtful and revealing descriptions of the reading/listening process. In his opening apologia, he contrasts cleverly "colored" *gestes* and rhymes with his own supposedly unadorned but more substantial prose treatise. In vivid terms that transcend the merely conventional, he makes it clear that both forms of writing would normally be heard:

> Many men there ben that, with eeres openly sprad, so moche swalowen the deliciousnesse of jestes and of ryme, by queynt knitting coloures, that of the goodnesse or of the badnesse of the sentence take they litel hede or els non.
>
> Soothly, dul wit and a thoughtful soule so sore have myned and graffed in my spirites, that suche craft of endyting wol not ben of myn acqueyntaunce. And, for rude wordes and boystous percen the herte of the herer to the in[ne]rest point, and planten there the sentence of thinges, so that with litel helpe it is able to springe; this book, that nothing hath of the greet flode of wit ne of semelich colours, is dolven with rude wordes and boystous, and so drawe togider, to maken the cacchers therof ben the more redy to hente sentence. (p. 1)

At a later point, Love instructs Usk that "bookes written neyther dreden ne shamen, ne stryve conne; but only shewen the entente of the wryter, and yeve remembraunce to the herer" (p. 14). In such a context, the occasional reference to readers alone – including a "thou reder" (p. 3) reminiscent of Chaucer – must probably be classified as "format-neutral."

Usk goes beyond Chaucer, however, in offering the beginnings of a phenomenology of aural reading. The "eeres openly sprad" that take in the *gestes* and rhymes but miss the *sentence* if any are contrasted to the hearer's heart pierced and implanted with the *sentence* of rude words, which in another striking image is to be "hente" by word-"cacchers." Further into his text, Usk asks for the prayers of "every inseer and herer of this leude fantasye" (p. 145). This word "inseeing" seems a very apt term for the process of absorbing the deep meaning of a work; it also seems, if not to be synonymous with hearing, at least not to be antagonistic to it. The sort of deeply internalized engagement with texts that is sometimes thought to rely on private reading seems here to be attributed to aural reception. Aurality also co-exists, in Usk as in Gower, with invocations of "scholastic literary theory" – specifically, an explication of the *titulus libri* and of final causality (Minnis 1988: 163–64).

This survey of Chaucer's contemporaries has revealed a general acceptance of public reading as a means of experiencing both frivolous and serious literature. Only "professional" readers such as Gower's Socrates, Diogenes, and Nectanebus are depicted reading privately. A less brilliant, and accordingly less argued-over, author than Chaucer, Gower organizes his narratives with the same hearing phrases that Chaucer does, assumes books are heard as often as Chaucer does, and evokes or depicts public recreational reading as regularly as Chaucer does. Few scholars have remarked on this parallelism; if they had, would they argue that Gower too was trying to promote a fictive orality, or carrying over minstrel phrases? How would such an argument take in Usk's far from conventional aural phraseology, and Youth's reading habits? And is it far-fetched to think Chandos Herald really expected his audience to be hearing him, when the squires of Edward IV's (and, retroactively, Edward III's) court would be described, *c.* 1471, as "talking of" just his kind of knightly chronicle? The evidence from Chaucer's more obscure contemporaries, writing in a variety of languages and genres, thus seems to support the hypothesis that his references to public reading simply recorded a current reality.

AUTHORS IN THE FIFTY YEARS AFTER CHAUCER'S DEATH (1400–1450)

The first half of the fifteenth century continued and intensified themes present in the time of Chaucer, in particular the importation into vernacular literature of scholarly procedures and language. Some writers follow Gower in making an ostentatious display of their academicism, while others follow Chaucer in focusing on their process in recreating their specialized sources as new works of literature. Whether with authorial input or not, scholarly organization and apparatus (especially glosses) are added to manuscripts of vernacular literary works.

The audience in this period was evolving as well. The fifteenth century is noted as a period of rising literacy and increasing availability of books (see, e.g., Owst 1961: 8–9; Edwards and Pearsall 1989: 257). Humanism was also filtering into England through such figures as Humphrey, duke of Gloucester. It is not surprising, then, that for the first time the texts we will survey occasionally conceive of the audience (sometimes as a general entity, and sometimes as a particular patron) reading in a studious, scholarly, and possibly private fashion.

Yet despite such incipient realignments, texts from the first half of the fifteenth century continue to manifest the aural-narrative constellation of phrases and references. Authors continue to address their "readers and/or hearers," while the occasional unconventional reference makes it clear that these usages are not mere formalisms. Even when academic vocabulary and procedures abound (as in *Mum and the Sothsegger*), the nature of these references and the invocations of hearing that accompany them remind us that scholarly-professional reading was as strongly aural as dividual.

This period does present one anomalous text in the prologue to *Partonope of Blois*, which makes a precocious distinction between literate readers and illiterate hearers. This passage (see below) must be accepted as evidence that a recognizably modern conception of reception modalities had been formulated before the close of the Middle Ages in England. Since, however (as far as my research extended), no other vernacular author made a similar distinction until the early sixteenth century, the *Partonope* prologue remains an intriguing but isolated case.

Reading events

This period provides two cases each of dramatized literary-professional and recreational reading.

Thomas Hoccleve's *Series* (1421–22) is an odd assortment of autobiography, stories, and *memento mori*, with connecting links. As J. A. Burrow (1984) has persuasively hypothesized, the compilation represents Hoccleve's attempt to demonstrate his return to normality and competence following on the mental breakdown recalled in the opening "Complaint." One way Hoccleve seeks to prove his competence as a poet is to give us many scenes of himself and a friend reading and discussing his source-texts.

This friend enters the poem knocking and hallooing at Hoccleve's door, demanding to know what he was doing. For reply, Hoccleve says, "right anon I redd hym my 'complaynt'" ("Dialogue," line 17). The two then decide that Hoccleve's next project should be a translation of a tale from the *Gesta Romanorum*. In the epilogue to this translation, the friend turns up again to read it – to himself, it seems, since "he it nam / In-to his hand and it al ouersy" (epilogue to

"Jereslaus' wife," lines 6–7). Missing the moralization, he goes home to fetch his copy of the *Gesta*, then "cam ther-with and it vn-to me redde" (line 22). After a translation of the *Ars moriendi* ("Lerne to dye"), the friend advises Hoccleve to translate a tale he had "redde" ("Jonathas," line 5) and Hoccleve "red haue on rowe" (line 33). He brings Hoccleve the book, and the poet duly translates it.

The overseeing friend, whether or not he ever existed, allows Hoccleve to air his poetic rationales and self-defenses, and, in their interdigitating readings, "redings" (in the sense of advice-giving), and lendings of books, creates a strong impression of the professionalism of Hoccleve's activities. This professionalism presupposes private reading but also moves easily into public reading, as the two friends alternately read to each other and to themselves.

The *Kingis Quair* (*c.* 1435) of James I of Scotland provides a less manic, more traditional example of Chaucerian literary-professional reading. Unable to sleep, the king takes up a copy of Boethius and reads the night away (stanzas 2–7), until

> The long nyght beholding, as I saide,
> Myn eyen gan to smert for studying,
> My buke I schet and at my hede it laide.
> (stanza 8, lines 1–3)

James diverges from Chaucer only in that his reading is the prelude not to a dream but to a decision to write another book, which relates a dream-vision he had in the past. In sending this "litill tretisse" out once written, James gives clear evidence that he, also like Chaucer, expected it to be read aloud. He asks

> the reder to haue pacience
> Of thy defaute, and to supporten it,
> Of his gudnesse thy brukilnesse to knytt,
> And his tong for to reule and to stere
> That thy defautis helit may bene here.
> (stanza 194)

Here "reder" must mean reader-aloud.

The first example of recreational reading from this period is also the first case of recreational private reading. The passage comes from a work now labeled *Mum and the Sothsegger*, which incorporates two fragments: the first called *Richard the Redeless* (before 1400), addressed to Richard II shortly before his deposition; and the second being *Mum and the Sothsegger* proper (1403–6), which continues the argument for the benefit of Henry IV. In the prologue to the first fragment the author anxiously asserts his loyalty and good intentions. Young men may pick holes in his logic, he says, but if

> elde opyn it [his book] other-while amonge,
> And poure on it preuyly and preue it well after,
> And constrewe ich clause with the culorum [conclusion],
> It shulde not apeire [injure] hem a peere a prynce though he were.
> (R prol.: 70–73)

In a poem full of the imagery of construing or poring over texts, this is the clearest invocation of private reading, complete with the word "preuyly."

Whereas Hoccleve and James I, like Chaucer, depict themselves as literary-professional readers with no apparent expectation that their audience will imitate them, the author of *Mum* not only attaches scholarly attributes to himself but seems eager to induce his audience to study his own work in a serious, scholarly manner.

The second piece of dramatized reading comes from a poem that could also be categorized as a speculum principis. Called by Robbins "The crowned king: on the art of governing" (1415), the poem contains useful if unsolicited advice for Henry V, communicated to the author in a dream-vision. What sent the poet into such admonitory slumbers, however, was an all-night celebration that included the public reading of romances. "And ye like to leer & listen awhile" (line 13), he notes, he will tell how the dream came to him:

> Ones y me ordeyned, as y haue ofte doon,
> With frendes and felawes, frendemen and other,
> And caught me in a company on corpus cristi even
> Six other vij myle oute of Suthampton,
> To take melodye and mirthes among my makes,
> With redyng of romaunces, and reuelyng among.
> (lines 17–22; Robbins 1959 no. 95)

Only with the dawn did the poet finally go to bed and dream the rest of his poem.

Whether a night like this really was involved in the poem's composition, the author clearly considers it a likely enough way for not just one but many nights to be spent (as per line 17). Like the historical reports of British prelection reviewed in the previous chapter, this account mingles music and singing with public reading as delightful activities carried on among a loose assortment of friendly people.

This group obviously contained literate members, including the poet – not surprisingly, since to sustain such festive occasions they must have been fairly wealthy. If not from the ranks of the nobility that entertained themselves at court with similar fare, these men were surely from at least the upper-middle classes, a hypothesis sustained by the poet's desire to address the king on serious issues of national governance. In invoking the sort of reception environment characteristic of the English public-sphere setting (see chapter 4), the author may be implicitly directing his speculum into a similar context of intimate, discursive aurality. It is not surprising, if so, that the author restores the enjoyable activity of shared vernacular literature to a positive valuation – and to an apparently woman-less context – nor that he bypasses the associations with sloth and temptation that Gower, Langland, and the *Parlement* author had built around such "rioting with renkes."

Partitioned modalities in Partonope of Blois

As noted above, one text stands out in this period for its idiosyncratic adherence to the "deficiency" principles considered by many modern scholars to explain medieval aurality. After discussing the usefulness of books, the prologue to the romance *Partonope of Blois* advises:

> And ther-fore Stories for to rede
> Wolle I conselle, wyth-owten drede,
> Bothe olde and yonge that letteryd be.
> To the lewed also, parde,
> Is goode sum-tyme for to here.
> For by herynge he may lere
> Thynge that fryste he ne knewe;
> And to soche folke olde thynge ys new,
> Whanne hyt ys in gestes songe,
> Or els in prose tolde wyth tonge.
> (lines 18–27)

The author implies that Latinate or literate people (the distinction doesn't seem to be relevant here) would read texts privately. The "lewed," on the other hand, might occasionally benefit from hearing, because they might hear things they didn't know before. In any case, "soche folke" are so naïve as to enjoy hearing old material recycled, in the form of sung *gestes* or prose tales read aloud.

Like many modern critics, the author of *Partonope* does, indeed, seem to associate literacy with enfranchisement and hearing with a variety of deficiencies. Moreover, he seems to have added this passage himself: while his immediate source-text has not survived, the corresponding passage in the existing French versions of the romance is concerned only with justifying the author's decision to write in the vernacular (ed. Gildea, lines 77–92). This reconfiguration of modalities is so striking in the time-context assigned to this text – the second quarter of the fifteenth century – that one is tempted to consider a later date, especially as the unique manuscript is dated between 1475 and 1520. The consensus among scholars seems to be that the language of the text fixes it to an earlier period, however, although the heavy influence of Chaucer noticeable throughout might perhaps have also affected the poet's diction (see, e.g., Windeatt 1990).

The prologue to a fantastical romance, therefore, provides an unexpected, and unexpectedly early, context for an explicit identification of dividuality with literacy and of aurality and orality with illiteracy, ignorance, and naïveté. As far as I could discover, no other author made a similar statement until Gavin Douglas in 1513. For the period between *Partonope* and Douglas, both literary and historical records continue to attribute a very positively valued aurality to the uppermost classes of society. Thus, while it is undeniably an important and interesting text, the *Partonope* prologue cannot be said to have inaugurated a major new conception of literary modality.

Reading channels

The rest of this section will return from the hierarchies of *Partonope* to the persistent, unstigmatized bimodality of its contemporary texts. In the following analysis I will begin with some more or less simple examples of the "classic" aural-narrative constellation, then move on to a detailed look at one text.

Many texts from the first half of the fifteenth century exhibit the familiar reliance on standard aural phrases. The anonymous author of the prologue to the *Tale of Beryn* (bet. 1400–50), which brings Chaucer's pilgrims to Canterbury, uses "as ye shall hear" (prol., lines

122, 127, 303, 397) and "as ye have heard" (prol., lines 2, 15, 435) phrases to advance his narration. One translator of "Sir John Mandeville" prays to God on behalf of "alle tho that this bok redith or herith it to be red" (bet. 1390–1425; ed. Seymour, p. 147). Similarly, a headnote to a mid fifteenth-century copy of the General Prologue (to the *Canterbury Tales*) shows that its scribe, John Shirley, still considered aurality a likely means of experiencing Chaucer. He addresses the text to "yee so noble and worthi pryncis and princesse other estatis or degrees what euer yee beo that haue disposicione or plesaunce to rede or here the stories of olde tymis passed" (BL Harley 7333, f. 37). The placing of a "read and/or hear" in a "sweep" position – towards the end of a prologue or epilogue, to include all possible readers in all possible formats – is a pattern that will become increasingly familiar.

A passage in Lydgate's "Complaint of the Black Knight" (*c.* 1402) freely mixes references to his own writing, his audience's hearing, and a scribe's writing to another author's oral dictation:

> But I, alas! that am of witte but dulle,
> And have no knowing of such matere,
> For to discryve and wryten at the fulle
> The woful complaynt, which that ye shal here,
> But even-lyk as doth a skrivenere
> That can no more what that he shal wryte,
> But as his maister besyde doth endyte
> (lines 190–96; Skeat 1897 no. 8)

In Scotland, the author of the *Buik of the Most Noble and Valiant Conquerour Alexander the Grit* (1438) shows that some of the self-consciousness of the court writer is penetrating into the work of the aural romancers (at 11,138 lines, the *Buik of Alexander* is clearly not meant for memorization). He offers some of the standard topoi about writing as a cure for love-sickness (pt. 2, lines 17–28) and about his inadequacy as a translator (ep., lines 1–20). Nevertheless, his transmission–reception system is still heavily aural, at both ends. Like the *Gawain*-poet but more unequivocally, the author claims to have heard his source; he has, he says,

> translait in inglis leid
> Ane romans quhilk that I hard reid.
> (pt. 2, lines 21–22)

He apparently even wrote by dictating his translation to himself; he notes that he

> Bot said [the text] furth as me come to mouth,
> And as I said, richt sa I wrait.
> (ep., lines 14–15)

Finally, he juxtaposes a format-neutral "read" with a "hear" to describe his audience's reception:

> Quhairfoir I pray baith young and ald
> That yarnis this romanis for to reid,
> For to amend quhair I mysyeid!
> Ye that haue hard this romanis heir
> May sumdeill by exampill leir.
> (ep., lines 18–22)

An example of an ostentatiously scholarly author is Osbern Bokenham, who begins his *Legendys of Hooly Wummen* (1443–47) with a standard Aristotelian prologue, giving the four causes for the production of his book (lines 1–28; see Minnis 1988: 164–65). Nonetheless, Bokenham consistently anticipates a listening audience for his saints' lives. He gives the full complement of "as ye shall hear" (lines 82, 132, 1225, 5309, 9987); "as ye have heard" (line 9946); "whoso list to hear" (lines 31, 3140–41, 3465); and "read or hear" (line 6347). The prologue to Mary Magdalene's "Life" envisages an audience convened to hear the tale read aloud:

> Aftyr hyr conuersyoun eek in goostly grace
> How strong she wex & how myhty,
> Who lyst know, he not hens pace
> Tyl completly rede be this story.
> (LHW: 5343–46; see also 9505–7)

Even in his more intellectual *Mappula Angliae* (*c.* 1445), a prose geography of England translated from Ralph Higden's *Polychronicon*, Bokenham speaks confidently to his audience's ear. In his epilogue he addresses three apologiae to, in turn, "yche man that schalle be redere or herere ther-of," "my reder of or the herere," and "the redere or the herer of this seyde treetys" (ed. Horstmann, p. 34).

John Shirley, in a version of the *Secretum secretorum* that he claims to have translated, explains that "Daun Aristotles" wrote the book "at the request of Alexandre the Grete, for naturall disciplyne of hem that list to here and rede" (*The Governance of Kynges and of Prynces* [*c.* 1450], ed. Manzalaoui, pp. 267, 269). In copying out another version, which he calls the *Decretum Aristotelis* (bet. 1447–56), Shirley associates prelection with highly exclusive and elite audiences. His book, he warns,

> is nought to shewe to comvne, ne to rede to every man opunly, but secretly to kepe it and to rede it to-fore thestatly princes of the worlde. (ed. Manzalaoui, p. 203)

From the end of this period comes a work that reveals an interesting new patterning of "reads" and "hears." In his *Amoryus and Cleopes* (1448–49), John Metham deploys two "as ye shall hear" phrases (lines 1645, 1861) in the text proper, and in one metatextual statement beseeches Fame to favor him "qwere this boke in chambyr or halle / Be herd or red" (lines 242–43). His epilogue, however, speaks only of "reading"; he suggests, for example, that

> For tyme on-ocupyid, qwan folk haue lytyl to do,
> On haly-dayis to rede, me thynk yt best so.
> (lines 2210–11; see also 2137, 2138, 2157, 2205)

Although Derek Pearsall cites this passage as an example of private reading (1976: 69), it may, like the other "reads" in the epilogue, be classifiable as "format-neutral." Since Metham envisages a form of group inactivity ("qwan folk haue lytyl to do"), he may conceive of the remedy as a form of group activity – reading aloud. Nonetheless, the absence of any clear invocation of hearing marks somewhat of a departure from the standard distribution of modalities. This compartmentalization of reception-verbs – "hears" in the text, mostly "reads" with perhaps one "read and/or hear" in the metatext – is a pattern that we will note more fully below, in Lydgate's *Fall of Princes*.

As a more detailed illustration of the aural-narrative constellation ticking along as usual post-Chaucer, we can look at the *Siege of Thebes* (*c.* 1420). Lydgate gives this story as the one he supposedly tells Chaucer's pilgrims, after chancing to fall in with them as they set out to return to London. In the *Siege* we see Lydgate writing to his own sense of how literature functions, since, as the editors of this text note, "the *Siege of Thebes* was not, like the *Troy Book* and the *Fall of Princes*, made to order, for the pleasure of some noble patron" (ed. Erdmann and Ekwall: 9).

Along the lines laid out in chapter 4, we can note in Lydgate's non-bespoke text some ten references to written sources, e.g., "As Stace of Thebes writ the manere howe" (line 1272).[5] He mentions himself as reading in his source eleven times, in many variations of the basic "as I read" phrase, e.g., "And as I rede, Spynx this monstre hight" (line 624). As narrator of his story to the pilgrims, Lydgate urges them eight times to read his or other sources. Like Chaucer, he uses these references to bolster his authority ("But the truth yif ye lyst verryfie, / Rede of goddes the Genologye"; lines 3537–38); to get out of telling a bit of the story ("But ye may reden in a Tragedye / Of Moral Senyk fully his [Oedipus'] endynge"; line 994); and in general to dazzle his fictional or real audience with his erudition.

There are no format-specific references to the audience reading privately, but Lydgate mentions a hearing audience twice. The first time is in the last two lines of the prologue, and therefore directed to his real future audience:

> And as I coude with a pale cheere,
> My tale I gan anon as ye shal here.
> (lines 175–76)

A second reference by Lydgate occurs, rather confusingly, within the frame of his fictional oral narration. Citing the earlier part of his own story, he tells the pilgrims:

> And of his exile the soth he [Tideus] told also,
> As ye han herde in the storye rad.
> (lines 1406–7)

There are no references to the text existing in manuscript or to the audience handling it, perhaps because, as noted, the work was not written to a commission; thus it has only a short prologue that does not imagine an audience. Lydgate does, however, exhibit in full Chaucer's habit of using the standard aural phrases to carry his in-frame narration. Lydgate as in-frame narrator uses variants on "as ye shall hear" and "as ye have heard" some eleven times. Since he is supposed to be narrating orally, these phrases are clearly appropriate.

Less obviously appropriate are the cases in which in-frame oral narration uses phrases that properly belong to the author. Lydgate's mentions of his own writing occur, confusingly, when he is supposedly narrating his tale to the pilgrims. This fictive performance situation does not stop him from stating:

> I am wery mor therof [Oedipus marrying Jocasta] to write.

> The hatful processe also to endyte
> I pass ouer, fully of entent.
> (lines 823–25; see also lines 2433–34)

As Chaucerian epigone both in the matter and manner of his narration, Lydgate in the *Siege of Thebes* seems well content to carry on a clearly aural frame of narration. He writes from written sources for a hearing audience, a situation so familiar to him that he carries it over even into his fictional self's supposedly oral narration.

The incipient privatization of "read"

Mixed in with the continuing aurality of works such as those reviewed above, the first half of the fifteenth century also shows signs of a subtle connotative shift in the meaning of "read." Gradually, "read" began acquiring a sense of serious – and thus, at least potentially, private – engagement with the text. The literary factor that seems most implicated in this trend is not, perhaps surprisingly, the literary-professional reading modeled by Chaucer and imitated by Hoccleve, Lydgate, Henryson (see below), and others. Rather, it seems more indebted to the apparently more conservative model of scholarly-professional authorship initiated by Gower, via the Latin apparatus and verses of his *Confessio*.

The explanation lies in the educational agenda of scholarly writing: a master, that is, speaks to students who may by careful reading become masters themselves, whereas a literary author does not usually envision his audience conning over his text in the expectation of becoming authors in turn. Although the academic model sometimes seems to evoke private reading, however, it retains an imagery and practice of aurality as well, based on the lectures and disputations that were an equally important part of scholarly life.

As absorbed into the vernacular genre with which it had the greatest affinity – the speculum principis – the scholarly-professional model also intersected with the sociopolitical aurality of the public sphere (see chapter 4). As teacher, the speculum author would encourage his audience to study his doctrine; as mediator of the "public voice," he would encourage them to transform that doctrine into social reality by discussion.

Three specula from the early fifteenth century reflect a range of responses to this generic potential. The first in time is the most academic in tone; the second is more Chaucerian; and the third reveals an odd intersection of an author at home with a public-sphere aurality writing for a patron who embraced a humanistic version of scholarly dividuality.

As noted above, *Mum and the Sothsegger* (1400–6) is composed of two fragments written just before and soon after the fall of Richard II. Although the poem's editors claim that the author "shows no traces of exceptionally wide reading or of university training" (p. xxiv), he makes extensive use of the paraphernalia of academic reading. In seeking to understand society, he finds nothing useful in the works of Sidrac, Solomon, and Seneca:

> But glymsyng on the glose, a general revle
> Of al maniere mischief I merkid and radde:
> That who-so were in wire and wold be y-easid
> Moste shewe the sore there the salue were.
> (M: 314–17)

The successful glossator interprets this to mean he should "cunne of clergie to knowe the sothe," so he heads off to "Cambrigge, ... Oxenford and Orleance and many other places" (M: 319, 322–23). Although the seven liberal arts (personified) can do little to help him, he does not abandon his fondness for academic terms – e.g., "disputeson" (M: 242), "texte" and "glose" (M: 388), and "the pro and the contra as clergie askith" (M: 300).

As he is busily marking and reading his way through the text of society, the author readily applies the same imagery when suggesting how his audience should read his text. He comments that young men might benefit if they were to "mvse" on his book (R prol.: 67), while "elde" (old age), as quoted above, might wish to "opyn" his text

> And poure on it preuyly and preue it well after,
> And constrewe ich clause with the culorum.
> (R prol.: 71–72; see also 1: 82–84)

Despite the prevalent academic metaphors, however, the text abounds as well in references to hearing audiences. The author requests them to "listen" or "herken ane hande-while" (M: 106, 167, 656, 865), and he intends to withhold distribution of his poem, he says, until "it be lore laweffull and lusty to here" (R prol.: 63). Later, he delivers a spirited rebuke to the imagined reader who has not understood his allegory about a partridge:

A! Hicke Heuyheed! hard is thi nolle
To cacche ony kunynge but cautell [deceit] bigynne!
Herdist thou not with eeris how that I er tellde
How the egle in the est entrid his owen . . .?
(R 3: 66–69)

As with Usk, these phrases are not standard tags; the poet's easy mingling of academic terminology with ears that do or do not attend to his doctrine reminds us that most of his academic terms are based on public forms of scholarly reading: i.e., construing, in the form of lectures, and disputations.

Aurality, in fact, is not a relatively extrinsic issue to *Mum*; the question the poet and the poem ask so insistently is, precisely, should the wise man, the sooth-*sayer*, speak or keep *mum*? To speak is to bring the poet's – and the country's – concerns into the public sphere; to keep mum (perhaps, even, to read privately) is to keep these vital truths privatized, ensuring the sothsegger's personal safety but exposing the polity to manifold dangers. Of course, *Mum* resolves its dilemma in the very act of recounting it: by writing the poem the poet has chosen publication, has put his constructions of society into the public record, and voice. Appropriately, his closing comprehensive indictment of that society is delivered in the form of the public reading of a series of writs.

A more traditional form of speculum principis, based on the *Secretum secretorum* and two other specula, Thomas Hoccleve's *Regement of Princes* (1411) was written for Henry V when he was still Prince Henry. Although Hoccleve eschews any academic metaphors, he is very conscious of his authorship, which he models along the lines laid out by Chaucer. To the standard "I write" phrases of that model – e.g., "I write as my symple conceyt may peyse" (line 4401) – he adds his well-known, plangent description of the "trauaillous stilnesse" (line 1013) and aching body attendant on scribal work (lines 989–1022).

At the same time, he uses standard hearing phrases in referring to his audience – e.g., "as ye herd me seye" (line 136) and "as ye schulle here" (line 3395). Some passages even suggest that Hoccleve may have written for his own delivery before the prince (cf. Seymour 1981: xxv). "Yf your plesaunce it be to here, / A kynges draught, reporte I shall now here" (lines 2127–28), he offers, in the proem to the

Regement proper. "I beseche your magnificence," he concludes, "Yeve vnto me benigne audience" (lines 2148–49).

Besides any such possible command performance, Hoccleve also seems to imply a future in which the *Regement* has become part of the prince's library, a book he may read or have read to him for didactic purposes (in an unspecified setting) or may choose to hear for simple pleasure in his chamber (cf. R. F. Green 1980: 38):

> Yf that you liste of stories to take hede,
> Somwhat it [his book] may profite, by your leve:
> At hardest, when that ye ben in Chambre at eve,
> They ben goode to drive forth the nyght;
> They shull not harme, yf they be herd a-right.
> (lines 2138–42)

While tentatively suggesting a more studious, possibly private perusal of his text, Hoccleve – perhaps remembering the purported character of his royal addressee – reverts quickly to the sort of gregarious readings-for-entertainment characteristic of the historical reports reviewed in chapter 5. Yet, as suggested in that chapter, the informal and diffuse British prelections were in fact ideally conducive to general discussions constitutive of the public sphere.

Finally, John Lydgate's *The Fall of Princes* (1431–38) offers an alternate construct, in which the patron's scholarly tendencies seem to outstrip the author's. Written at the request of Humphrey, duke of Gloucester, it begins with a prologue invoking a scholarly, apparently private reader (with many "see" phrases), while the body of the text contains many references to aural reading. The epilogue, in the form of an envoy to Humphrey, reverts to the more "visual" world of the prologue. This is a pattern already encountered, in less rarefied form, in Metham's *Amoryus and Cleopes*.

Lydgate first draws a picture of the "old tyme" (1: 359) when

> lordis hadde plesance for to see,
> To studie a-mong, and to caste ther lookis
> At good leiser vpon wise bookis.
> (1: 362–64)

After this, the clearest suggestion of private recreational reading, Lydgate eulogizes Duke Humphrey, who

> hath gret ioie with clerkis to comune:
> And no man is mor expert off language,
> Stable in study alwey he doth contune . . .
> His corage neuer doth appalle
> To studie in bookis off antiquite,
> Therin he hath so gret felicite
> (1: 387–89, 395–97)

This stress on apparently private study goes with reception-phrases such as "Off sundry pryncis to beholde & reede" (1: 105) and "as men may reede & see" (1: 285).

Once into his narration, however, Lydgate makes heavy use of the standard aural phrases common in his other works and in many other English poets; variations on "as ye shall hear" and "as ye have heard devise" occur dozens of times.[6] One three-line passage manages to lay out the complete aural-narrative constellation, in which a written source (Boccaccio's *De casibus virorum illustrium*) passes from a (re)writing author to a listening audience:

> How it [the Roman triumph] was vsid, he [Boccaccio] maketh mencioun,
> Ceriousli reherseth the manere,
> Which I shal write, yif ye list to heere.
> (4: 516–18; see also 4: 3064–65, 3862, 3955–57; 6: 987; 7: 74–77; 8: 3029–31)

In his epilogue, Lydgate reverts to a more "visual" sensibility, apostrophizing the duke, "Whan this translacioun ye haue rad and seyn" (9: 3369), and asking correction from those who will "rede" (9: 3378) or "be-holde" (9: 3394) the book – although one line does note that the book's matter has been "Lamentable and doolful for to here" (9: 3502).

Conclusion: reception-verbs in a shifting semantic field

The material analyzed here seems to support a conclusion that, despite an association of learnedness and prestige that was investing "read" with some sense of private reading, aurality was still thriving. The fact of its persistence seems well supported by the many conventional and unconventional literary passages that invoke the hearing of books, as well as by the historical texts reviewed in chapter 5.

Apart from the anomalous and isolated "deficiency" perspective of the *Partonope* prologue, the most significant new player in the modality schema is the humanism represented here by Humphrey of Gloucester. The figure of the scholar-prince casts a new aura of glamour and fashion over the pedantries of "Gowerian" scholarly-professional reading, diverting reception-phrases from the habitual channels of the aural-narrative constellation.

It may be that in this time a prefatory implication of scholarly intensity was becoming one way of flattering patrons and audience as the author eased them into the book he had prepared for them. This is much the likeliest explanation for Metham's procedure; it is improbable that the Stapletons, his patrons, were eagerly importing Italian reading styles to the wilds of Norfolk. In such cases, a reversion to "hear" phrases in the text would suggest everyone relaxing into their accustomed relationship to reading.

Overall, the authors of courtly literature, and even of the specula principis, continue to endorse the bimodality of their literate audiences' reading. The default expectation seems to be that the audience would hear the text, while private, or at least studious, reading would be in order if someone wanted to get the full didactic benefit out of the work.

AUTHORS IN THE "AGE OF INCUNABULA" (1450–1491)

The second half of the fifteenth century is a period of sparse evidence and much importance for the history of medieval modalities. Unlike Chaucer and Gower or Hoccleve and Lydgate in the previous periods, no author emerges from this one with a corpus of works reflecting a significant interest in reception channels, although Malory's single work does raise interesting issues. However, we do have, in Caxton's prologues and epilogues, the comments of a man who must be judged the preeminent expert on the reading modalities of the English upper and upper-middle classes.

The texts written during this period corroborate Robert Yeager's comparison of the fifteenth century to a "crossroads nation" (1984: vii). Certain works manifest traits often associated with humanism and the English Renaissance; others seem more classically "medieval." During this time of cultural flux a privatized sense and to some extent practice of "reading" seem to be taking hold, balanced by a persistent aurality. The texts show an increasing reliance on "read" and the "look" verbs, as humanism adds its influence to, or crosscuts the crossover influence of, traditional scholarly-professional reading. That pattern, however, is usually offset by at least one metatextual "read and/or hear" and, often, by a textual "hear" or two or by an invocation of the hearing of books. This seems a further development of the pattern that the previous section noted in Metham and in Lydgate's *Fall of Princes*, in which metatextual "reads" were countered by a strong presence of textual "hears." In the latter half of the century the "reads" have colonized the text as well, but still without eradicating the "hears." Some texts remain as "ear"-oriented as ever, and to the end of his career Caxton takes frequent note of potential hearers.

Although such uses of "hear" verbs, occurring out of synch with the putative linear evolution from "oral" to "literate," are often dismissed as archaisms (see, e.g., Pearsall's edition of *The Floure and the Leafe*, pp. 17, 49, 67), I see no reason to discount data with such preemptive interpretations. As will emerge in the discussion of Malory, for instance, the hearing of books may be invoked in a context explicitly identified as current. The implication is that the slow ascendency of a privatized sense of reading coexisted throughout the latter half of the fifteenth century with a persistent, unstigmatized aurality. People who wanted to read books may have just gone ahead and read them, privately, more often than before. But another time they might just as well have chosen to read the books aloud with their household, for mutual entertainment and/or instruction. With the exception of the *Partonope* prologue (discussed in the previous section but only recorded in a manuscript dated between 1475 and 1520), I came across no text within this period that attaches any negative connotations – of either illiteracy or unfashionability – to the hearing of literature.

Reading events

Several instances of both private and public scholarly-professional reading are provided in an anonymous text known as the *Court of Sapience*. In his search for wisdom, the narrator visits the courts of various allegorized females, in several of which he witnesses the appropriate form of reading. In the court of Dame Intelligence (inner knowledge), for example, he sees a collection of church fathers and is ravished

to byhold how fresshe, lusty, and grene
Was theyr desyre to loke on bookes clene,
And hevenly thyng with eye mental to see.
(lines 1719–21)

At Sapience's own court, "Theologye" reads from a Bible to the four evangelists, among others, while a variety of theologians "studyed upon" other books, apparently privately (lines 1793–1806). In a parlor Dialectic "red," i.e., lectured, to "many clerk and scoler of yong age" (lines 1842–45), while in another parlor Rhetoric delighted an audience of clerks with her "beauperlaunce" (lines 1891–1904). This set of descriptions offers a cross-section of scholarly reading practices, from private study-reading through aural lecturing and oral/rhetorical improvisation.

A more famous instance of professional reading is Robert Henryson's perusal of Chaucer's *Troilus and Criseyde*, described in the opening of his *Testament of Cresseid* (before 1492). Chilled by a vigil in his cold "oratur," the poet enters his "chalmer," mends the fire, takes a drink, and

To cut the winter nicht and mak it schort
I tuik ane quair – and left all vther sport –
Writtin be worthie Chaucer glorious
Of fair Creisseid and worthie Troylus.
(lines 39–42)

After summarizing Chaucer's plot, Henryson takes up "ane vther quair" (line 61); it tells, he claims, the story of Cresseid's demise, and his retelling of that story forms the substance of the poem that follows.

Like Chaucer, Henryson sets up a situation that seems paradigmatic of leisure reading, then passes smoothly into a retelling of his reading material that, retrospectively, defines it as a source-text and himself as a poet – an identification strengthened by his coy doubt "gif this narratioun / Be authoreist, or fenyeit of the new / Be sum poeit" (lines 65–67). Finally, Henryson exophorically effaces his contribution by retrofitting his narrative into the tradition, as a retelling of a nonexistent continuation to Chaucer's *Troilus*.

Another author-narrator of this period provides the first British example of private recreational reading of romances. In *The Isle of Ladies* (*c.* 1475), the ladies (and the stowaway author, as a male acolyte who has dreamed his way onto the island) are awaiting the decisions of the God of Love, who has just conquered their land:

> Well semed yt they had great feare.
> And toke lodginge every wyght;
> Was none departed of that night.
> And some to reade old romansys
> Hem occupied for ther pleasaunces [entertainment],
> Some to make virleyes & leyes,
> And some to other diuerse pleyes.
> And I to me a romaunse toke,
> And as I readinge was the booke,
> Me thowght the spere had so rone
> That it was risinge of the sonne.
> (lines 970–80)

The emphasis on "pleasaunce" and the plural pronouns seem to suggest that the ladies' "diuerse pleyes" – even the composition of virelays and lays – were undertaken in small groups. The author, on the other hand, isolated by his sex, resorts to what may be a second-best choice: private reading. Although this reading recalls Chaucer's similar taking of a romance "To rede and drive the night away" (BD: 49), the author in this case is merely a recreational reader, since his romance does not provide him with any subject-matter for his story.

A century after Froissart's demoiselle, therefore (see chapter 5), we finally see a British reader reading privately for fun; but, just as in the *Espinette amoureuse*, that behavior coexists easily, among a courtly elite, with public reading. Indeed, in both texts there is an implication that one reads alone only when, for one reason or another, there's no one else to read with.

Reading channels

In this section, I will first group together all the more minor witnesses to reception, after which I will look in greater detail at the two most forthcoming sources, Malory and Caxton.

Sir Gilbert Hay's *Buke of the Governaunce of Princis* (1456), translated from the *Secretum secretorum* for the chancellor of Scotland, shows aurality still in full flower. Like John Shirley, Hay emphasizes both the exclusively upper-class and the aural nature of his version of the *Secretum*. Hay introduces one section, for example, with a rubric explaining:

> Here declaris the noble philosophour how it efferis wele to kingis and princis to have and ger rede before thame oft tymes alde ancienne noble stories.

Hay's text goes on to recommend that the ruler "ger rede in thy presence bath cronykis and histories" (ed. Stevenson 2: 103–4).

The author of the *Court of Sapience* (mid 15th c.), while favoring "look" and "see" when referring his audience to sources (e.g., "Gay thinges y-made eke yf the lust to see / Goo loke the *Code* also, the *Dygestes* thre"; lines 1922–23), relates in his prohemium that he dreamt he met Wisdom in a meadow and "spak with her, as ye may here and rede" (line 13). In *Knyghthode and Bataile* (1458–59), an anonymous translation of Vegetius' *De re militari*, a preponderance of "reads" mixes with references to aural reception. The author claims, for example, discussing "chiualeres,"

> that daily wil thei lere,
> And of antiquitee the bokys here.
> (lines 1693–96)

A listening audience is also invoked via direct address, e.g., "That archery is grete vtilitee, / It nedeth not to telle eny that here is" (lines 446–47).

The dreamer-poet in *The Floure and the Leafe* (3d qtr. 15th c.) seems equally committed to a "read"-biased bimodality. She writes her tale for "them that lust it to rede" and worries "who shall behold" her book's "rude langage" (lines 590, 594–95). Yet the text of this elegant dream-vision also includes two standard aural phrases – a "who-so list heare" (line 204) and an "as ye have herd" (line 228) – along with a possibly format-neutral "As ye may in your old bookes rede" (line 509). The author of the *Isle of Ladies* (*c.* 1475), despite his penchant for private reading, makes frequent use of aural forward- and back-references ("as ye shall hear," lines 57, 70, 228, 949, 1439; "as ye have heard," lines 52, 998, 1340). This aurality constellates unconcernedly, according to the familiar pattern, with the text's writtenness: e.g., the author's offer to relate his dream "Wiche ye shall here and all the wise / As holly as I cane devise / In playne englishe, evell writton" (lines 57–59).

In his speculum principis, *Active Policy of a Prince* (*c.* 1470), George Ashby advises Henry VI's son, Edward, to "rede in cronicles the ruine / Of high estates and translacion" (lines 155–56), while by "Redyng the bible & holy scripture" (line 128), he may learn the value of virtuous conduct.[7] Ashby anticipates great benefit if Edward will educate his children:

> Do theim to be lettred right famously
> Wherby thei shall reule bi Reason and skele.
> (lines 648–49)

Yet literacy per se is not the key to such wise rule, for it can come as well from hearing:

> Who that herith many Cronicles olde,
> And redithe other blessid Scripture,
> Shall excede al other bi manyfolde
> Resons, and his discrecions ful sure ...
> (lines 204–7)

Robert Henryson refers a few times to reading, along lines familiar from the aural-narrative constellation: his reading as author ("Of Ixione, that in the quhele was spred, / I sall the tell sum part, as I haue red"; *Orpheus and Eurydice* [last qtr. 15th c.], lines 489–90); the reading of other professionals ("With quhome the Feynd falt findes, as clerkis reids"; *Moral Fables of Aesop* [last qtr. 15th c.], line 2435; see also *Orpheus*, line 477); and source-reading recommended to his audience ("And Solomon sayis, gif that thow will reid"; *Fables*, line 391). With an equal sparseness, however, Henryson also invokes the standard auralities. Apart from the rhetorical flourish in the prologue to the *Fables*, which notes that their "polite termes of sweit rhetore / Richt plesand ar vnto the eir of man" (prol.: 4–5), he uses the familiar phrase "as ye shall hear" three times, e.g., "Of quhome [the cock] the fabill ye sall heir anone" (prol.: 63; see also line 1208; *Orpheus*, line 260). The *Orpheus and Eurydice* opens, moreover, by noting that praise of a lord's ancestors will incline his heart "The more to vertu and to worthynes, / Herand reherse his eldirs gentilnes" (lines 6–7). For all his aureation and scholarly terminology, therefore, Henryson does not seem inclined to exit from the aural-narrative matrix of professional private reading and reception via hearing or format-neutral reading.

The "prosification" of the medieval romance is often cited as evidence of the victory of private reading. "The spread of the custom of reading to oneself had already favoured the practice of retelling inherited romances in prose versions, beginning in French as early as the thirteenth century," notes Schlauch (1963: 5), for example. This argument is based on the familiar polarization of conflated modalities (see chapter 1). Verse romances are identified with "oral" performance – meaning, really, memorial or minstrel performance, but tending to sweep in aural reading as well. Since prose, especially prose of any length, was much harder to memorize – and since prelection has been effaced from the argument – scholars easily conclude that prosified romances could only have been intended for private reading.

Since Sir Thomas Malory's prose romance, *Le Morte Darthur* (1470), is 1,260 pages long in Vinaver's edition, it must by this argument have been written for a privately reading audience. Malory, however, gives quite a lot of evidence that he is writing for listeners. His standard back-reference is the familiar "as ye have heard before," e.g., "So sir Trystram tolde La Beall Isode of all this adventure as ye have harde toforne" (p. 692).[8] He effuses that as a youth Tristram "laboured in huntynge and in hawkynge – never jantylman more that ever we herde rede of" (p. 375). In the famous bibliography-dirge with which he closes out Arthur's worldly life, Malory declares:

> Thus of Arthur I fynde no more wrytten in bokis that bene auctorysed, nothir more of the verry sertaynté of hys dethe harde I never rede, but thus was he lad away in a shyp wherein were three quenys . . . (p. 1242)

Mark Lambert has pointed out that references to historical remains, including textual sources, escalate abruptly in the *Morte*'s last two books. The effect is to create a cumulative sense of Arthur and his age slipping into the past, further and further away from the reader's present (Lambert 1975: 125–38). That effect reaches a climax in the description of Arthur's passing. Here if anywhere – if private reading were indeed a key index of the post-Arthurian, post-oral, endophoric new order – Malory might have signaled a transition into this new means of transmitting and interpreting source-tradition. Instead, he seamlessly connects aurality with his latter-day research efforts and with the authenticating textuality of books.

Malory's depictions of reading are also instructive. His upper-class protagonists, male and female, all seem to be literate: they read a fair number of letters, not to mention the occasional magic sword. In one episode in the "Tristram" (pp. 615–18), for example, slanders are promulgated and loyalties asserted in a set of letters that circulate energetically among Lancelot, Isode, Tristram, Mark, Guenevere, and

Arthur. The private reading of these letters is emphasized by the repetition of the ominous word "privy." Arthur and Guenevere, for example, "opened the lettirs prevayly" that each had received from Mark; the enraged Guenevere sent hers on, "prevayly," to Lancelot (p. 617). The privacy in which these letters are read signals a privatization of experience, but for Malory this is an entirely threatening development, symptomatic of the oncoming factionalization of the court and of the dangers of over-privatized behavior – i.e., the parallel adulteries of Cornwall and Camelot. Significantly, this particular episode is resolved when Lancelot's friend Dinadan punishes Mark's privy scandal-mongering by composing a scurrilous lay and commissioning minstrels to perform it throughout Wales and Cornwall (p. 618). Thus public sanctions contain private mischief – for the time being.

By contrast, when Arthur took Elaine of Astolat's last letter to his chamber, "he called many knyghtes aboute hym and seyde that he wolde wete opynly what was wryten within that lettir. Than the kynge brake hit and made a clerke to rede hit" (p. 1096). This public process leads to a public explanation from Lancelot that removes any dangers of misinterpretation and allows the episode to resolve itself successfully.

Malory's personal reading map, therefore, seems to regard private reading as suspect and public reading as socially restorative. Rather like Plato regretting that writing will sap the powers of memory (*Phaedrus*, pp. 560–71), Malory sees unexpected disadvantages to a development we are accustomed to think of as entirely positive. In anticipating his readers' behavior or reporting his own, moreover, Malory repeatedly assumes aurality as the channel.

Whatever the aged, idealistic, and probably incarcerated Malory did or did not know about reading behavior in 1470, William Caxton surely knew what he was about in 1485, when he directed his first edition of Malory "unto alle noble prynces, lordes and ladyes, gentylmen or gentylwymmen, that desyre to rede or here redde of" Arthur (ed. Blake: 109).[9]

I have already analyzed, in a previous article, the uniquely significant set of prologues, epilogues, and other comments appended by Caxton to some 41 of the 100 or so books he published between 1473 and the year of his death, 1491 (Coleman 1990a). One conclusion presented there was that 60 percent of Caxton's references to his audience's reception used the word "read," while 40 percent used "hear." Moreover, the context of some of these "reads" in fact designates public reading, which suggests that other "reads" as well may be format-neutral. A breakdown of Caxton's publishing career into three periods (pp. 96–97) showed the proportion of "reads" to "hears" highest from *c.* 1473 to 1479 (73%–27%), nearest the mean from 1480 to 1485 (56%–44%), and rising again from 1486 to 1491 (67%–33%). This pattern may reflect a heightened interest in reading both at the beginning of Caxton's venture into publishing and as he came under the influence of the humanists (see below). It certainly does not show the steady rise in "reads" one might expect as printing began to transform the relationship of text and audience.

Many of Caxton's "hears" come as half of the familiar pair "read and/or hear." Like Shirley, for example, Caxton introduces the *Canterbury Tales* (2d ed., 1484) with an "alle ye that shal in thys book rede or heere" (ed. Blake: 62). Very commonly, the "read and/or hear" comes in the final statement to the audience, after a series of "reads" that may have been either format-neutral or privacy-biased. These "sweep" statements seek to pull in, or make explicit, all possible reading formats and every conceivable reader, and they usually introduce a request for correction. Thus, in the epilogue to Earl Rivers' translation of the *Dicts and Sayings of the Philosophers* (1st ed., 1477), Caxton refers twice to his own reading (p. 73), then to "al them that shal rede this lytyl rehersayll" (p. 75) and to persons "that have red this booke in Frensshe" (p. 76). His final statement sweeps in "my sayd lord or ony other persone whatsomever he or she be that shal rede or here it" (p. 76).

One might conclude that for Caxton, "read" had begun to take on its modern connotation of private reading, and that his use of "read and/or hear" in the "sweep" position represented a politic nod in the direction of those still attached, for whatever reason, to the old-style reception format. Nonetheless, there are texts where all the reception-statements are of the "read and/or hear" form: the prologue to *Charles the Great* (1485) has three in a row (p. 67), with one in the epilogue (p. 68); the prologue to the *Book of Good Manners* (1487) also has three in a row (pp. 60–61). And in other cases, public reading is explicitly invoked.

The most significant example of the latter point, and a generally important and interesting invocation of late fifteenth-century reading modalities, is Caxton's statement in the prologue to his translation

Eneydos (1490). In this, one of the last books he published, Caxton mentions his own professional reading twice (pp. 78–79). Reflecting the influence of humanistic ideas about text-editing, he claims to have even invoked the help of John Skelton – who "hath redde" not only "Vyrgyle" (p. 80) but even "the ix muses" (p. 81) – in establishing his text. After these flights of professional reading, it is not surprising to find Caxton emphasizing that the *Eneydos* "is not for a rude, uplondyssh man to laboure therin ne rede it, but onely for a clerke and a noble gentylman." He goes on to suggest to these learned men a subsidiary research project: "And yf ony man wyll entermete in redyng of hit late hym goo rede and lerne Vyrgyll or . . . Ovyde." But the final end of all this upmarket reading is that the willing scholar "shall see and understonde lyghtly all yf he have a good redar and enformer" (p. 80). Caxton's source, the late fourteenth-century *Livre des Enéides*, had merely advised: "Who that will know how Aeneas went to hell, let him read Virgil, Claudian or the Epistles of Ovid and there he shall find more than truth" (quoted in Painter 1976: 176 n. 2) – with no "redar and enformer" in sight.

Caxton, as sensitive to the times as ever, has caught the sense of the oncoming humanistic revolution, while retaining his more traditional roots (and potential audience). The description of his target reader – "a clerke and a noble gentylman" – recalls the figure of the scholar-prince then being formulated as the archetypal patron of the literary humanist. Yet deeds of arms, love, and noble chivalry – the subject-matter that Caxton describes as of interest to this reader (p. 80), and indirectly as the topics of the *Eneydos* – are standard medieval preoccupations. Caxton thus seems to visualize readers on the cusp, still happy to read his vulgate *Aeneid* as a "ripping tale" but also potentially aware of its role as a key humanistic text that they can master as part of a program of self-education and improvement.

But while, like Malory, accelerating us away from the past and the passé, Caxton, also like Malory, fails to make the persistent modern connection between this new age and private reading. Rather, he presents us with an aurality repackaged. His prologue's closing reference to a "redar" makes it clear that the preceding "reads," not to mention the "see and understonde," are suggesting a research project conducted by means of a trained reader (a Skeltonian reader of the muses) prelecting and expounding the Latin sources. Such reading is presented as elite, fashionable behavior (not for a "rude uplondyssh man"); the reader is flatteringly assumed to have the time, the competence, and the texts on hand to do follow-up reading in important Latin sources, as well as to be wealthy enough to employ a scholar-prelector. This scenario recalls the fashion, noted in chapter 5, of royal or noble sixteenth-century households maintaining readers for just such purposes – to read and expound the classics.

A review of Caxton's "reads" and "hears" thus leaves one with a sense of bimodal reading still a well-entrenched reception format among English audiences. In one of his very last reception-statements, from the last year of his life, Caxton explains that "wel-disposed persones that desiren to here or rede ghostly informacions maye the sooner knowe by this lityll intytelyng th'effectis of this sayd lytyll volume" (*Horologium sapientiae* [*c.* 1491], p. 102). A century after Chaucer stumped his (future) critics by telling people who didn't want to hear a story to turn the page, Caxton is thus unconcernedly telling people who do want to hear "ghostly informacions" to look at the table of contents. Aurality remains as much, or as little, of a conundrum on the threshold of the English Renaissance as in the reign of Richard II.

Rather than any radical reorientation of reception channels, thus, the modality shift of the late fifteenth and early sixteenth century shows public reading slowly becoming relatively less common and private reading relatively more so. The change comes less in the abandonment of oral performance – which did not occur – than in the slow absorption by a growing number of people of a sense that studious – and thus, potentially, private – reading was a fashionably meritorious way to experience serious vernacular literature.

That this fashion had become well enough entrenched to invite ridicule is suggested in Caxton's *History of Reynard the Fox* (1481). As Caxton translates his closely contemporary Dutch source (printed 1479), the prologue advises:

> Thenne who that wyll haue the very vnderstandyng of this mater / he muste ofte and many tymes rede in thys boke and ernestly and diligently marke wel that he redeth / ffor it is sette subtylly / lyke as ye shal see in redyng of it / and not ones to rede it ffor a man shal not wyth ones ouer redyng fynde the ryght vnderstanding ne comprise it well / but oftymes to rede it shal cause it wel to be vnderstande. (ed. Goldsmid, p. 16)

In piling on the "reads," in urging multiple, studious perusals of the text, this stutteringly pro-"literacy" passage (not present in the century-old verse original from which the Dutch prosifier had been working; see *Van den Vos Reynaerde*, ed. Hellinga) willfully communicates the exact opposite of what it says. Who needs all this scholarly head-butting to understand a story about a fox and a lion? *Reynard* is a narrative meant to amuse its audience, and perhaps to pique them with its easy-to-follow political overtones, but not to challenge them with arduous semantic opacities. Evidently, the Boccaccian call to "read, ... persevere, ... sit up nights, ... inquire, and exert the utmost power of your mind" (in Hardison et al. 1974: 208) had become enough of a commonplace by this time to merit debunking.

CODA: AUTHORS IN THE "AGE OF TRANSITION" (1495–1525)

To my own surprise, in my initial analysis I reached the end of the period I'd set myself to cover without finding any evidence that clearly manifested the ascendancy of dividuality over aurality. Peering just beyond that boundary, however, I discovered two texts that reveal some remarkably different formulations of literary transmission and reception. These seem to signal the final archaizing of the long-running aural-narrative constellation, in favor of a more individualistic, endophoric relationship to tradition.

A striking departure from the medieval norm comes in John Skelton's *Garlande or Chapelet of Laurell* (*c.* 1495). Skelton takes up Chaucer's conceit of the House of Fame, peopling it with a large assembly of poets, classical and medieval. To the unlaureled Chaucer, Gower, and Lydgate are assigned the task of introducing Skelton to Fame, who will confer the laurel on him; the implication is, clearly, that Skelton represents the culmination of the poetic enterprise initiated by these musty old *auctores* (cf. Spearing 1985: 243). Skelton describes how the three poets approached him:

> And of there bounte they made me godely chere
> In maner and forme as ye shall after here.
> (lines 398–99)

This, the only time Skelton ever uses this most familiar of aural phrases, registers resoundingly as a quote, an invocation of the now-outmoded phraseology and modality associated with his poetic predecessors. Like Chaucer's quotes from memorial romance in "Sir

Thopas," Skelton's conscious and implicitly ironic "as ye shall after here" seems to signal the effective cessation of the modality system that it had served so long.

Another symptomatic text comes from Gavin Douglas. In congratulating himself on finishing his translation of Virgil, in 1513, Douglas assures his book:

> Now salt thou with euery gentill Scot be kend,
> And to onletterit folk be red on hight,
> That erst was bot with clerkis comprehend.
> ("Ane exclamatioun," lines 43–45)

In such contexts, medieval translators had usually congratulated themselves for having made a work previously available only to clerks accessible for reading or hearing by English-speakers. Douglas refines, and redefines, this convention by apparently introducing a hierarchical distinction between the vernacular audience's modalities. Instead of employing the indifferently bimodal "read and/or hear," he suggests that the "gentill," or upper-class, Scots will read privately, while the unlettered folk will be able to have the book read to them. Even the phrase "red on hight" is a new one; by providing a term explicitly designating aural reading, it implies that the word "read," when left unmodified, refers only to private reading. And indeed, except for one or two rhetorical "hears," Douglas' standard reception-verbs, in his many metatextual statements, are "read" and "see." Thus, it seems, he expected all but the illiterate among his audience to read his text privately.

Despite such shots across the bow of the aural-narrative constellation, however, other, less avant-garde writers of the early Renaissance went right on using "read and/or hear" and speaking of the hearing of books. Stephen Hawes, for example, fits into the pattern noted in the last section, mixing a dominant "read" with persistent aural phrases. He adapts a standard "hear" phrase to be used with "read," for instance, in *The Example of Vertu* (1509):

> Dame dyscrecyon ferther me brought
> Into a fayre chambre as ye may rede.
> (lines 534–35)

Yet he is no less ready, when speaking of the behavior suited to "hye degre and lowe" (*The Conforte of Louers* [1509], line 112), to declare that

> The lorde and knyght delyteth for to here
> Cronycles and storyes of noble chyualry.
> (lines 106–7)

As late as 1524–25, John Bourchier, Lord Berners, introduced his translation of the *Chronicles of Froissart* with a pattern very familiar from Caxton: a host of "reads" capped by, in sweep position, a "read and hear." Berners expects his audience to "se, beholde, and rede" his text, for example, and deploys seven further "reads" to describe his practice and that of "the noble gentylmen of England." Yet he concludes with a request to "all the reders and herers therof to take this my rude translacion in gre" (I: xxvii–xxviii).

CONCLUSION: DECONSTELLATED AURALITY

From the time of Chaucer through the late fifteenth century, the presence of aurality and of the aural-narrative constellation was clear and unambiguous, although a privatized sense of "read" was gathering force. In this last coda section, we've seen the aural-narrative constellation in decline at last, with "read" apparently privatized and "hear" persisting only among the more conservative writers and the more traditional genres.

With the extinction of the aural-narrative constellation went the exophoric encoding of relationships among sources, authors, and audience that had dominated secular vernacular writings since the time of Chaucer. Literary texts over the late fifteenth and early sixteenth century reflect authors slowly centralizing prestige on their own function, departing from the self-effacement of the status-diffusing "public voice" in favor of the dominant tones associated with, originally, the scholarly lecturer and, later, the laureled humanist. This new wave of authors seems to write either for studious private reading or for a public reading more along the lines we are familiar with today – to the sorts of respectful, passive audiences V. A. Kolve envisaged, anachronistically, as listening to Chaucer (1984: 15–16; quoted in chapter 3).

Whatever style of reading the more ambitious early Renaissance authors craved, however, more evidence is needed before we can know what style of reading they actually received. The historical and literary material reviewed at the end of chapter 5 suggests that aurality re-emerged in the Renaissance in a variety of new forms, unhindered by an increasing reliance on private reading as a norm.

Conclusion

After so much chronology traversed, and so much variety encompassed, I lay down my ethnographer's staff. The voyage – touted in all the literary travel brochures as a thrilling ascent from the stumbly foothills of orality to the soaring alps of literacy – has turned out, in practice, to be at once less glorious and more interesting. The simplistic alignments have not held, and the readers have, persistently, defied the rules codified six centuries after their demise.

The evidence shows that the hearing of books continued to be a favored mode of reading well past the expiration date dictated by purely technological, evolutionary premises. Despite the Great Divide mandated by "strong" theorists, aurality mixed the two poles of orality and literacy in a long-term, stable relationship that can be meaningfully described as "transitional" only from the perspective of a half-millennium. Although the logic of unilinear evolution would associate "orality" in an age of literacy with poverty, ignorance, and low status, almost every aural reader we have encountered was wealthy, literate, and powerful. Reductive essentialist generalizations are further invalidated by the finding that, while the French and the British both favored public reading, they distinguished among genres and conducted their reading sessions very differently. Factors ignored by the standard theories have proved more crucial in influencing such behavior than the technological achievements those theories fetishize. Above all, medieval readers chose to share their experience of literature because they valued shared experience. For them, a book read aloud came alive not only with the performer's voice but with the listeners' reactions and responses, with their concentration, their tears and applause, their philosophical or political debates, and their demands that the page be turned.

Books written for such reading came out of and fed back into an exophoric, communalizing impulse that bound author to audience in mutual dependency and respect. It is traditional to assume that such a literary matrix could only hamper creativity – and thus (circularly) that Chaucer could not have been writing for aural reception. Since the evidence suggests strongly that Chaucer *was* writing for aural reception, however, we may have to revise our opinion of the constraints that situation imposed. While oral or aural literature, when mediocre, may have been mediocre in certain characteristic ways, the modalities themselves did not mandate literary failure – any more than dividuality guarantees literary success. In fact, writing for a listening audience may have presented an exciting challenge: the author had time to reflect on and polish his words knowing that they would take on life and vigor from the dynamics of presentation before an audiate audience. Similar conditions, after all, seem not to have hampered Shakespeare's creativity.

The energetic imposition of twentieth-century values misrepresents and disenfranchises the realities of late medieval reading, substituting for the complex interlinking and differentiation of modalities the clear, well-lit progression from "orality" to "literacy." Many scholars, convinced of the "strong" model's validity, devote themselves to self-fulfilling explications of the transforming powers of literary literacy. Buttressed by the survivalist logic of evolutionism, they have institutionalized the view that Chaucer's references to hearing represent a nostalgic carry-over from bygone oral days. They have further shut their ears to the persistent "hears" of Chaucer's contemporaries and successors, only reiterating at times the timeworn characterization of such references as "archaisms."

I hope that the evidence assembled in this book will contribute to the archaizing of such arguments. The time has come to prize open the doors of critical perception, to make room for a more nuanced and conceivably more accurate conception of the cultural matrix within which medieval authors worked. Further investigations along the lines of the one conducted here might considerably enlarge our understanding of medieval reading practices and of the complex relationships among various genres, areas, and periods.

Notes

1. ON BEYOND ONG: THE BASES OF A REVISED THEORY OF ORALITY AND LITERACY

1 In quotation marks, as here, these two terms may be understood to mean "orality and literacy as defined by the proponents of standard orality/literacy theory." The discussion below will suggest some of the problems involved in this theory and the many confusions attendant on the key terms "orality" and "literacy." Since these confusions affect "literacy" and "literate" in particular, these terms will more often be found placed in quotation marks.

2 See Dorson 1968: chap. 6 for a discussion of anthropological Darwinism.

3 See chapters 4 and 5 for evidence that almost all the late medieval public readers of whom record survives (in France and Britain, at least) were "amateur" readers, not professional minstrels.

4 In the following discussion it will sometimes be difficult to keep my sights on "aurality," since the authors I cite tend to sweep it in with a variety of other phenomena under such terms as "oral delivery," "orality," and even "literacy."

5 For a more ideological statement of the vested interest of academics in validating their own subculture, see Street 1984: 38–39, 224; see also Finnegan 1994.

2. TAXONOMIES AND TERMINOLOGY: THE PURSUIT OF DISAMBIGUITY

1 Although some theorists reserve "text" for written material (see, e.g., D. R. Olson 1977: 258), I will use it to designate any assemblage of words shaped into a communicative genre, whether written or not.

2 Joseph J. Duggan (1989) tries out "ocular" reception, and Carl Lindahl (1987) plumps for "optical." Both terms, it seems to me, carry too strong a flavor of the eye chart.

3 I do not consider literary style in this book, since a proper exploration, deconstruction, and reconstruction of our concepts of "oral" and "literate" style would require a book-length study of its own. No such exploration can properly begin, moreover, until investigations such as the one attempted here have been examined, revised, and assimilated.

4 "Restricted" and "elaborated" codes are terms devised by the sociolinguist Basil Bernstein (1964, 1972), designating context-bound and context-free modes of speech.

5 Indeed, education within a repressive system can be an effective means of maintaining control over potentially dissident groups. A girl subjected to the standard medieval education, for example, would be led to internalize many misogynistic messages, rendering her, perhaps, more docile and manageable than an illiterate woman (compare Julian of Norwich and Margery Kempe).

3. A REVIEW OF THE SECONDARY LITERATURE

1 See the Glossary for definitions of this and other terms I have either borrowed from other writers or introduced myself.

2 As John Fleming remarked in a symposium on Chaucer's audience, "The middle classes have been rising for so long in Chaucerian scholarship that they are by now observable only with the most powerful optical instruments" ("Chaucer's audience," 1983: 179).

3 So far I have collected sixteen citations of this passage that interpret it in the manner described below; those not quoted here are (in chronological order) Bronson 1940: 3; Muscatine 1966: 89; Brewer 1974: 75; Mehl 1974: 174 (cited above in another context); "Chaucer's audience," 1983: 177; Fisher 1985: 243; Brewer 1988: 86, 108; McKenna 1988: 41–42; Schibanoff 1988: 101–2; De Looze 1991: 168, 177; and Pearsall 1992: 187.

4 The poem's first editor, Sir Israel Gollancz (rev. ed., 1930), dealt with the lack of a reference to writing by inserting one. His "makers of myrthes" carry "Wyse wordes with-inn, that wr[iten] were neuer" (line 22); the actual manuscript reading, which has been restored by later editors (e.g., Trigg), is "that wroghte were neuer." Coleman, however, reproduces Gollancz's reading, with the brackets removed (1981: 56).

4. THE SOCIAL CONTEXT OF MEDIEVAL AURALITY: INTRODUCTORY GENERALIZATIONS FROM THE DATA

1 The discussion of "the ethnography of reading" here and in the following chapters was written before the publication of Jonathan Boyarin's excellent *Ethnography of Reading* (1993), a collection of articles applying an interdisciplinary, post-Great Divide approach to the study of texts and cultures.

2 See the Glossary for definitions of this and other terms I have either borrowed from other writers or introduced myself.

3 I cannot close this section without noting A. C. Baugh's (1967) influential discussion of "the question whether professional entertainers – minstrels – ever read aloud from a written text" (p. 21). Baugh's citations seem to support his conclusion "that romances were sometimes sung, sometimes recited, and sometimes read from a book" (p. 23), but it is significant that in making this statement Baugh has fallen into the passive voice. Apart from the *Havelok* passage quoted above, Baugh does not find any text that seems to identify a minstrel as the person reading the book aloud. Addresses to those "That herken to mi romaunce rede" (*Guy of Warwick*, *c.* 1300; quoted in Baugh 1967: 22) are inconclusive and, as Baugh notes, often complicated by the tendency for "read" to mean "relate, tell a story" (p. 21).

One work not cited by Baugh – *Sir Eglamour of Artois*, in the Cotton manuscript version (*c.* 1446–60) – summarizes a typical piece of romance mismating with the comment:

> Thus gracyously he [Eglamour] hase sped
> Hys owen modyr hase he wed,
> As I herde a clerke rede.
> (lines 1141–43)

This last line may suggest that when romances were read aloud, the prelector would be not a minstrel – whose expertise lay primarily in harp-playing, singing, and memory – but a cleric, one trained in the intelligent decoding of written texts (which involved both private and public reading). Since, however, I have largely excluded romances from my corpus of investigation, I would hesitate to make any definitive statement other than that if minstrels did sometimes read books aloud, they probably confined themselves to popular romances.

4 I realize that these miniatures cannot be considered in any case to present an exact record of "real-life" reading behavior. At a minimum, however, they indicate how a contemporary artist found it plausible or meaningful to represent the relationship among author, text, and audience.

5 Paul Strohm (1989: 22) feels that this description is anachronistic for Edward IV's time; see chapter 5 for my attempt to refute Strohm's argument.

6 This is the interpretation favored by D. H. Green (1994: 174).

7 The Valenciennes illumination was unfortunately unavailable for reproduction, but figure 11 presents a substantially identical illumination from another manuscript of the *Chroniques*.

8 The relevant lines are:

the Knight: "But of that storie list me nat to write" (CT 1: 1201);
the Franklin: "he was so weel apayd / That it were impossible me to wryte" (5: 1548–49);
Chaucer-the-pilgrim: "Shul ye nowher fynden difference / Fro the sentence of this tretys lyte / After the which this murye tale ['Melibee'] I write" (7: 962–64);
the Monk: "For though I write or tolde yow everemo / Of his knyghthod, it myghte nat suffise" (7: 2653–54).

5. AURAL HISTORY

1 For convenience, the category "devotional" will be understood to include religious material such as the Bible, biblical commentaries, devotional manuals, saints' lives, and so on.

2 See the Glossary for definitions of this and other terms I have either borrowed from other writers or introduced myself.

3 The count was not an insomniac, as William Nelson assumes (1976/77: 112); he was simply a "night person." "The habit of the count of Foix," notes Froissart, "is such or was then, and had always been in childhood, that he rose at high noon and supped at midnight" (*Chroniques*, ed. de Lettenhove, XI, 85). Latter-

day "night people" will envy the count's power to make everyone else live according to his own internal clock!

4 Among the thirty-eight books that Janet Backhouse (1987: 39–41) lists as owned by or associated with Edward IV, for example, only five offer any English history – and these were written by foreigners (Jean Froissart and Jean de Wavrin) for French or Burgundian patrons.

5 The stronger English association of chronicles with entertainment makes some sense, given that these works tended to devote considerable space to the romanticized adventures of Arthur and his court. Philippe de Mézières, in recommending a course of chronicle-reading to Charles VI, feels compelled to note: "The equally well-known valor of King Arthur was full great, but the history of him and his followers is so full of fictions that his history must remain suspect" (II, 222).

6 In 1407, the latest possible date for the poem's composition and performance, the princes were, respectively, nineteen, eighteen, seventeen, and sixteen.

7 Froissart had collected materials for his chronicle when he was in England but wrote it on the Continent, while under the patronage of a variety of French and Burgundian nobles (Reid 1976: 245–46).

8 I am much indebted to Jennifer Richards for directing me to many of the sources cited in this discussion.

6. AN "ETHNOGRAPHY OF READING" IN CHAUCER

1 See the Glossary for definitions of these and other terms I have either borrowed from other writers or introduced myself.

2 Against this picture of the Monk as a hypothetical private reader we should balance his claim to have "an hundred [tragedies] in my celle" (CT 7: 1972).

3 Sylvia Thrupp points out: "Even in the fifteenth century, when appreciation of Chaucer was growing, an immoderate literary enthusiasm stood out as a little peculiar, as in the figure of William of Worcester, Sir John Fastolf's secretary, of whom a friend wrote that he was 'as glad and as feyn of a good boke of Frensh or of poetre as my Mastr Fastolf wold be to purchace a faire manoir'" (1948: 248–49).

7. AN "ETHNOGRAPHY OF READING" IN NON-CHAUCERIAN ENGLISH LITERATURE

1 See the Glossary for definitions of these and other terms I have either borrowed from other writers or introduced myself.

2 Although Gower is content (unlike Chaucer) to isolate this reading process from any mention of the book it might lead to, the painter of the delightful Morgan 126 illustration obviously rejected the idea of depicting Socrates in the (iconographically rare) pose of a "passive," private reader. Rather, the painter reverted to the familiar, socially interactive iconography of the author writing at a "table full of books" (see chapter 4). Xantippe, clearly, remains unimpressed.

3 Similar phrases occur throughout the *Speculum meditantis*, e.g.: "[The devil] engendered then full false offspring, / As you will hear, if you keep peace" ("[Le

diable] Lors engendra tieu fals encress, / Come vous orretz, si faitez pes"; lines 202–3) or "Then they began to argue, / As you have heard spoken before" ("Si les commence a resonner, / Comme vous orretz parler avant"; lines 9753–54). See also lines 203, 324, 838, 1044, 1334, 3678, 9688, 9756, 10031, 10033, 10063, 11430, 12024. Gower clearly considered that an audience fluent in Anglo-Norman, the language of the elite classes of English society, would still be hearing his text.

4 Interestingly, and not atypically, the editors of this text delete its aurality in their translation of line 197: "Bot never yet in no boke breved I herde" becomes "but I have not yet found written down in any book" (ed. Cawley and Anderson: 59, note to lines 196–204).

5 To consolidate all the bulkier line-references in one note, these are the citations pertinent to the forthcoming discussion:

references to written sources: lines 199, 1272, 1505, 1679, 2599, 3839, 3848, 3971–72, 4235, 4501;

Lydgate reading in his sources: lines 335, 452, 624, 1151, 1303, 2597, 2767, 3034, 3522, 3563, 4417;

urging audience to read sources: lines 200, 994, 1015, 1753, 3157, 3193–3203, 3538, 4679;

in-frame narrator using "hear" phrases: lines 658, 1103, 1407, 1900, 2447, 2535, 2552, 2736, 3314, 3519, 3929.

6 *Fall of Princes*, variants of "as ye shall hear": 1: 1210; 2: 763, 1379; 3: 4775; 4: 518, 3064, 3956; 5: 1803; 6: 987; 7: 77, 329; 8: 11, 1426. Variants of "as ye have heard devise": 1: 1741, 2081, 3468, 3656; 2: 7, 3134, 4323; 3: 1703, 2600, 3062, 3908; 4: 2134, 2144, 2498, 2879, 3562, 3570, 3862; 5: 1727; 6: 2749; 7: 132, 278; 8: 1878, 2151; 9: 1101.

7 Like Blacman and Fortescue, both also dependents of Henry VI, Ashby associates the reading of chronicles and Scripture, on the Franco-Burgundian model (see chapter 5).

8 See also pp. 298, 318, 624, 637, 722, 776, 975, 1011, 1078, 1088, 1169, 1241; as often, the phrase does similar duty with in-frame narratives, e.g., Lancelot telling a hermit: "Holy fadir, … I mervayle of the voyce that seyde to me mervayles wordes, as ye have herde toforehonde" (p. 897).

9 All page-references for Caxton's prologues and epilogues refer to *Caxton's Own Prose*, ed. N. F. Blake (London, 1973).

Glossary

(Chapter references are to chapters in which the term being defined was first introduced.)

Audiate, audiacy: Applied to experienced and able hearers who are accustomed both to the matter and manner of traditional oral and aural literature. (Chapter 1.)

Aural, aurality: Applied to the reading aloud of a written text to one or a group of listeners. Cf. *dividuality*. (Chapter 1.)

Aural-narrative constellation: A complex system of reception-phrases in medieval texts, reflecting the interrelationships of professional and recreational, public and private reading. (Chapter 4.)

Bimodal, bimodality: Applied to texts written for an audience that might read them either publicly or privately. (Chapter 2.)

Conflation: The equation of aurality with either "orality" or "literacy." (Chapter 3.)

Deficiency theory: The idea that people read publicly only because they lack the literacy and books to do otherwise, and that, as soon as these deficiencies are removed, people will naturally and immediately turn to private reading. (Chapter 3.)

Dividual, dividuality: Applied to the private reading of written texts, whether the reader read in complete silence or voiced the text as he or she went along. (Chapter 2.)

Endoliterate, endoliteracy, endophoric literacy: Applied to forms of reading or thinking that exhibit the traits identified with endophoricity (q.v.). (Chapter 2.)

Endophoric, endophoricity: Applied to the cognitive and literary traits sometimes labeled "literate," i.e., that exhibit a separation between the self and the environment (e.g., autonomy, abstraction, a sense of the past, etc.). Cf. *exophoric*. (Chapter 2.)

Ethnography of reading: Systematic investigation, based on texts and on records contemporary with them, of the interactions of authors, traditions, texts, and audiences within certain clearly spelled-out boundaries of, e.g., time and place. (Chapter 4.)

Eureka topos: A scholarly trope in which some increment of technological improvement (e.g., rising literacy or the introduction of paper) is gleefully credited with inaugurating the age of private reading. (Chapter 3.)

Glossary

Exoliterate, exoliteracy, exophoric literacy: Applied to forms of reading or thinking that exhibit the traits identified with exophoricity (q.v.). (Chapter 2.)

Exophoric, exophoricity: Applied to the cognitive or literary traits sometimes labeled "oral," i.e., that exhibit an assimilation of the self to the environment (e.g., concreteness, traditionality, homeostatization of the past, etc.). Cf. *endophoric.* (Chapter 2.)

Fictive orality: The assertion that any references in a later medieval text to listening audiences can be explained as a deliberate or unconscious carry-over from the departed age of minstrel or bardic performance. (Chapter 3.)

Format: The means by which a medieval text was composed, communicated, or received. (Chapter 2.)

Format-neutral: Applied to a medieval use of the word "read" where the author does not specify, and may not care, whether public or private reading is meant. (Chapter 2.)

Great Divide: The rigid polarization of "orality" and "literacy" as envisioned by standard orality/literacy theory (q.v.). (Chapter 1.)

Literacy complex: The scholarly willingness to accept any supposed indication of "literacy" (e.g., the presence of a written text or the use of the word "read") as sufficient proof that the author was writing for private reading. (Chapter 3.)

Literate, literacy: Used in the text without quotation marks, these terms have two meanings: as a technological description, able to read and, possibly, write; as a cultural entity, applied to the experience of books as stored in writing. In the latter sense, "literacy" overlaps with "orality" in two areas: public reading and voiced private reading. Cf. *oral.*

Used in the text with quotation marks, these terms mean: demonstrating some or all of the cognitive and/or literary traits associated by orality/literacy theory (q.v.) with the introduction or expansion of writing-technologies. (Chapters 1 and 2.)

Memorial, memoriality: Applied to the performance of texts from memory; in the present book, this term will apply chiefly to minstrel performance. (Chapter 2.)

Metatext: The prologues, epilogues, and rubrics with which medieval authors framed their texts. (Chapter 4.)

Modality: The cultural matrix within which a mode or modes of reception operate; e.g., orality, aurality, dividuality (q.v.). (Chapters 1 and 2.)

Oral, orality: Used in the text without quotation marks, these terms have two meanings: as a technological description, unable to read or write; as a cultural entity, applied to the experience of books as presented orally. In the latter sense, "orality" overlaps with "literacy" in two areas: public reading and voiced private reading. Cf. *literate*.

Used in the text with quotation marks, these terms mean: demonstrating some or all of the cognitive and/or literary traits associated by orality/literacy theory (q.v.) with the lack of or deficiencies in writing-technologies. (Chapters 1 and 2.)

Orality/literacy theory: The theory – pioneered by Jack Goody and Ian Watt (1963) and Eric Havelock (1963), and elaborated by Walter Ong (esp. 1982) – that many cultural and literary factors are determined by the absence, presence, and degree of "internalization" of literacy. (Chapter 1.)

Peroral, perorality: Applied to texts composed, stored, and performed with no recourse to writing. (Chapter 2.)

Prelect, prelection: To read a written text aloud to one or more listeners; a term borrowed from John of Salisbury. (Chapter 2.)

Survival, survivalism: A corollary of the theory of unilinear evolution; it dismisses rituals, beliefs, and procedures that persist from one evolutionary stage into the next as inert vestiges with no power to define their context. (Chapter 1.)

Sweep position: The placement of the reception-phrase "read and/or hear" as the last in a series of "hears" or (especially) "reads" in a prologue or epilogue, perhaps as a final attempt to embrace all possible reception preferences. (Chapter 4.)

Technological determinism: The assumption that technological changes such as the introduction of writing, rising literacy, or improvements in book-production result directly in "literate" (q.v.) cognitive skills. (Chapter 1.)

Bibliography

PRIMARY SOURCES

(Note: Names such as Geoffrey of Vinsauf, Olivier de la Marche, or Vespasiano da Bisticci are alphabetized under the first name.
EETS OS/ES = Early English Text Society Old Series / Extra Series.)

Ascham, Roger, *The Schoolmaster*, ed. Lawrence V. Ryan (Ithaca, 1967).

Ashby, George, *Poems*, ed. Mary Bateson, EETS ES 76 (London, 1899).

Aubert, David, *Croniques et conquestes de Charlemaine*, ed. Robert Guiette, 3 vols. (Brussels, 1940, 1943, 1951).

Blacman, John, *Henry the Sixth: A Reprint of John Blacman's Memoir*, ed. and trans. M. R. James (Cambridge, 1919).

Bokenham, Osbern, *Legendys of Hooly Wummen*, ed. Mary S. Serjeantson, EETS OS 206 (London, 1938).

Mappula Angliae, ed. C. Horstmann, *Englische Studien*, 10 (1887), 1–34.

Le Bone Florence of Rome, ed. Wilhelm Vietor and Albert Knobbe (Marburg, 1899).

The Buik of Alexander or the Buik of the Most Noble and Valiant Conquerour Alexander the Grit, ed. R. L. Graeme Ritchie, 4 vols., Scottish Text Society nos. 17 (vol. I, 1925), 12 (vol. II, 1921), 21 (vol. III, 1927), 25 (vol. IV, 1929) (Edinburgh).

Caxton, William, *Caxton's Own Prose*, ed. N. F. Blake (London, 1973).

trans., *The History of Reynard the Fox*, ed. Edmund Goldsmid (Edinburgh, 1884).

Chandos Herald, *La Vie du Prince Noir*, ed. Diana B. Tyson (Tübingen, 1975).

Chaucer, Geoffrey, *The Riverside Chaucer*, ed. Larry D. Benson, 3d ed. (Oxford, 1988).

Li Chevaliers as deus espees, ed. Wendelin Foerster (Halle, 1877).

Chrétien de Troyes, *The Knight with the Lion, or Yvain (Le Chevalier au lion)*, ed. and trans. William W. Kibler (New York, 1985).

Christine de Pizan, *Les Epistres du débat sus "Le Rommant de la rose,"* in Eric Hicks, ed., *Le Débat sur le "Roman de la rose"* (Paris, 1977), pp. 5–26.

The "Livre de la paix" of Christine de Pisan, ed. Charity Cannon Willard (The Hague, 1958).

Le Livre des fais et bonnes meurs du sage roy Charles V, ed. Suzanne Solente, 2 vols. (Paris, 1936, 1940).

The Middle English Translation of Christine de Pisan's "Livre du corps de policie" [The Body of Polycye], ed. Diane Bernstein (Heidelberg, 1977).

Clifford, Lady Anne, *The Diary of the Lady Anne Clifford*, ed. V. Sackville-West (London, 1924).
The Court of Sapience, ed. E. Ruth Harvey (Toronto, 1984).
Cursor mundi, ed. Richard Morris, 2 vols., EETS OS 57, 68 (London 1874, 1878).
Deschamps, Eustache, *L'Art de dictier*, in *Oeuvres complètes*, vol. VII, ed. Gaston Raynaud (Paris, 1891), pp. 266–92.
Oeuvres complètes, vol. I, ed. Le Marquis de Queux de Saint-Hilaire (Paris, 1878).
Douglas, Gavin, *Virgil's "Aeneid" Translated into Scottish Verse* [*Eneados*], ed. David F. C. Coldwell, 4 vols., Scottish Text Society 3d ser., nos. 30 (vol. I, 1964), 25 (vol. II, 1957), 27 (vol. III, 1959), 28 (vol. IV, 1960) (Edinburgh).
Emaré, in Walter H. French and Charles B. Hale, eds., *Middle English Metrical Romances* (New York, 1930), pp. 423–55.
"The Floure and the Leafe" and "The Assembly of Ladies," ed. Derek Pearsall (London, 1962).
Fortescue, Sir John, *De laudibus legum Anglie*, ed. and trans. S. B. Chrimes (Cambridge, 1942).
Froissart, Jean, *Chroniques*, vol. VIII, pt. ii: *Texte et variantes*, ed. Gaston Raynaud, Société de l'Histoire de France 238 (Paris, 1888).
L'Espinette amoureuse, ed. Anthime Fourrier (Paris, 1963).
Meliador, ed. Auguste Longnon, 3 vols. (Paris, 1895, 1899).
Oeuvres: *Chroniques*, ed. Kervyn de Lettenhove, vols. XI, XV (Brussels, 1870–71).
Oeuvres: *Poésies*, vol. II: *Le Dit du florin*, ed. Auguste Scheler (Brussels, 1871).
Sir John Froissart's Chronicles of England, France, Spain, Portugal, Scotland, Brittany, Flanders, and the Adjoining Countries, trans. Lord Berners, 2 vols. (rpt. London, 1812).
[*Gawain*-poet], *Pearl, Cleanness, Patience, Sir Gawain and the Green Knight*, ed. A. C. Cawley and J. J. Anderson (London, 1985).
Sir Gawain and the Green Knight, ed. J. R. R. Tolkien and E. V. Gordon; rev. 2d ed., ed. Norman Davis (Oxford, 1970).
Geoffrey of Vinsauf, *The New Poetics* [*Poetria nova*], trans. Jane Baltzell Kopp, in James J. Murphy, ed., *Three Medieval Rhetorical Arts* (Berkeley, 1971), pp. 32–113.
Giraldus Cambrensis, *Opera*, vol. I: *De rebus a se gestis, etc.*, ed. J. S. Brewer, Rolls Series 21 (London, 1861).
Opera, vol. VI: *Itinerarium Kambriae*, ed. James F. Dimock, Rolls Series 21 (London, 1868).
Gower, John, *Complete Works*, vol. I: *The French Works*, ed. G. C. Macaulay (Oxford, 1899).
Complete Works, vols. II–III: *Confessio Amantis*, ed. G. C. Macaulay (Oxford, 1901).
[*Les Grands Chroniques de France*] *Chronique des règnes de Jean II et de Charles V*, ed. R. Delachenal, vol. II (1364–80), Société de l'Histoire de France 375 (Paris, 1916).
Guillaume de Machaut, *Le Livre du voir-dit*, ed. P. Paris (Paris, 1875).
Hardison, Jr., O. B., Alex Preminger, Kevin Kerrane, and Leon Golden, *Medieval Literary Criticism: Translations and Interpretations* (New York, 1974).
The Harley Lyrics, ed. G. L. Brook, 2d ed. (Manchester, 1956).

Havelok, ed. G. V. Smithers (Oxford, 1987).
Hawes, Stephen, *The Minor Poems*, ed. Florence W. Gluck and Alice B. Morgan, EETS 271 (London, 1974).
Hawthorne, Nathaniel, *The Blithedale Romance* (rpt. Columbus, 1964).
Hay, Sir Gilbert, *The Buik of King Alexander the Conqueror*, vol. II, ed. John Cartwright, Scottish Text Society 4th ser., no. 16 (Edinburgh, 1986).
The Buke of the Governaunce of Princis, in J. H. Stevenson, ed., *Gilbert of the Haye's Prose Manuscript*, vol. II, Scottish Text Society 62 (Edinburgh, 1914), pp. 71–165.
Henryson, Robert, *The Poems of Robert Henryson*, ed. Denton Fox (Oxford, 1981).
Hoby, Lady Margaret, *Diary of Lady Margaret Hoby, 1599–1605*, ed. Dorothy M. Meads (London, 1930).
Hoccleve, Thomas, *The Series*, in *Works*, vol. I: *The Minor Poems*, ed. Frederick J. Furnivall, EETS ES 61 (London, 1892), pp. 95–242.
Works, vol. III: *The Regement of Princes ... and Fourteen of Hoccleve's Minor Poems*, ed. Frederick J. Furnivall, EETS ES 72 (London, 1897).
Hume, Alexander, *Hymnes, or Sacred Songs, Wherein the Right Vse of Poesie May Be Espied*, Maitland Club 41 (Edinburgh, 1832).
"Instructions for a devout and literate layman," ed. and trans. William Abel Pantin, in J. J. G. Alexander and M. T. Gibson, eds., *Medieval Learning and Literature: Essays Presented to Richard William Hunt* (Oxford, 1976), pp. 398–422.
The Isle of Ladies, or The Ile of Pleasaunce, ed. Anthony Jenkins (New York, 1980).
Itinéraires de Philippe le Hardi et de Jean sans Peur, ducs de Bourgogne (1363–1419), ed. Ernest Petit, Collection de documents inédits sur l'histoire de France, vol. IX (Paris, 1888).
James I of Scotland, *The Kingis Quair*, ed. Matthew P. McDiarmid (London, 1973).
Jean Cabaret d'Orville, *La Chronique du bon duc Loys de Bourbon*, ed. A.-M. Chazaud (Paris, 1876).
John of Salisbury, *The Metalogicon*, ed. and trans. Daniel McGarry (Berkeley, 1955).
Opera omnia, vol. V: *Metalogicon*, ed. J. A. Giles (Oxford, 1848).
Kempe, Margery, *The Book of Margery Kempe*, ed. Sanford Brown Meech, vol. I, EETS OS 212 (London, 1940).
Knyghthode and Bataile, ed. R. Dyboski and Z. M. Arend, EETS OS 201 (London, 1935).
Langland, William, *The Vision of Piers Plowman*, ed. A. V. C. Schmidt (London, 1978).
The Laud Troy Book, ed. J. Ernst Wülfing, EETS 121–22 (London, 1902–3).
Liber custumarum, pts. 1–2 (*Munimenta Gildhallae Londoniensis*, vol. II), ed. Henry Thomas Riley, Rolls Series 12 (London, 1860).
[*Liber niger*] *The Household of Edward IV: The Black Book and the Ordinance of 1478*, ed. A. R. Myers (Manchester, 1959).
Le Livre des fais du bon messire Jehan le Maingre, dit Bouciquaut, mareschal de France et gouverneur de Jennes, ed. Denis Lalande (Paris, 1985).
Lydgate, John, *Lydgate's Fall of Princes*, ed. Henry Bergen, 4 vols., EETS ES 121–24 (London, 1924, 1927).

Lydgate's Siege of Thebes, vol. I [text], ed. Axel Erdmann, EETS ES 108 (London, 1911).

Lydgate's Siege of Thebes, vol. II [apparatus], ed. Axel Erdmann and Eilert Ekwall, EETS ES 125 (London, 1930).

Malory, Sir Thomas, *The Works of Sir Thomas Malory* [*Le Morte Darthur*], ed. Eugène Vinaver, 2d ed., 3 vols. (Oxford, 1967).

"Mandeville, Sir John," *The Bodley Version of Mandeville's Travels*, ed. M. C. Seymour, EETS 253 (London, 1963).

Mandeville's Travels, vol. I [text], ed. P. Hamelius, EETS OS 153 (London, 1919).

Mannyng, Robert, of Brunne, *Handlyng Synne*, ed. Idelle Sullens (Binghamton, 1983).

The Story of England [*Chronicle*], ed. Frederick J. Furnivall, Rolls Series 87 (London, 1887).

Manzalaoui, M. A., ed., *Secretum secretorum: Nine English Versions*, vol. I [text], EETS 276 (Oxford, 1977).

Metham, John, *The Works of John Metham*, ed. Hardin Craig, EETS OS 132 (London, 1916).

Mum and the Sothsegger, ed. Mabel Day and Robert Steele, EETS OS 199 (London, 1936).

Myers, A. R., ed., *English Historical Documents: 1327–1485* (London, 1969).

Olivier de la Marche, *Mémoires*, vol. II, ed. Henri Beaune and J. D'Arbaumont (Paris, 1884).

"Orders and rules of the house of the Princess Cecill, mother of King Edward IV," in *A Collection of Ordinances and Regulations for the Government of the Royal Household* (London, 1790), pp. *35–*39.

"Ordinances for the government of Prince Edward, son of Edward IV," in *A Collection of Ordinances and Regulations for the Government of the Royal Household* (London, 1790), pp. *27–*33.

Parlement of the Thre Ages, ed. M. Y. Offord, EETS 246 (London, 1959).

Partonopeu de Blois: A French Romance of the Twelfth Century, ed. Joseph Gildea, vol. I (Villanova, Pa., 1967).

[Partonope of Blois] The Middle-English Versions of Partonope of Blois, ed. A. Trampe Bödtker, EETS ES 109 (London, 1912).

Philippe de Commines, *Mémoires*, ed. Joseph Calmette, 2 vols. (Paris, 1924–25).

Philippe de Mézières, *Le Songe du vieil pelerin*, ed. G. W. Coopland, 2 vols. (Cambridge, 1969).

Plato, *Phaedrus*, in *Euthyphro, Apology, Crito, Phaedo, Phaedrus*, ed. and trans. Harold North Fowler, Loeb Classical Library Plato, vol. I (London, 1947), pp. 413–579.

Richard Aungerville de Bury, *Philobiblon*, trans. Archer Taylor (Berkeley, 1948).

Robbins, Rossell Hope, ed., *Historical Poems of the XIVth and XVth Centuries* (New York, 1959).

Scogan, Henry, "A moral balade," in Walter W. Skeat, ed., *The Complete Works of Geoffrey Chaucer*, vol. VII: *Chaucerian and Other Pieces* (Oxford, 1897), pp. 237–44.

Shirley, John, trans., "The dethe of the Kynge of Scotis," in Joseph Stevenson, ed.,

The Life and Death of King James the First of Scotland, Maitland Club 42 (Edinburgh, 1837), pp. 47–67.

Sidney, Sir Philip, *The Countess of Pembroke's Arcadia (The New Arcadia)*, ed. Victor Skretkowicz (Oxford, 1987).

Sir Eglamour of Artois, ed. Frances E. Richardson, EETS 256 (London, 1965).

Sir Tristrem, ed. Sir Walter Scott, 3d ed. (Edinburgh, 1811).

Skeat, Walter W., ed., *The Complete Works of Geoffrey Chaucer*, vol. VII: *Chaucerian and Other Pieces* (Oxford, 1897).

Skelton, John, *The Complete English Poems*, ed. John Scattergood (Harmondsworth, 1983).

Le Songe du vergier, ed. Marion Schnerb-Lièvre, 2 vols. (Paris, 1982).

Statutes of the Colleges of Oxford, vol. I (Oxford, 1853).

The Tale of Beryn, with a Prologue of the Merry Adventure of the Pardoner with a Tapster at Canterbury, ed. F. J. Furnivall and W. G. Stone, EETS ES 105 (London, 1890).

Turner, Thomas, *The Diary of Thomas Turner: 1754–1765*, ed. David Vaisey (Oxford, 1984).

Twyne, John, "To the redar," in Hugo of Caumpedene, *The History of Kyng Boccus and Sydracke* (London, ?1537), p. 2.

Usk, Thomas, *The Testament of Love*, in Walter W. Skeat, ed., *The Complete Works of Geoffrey Chaucer*, vol. VII: *Chaucerian and Other Pieces* (Oxford, 1897), pp. 1–145.

Van den Vos Reynaerde, I Teksten: Diplomatisch Uitgegeven naar de Bronnen Voor het Jaar 1500, ed. W. G. Hellinga (Zwolle, 1952).

Vespasiano da Bisticci, *The Vespasiano Memoirs: Lives of Illustrious Men of the Fifteenth Century*, trans. William George and Emily Waters (London, 1926).

Wace, *Le Roman de Rou*, vol. I, ed. A. J. Holden (Paris, 1970).

Ward, G. R. M., ed. and trans., *The Foundation Statutes of Bishop Fox for Corpus Christi College in the University of Oxford* (London, 1843).

The Wars of Alexander, ed. W. W. Skeat, EETS ES 47 (London, 1886).

William of Malmesbury, *Gesta regum anglorum*, ed. William Stubbs, Rolls Series 90, vol. II (London, 1889).

[*Winner and Waster*] *A Good Short Debate Between Winner and Waster*, ed. Sir Israel Gollancz, with Mabel Day, rev. ed. (London, 1930).

Wynnere and Wastoure, ed. Stephanie Trigg, EETS 297 (Oxford, 1990).

Ywain and Gawain, ed. Albert B. Friedman and Norman T. Harrington, EETS 254 (London, 1964).

SECONDARY SOURCES

Armstrong, C. A. J. 1942. "The piety of Cicely, duchess of York: A study in late medieval culture," in Douglas Woodruff, ed., *For Hilaire Belloc: Essays in Honor of His 71st Birthday* (rpt. 1969, New York), pp. 68–91.

Auerbach, Erich. 1965. *Literary Language and Its Public in Late Latin Antiquity and in the Middle Ages*, trans. Ralph Manheim (London).

Babcock, Barbara A. 1977. "The story in the story: Metanarration in folk narrative," in Bauman, ed., *Verbal Art as Performance*, pp. 61–79.

Bibliography

Backhouse, Janet. 1987. "Founders of the Royal Library: Edward IV and Henry VII as collectors of illuminated manuscripts," in Daniel Williams, ed., *England in the Fifteenth Century* (Woodbridge), pp. 23–41.

Basso, Keith H. 1974. "The ethnography of writing," in Richard Bauman and Joel Sherzer, eds., *Explorations in the Ethnography of Speaking* (Cambridge), pp. 425–32.

Baugh, Albert C. 1950. "The authorship of the Middle English romances," *Bulletin of the Modern Humanities Research Association*, 22, 13–28.

1959. "Improvisation in the Middle English romance," *Proceedings of the American Philosophical Society*, 103, 418–54.

1967. "The Middle English romance: Some questions of creation, presentation, and preservation," *Speculum*, 42, 1–31.

Bauman, Richard, ed. 1977. *Verbal Art as Performance* (Prospect Heights, Ill.).

Bäuml, Franz H. 1980. "Varieties and consequences of medieval literacy and illiteracy," *Speculum*, 55, 237–65.

and Edda Spielmann. 1975. "From illiteracy to literacy: Prolegomena to a study of the *Nibelungenlied*," in Joseph J. Duggan, ed., *Oral Literature: Seven Essays* (New York), pp. 62–73.

Beljame, Alexandre. 1948. *Men of Letters and the English Public in the Eighteenth Century: 1660–1744*, trans. E. O. Lorimer (London).

Benson, Larry D. 1965. *Art and Tradition in "Sir Gawain and the Green Knight"* (New Brunswick).

Bernstein, Basil. 1964. "Aspects of language and learning in the genesis of the social process," in Dell Hymes, ed., *Language in Culture and Society* (New York), pp. 251–60.

1972. "Social class, language and socialization," in Pier Paolo Giglioli, ed. *Language and Social Context* (Harmondsworth), pp. 157–78.

Bolton, W. F. 1970. "Introduction: The conditions of literary composition in medieval England," in Bolton, ed., *History of Literature in the English Language*, vol. I: *The Middle Ages* (London), pp. ix–xxxvi.

Bourrilly, V. L. 1905. *Jacques Colin, Abbé de Saint-Ambroise* (Paris).

Bowden, Betsy. 1987. *Chaucer Aloud: The Varieties of Textual Interpretation* (Philadelphia).

Boyarin, Jonathan, ed. 1993. *The Ethnography of Reading* (Berkeley).

Brand, Paul. 1987. "Courtroom and schoolroom: The education of lawyers in England prior to 1400," *Historical Research*, 60, 147–65.

Brewer, Derek. 1966. "The relationship of Chaucer to the English and European traditions," in Brewer, ed., *Chaucer and Chaucerians: Critical Studies in Middle English Literature* (London), pp. 1–38.

1974. "Towards a Chaucerian poetic," *Proceedings of the British Academy*, 60, 219–52; rpt. 1984 in Brewer, *Chaucer: The Poet as Storyteller* (London), pp. 54–79.

1978. *Chaucer and His World* (London).

1982. "The social context of medieval literature," in Boris Ford, ed., *Medieval Literature: Chaucer and the Alliterative Tradition*, rev. ed. (Harmondsworth), pp. 15–40.

1988. "Orality and literacy in Chaucer," in Willi Erzgräber and Sabine Volk, eds.,

Mündlichkeit und Schriftlichkeit im englischen Mittelalter (Tübingen), pp. 85–119.

Bronson, Bertrand H. 1940. "Chaucer's art in relation to his audience," *Five Studies in Literature*, University of California Publications in English 8 (Berkeley), pp. 1–53.

1960. *In Search of Chaucer* (Toronto).

Brunner, Karl. 1961. "Middle English metrical romances and their audience," in MacEdward Leach, ed., *Studies in Medieval Literature in Honor of Professor Albert Croll Baugh* (Philadelphia), pp. 219–27.

Burrow, J. A. 1971. *Ricardian Poetry* (London).

1973. "Bards, minstrels, and men of letters," in David Daiches and Anthony Thorlby, eds., *The Mediaeval World* (London), pp. 347–70.

1984. "Hoccleve's 'Series': Experience and books," in Robert F. Yeager, ed., *Fifteenth-Century Studies: Recent Essays* (Hamden), pp. 259–73.

Caie, Graham D. 1976. "The significance of the early Chaucer manuscript glosses (with special reference to the 'Wife of Bath's Prologue')," *Chaucer Review*, 10, 350–60.

Carruthers, Mary J. 1990. *The Book of Memory: A Study of Memory in Medieval Culture* (Cambridge).

Chafe, Wallace, and Deborah Tannen. 1987. "The relation between written and spoken language," *Annual Review of Anthropology*, 16, 383–407.

"Chaucer's audience: Discussion." 1983. *Chaucer Review*, 18, 175–81.

Chaytor, H. J. 1967. *From Script to Print: An Introduction to Medieval Vernacular Literature* (New York).

Chénu, M.-D. 1954. *Introduction à l'étude de Saint Thomas d'Aquin*, 2d ed. (Montreal).

Christianson, Paul. 1976/77. "Chaucer's literacy," *Chaucer Review*, 11, 112–27.

Clanchy, Michael T. 1979. *From Memory to Written Record: England 1066–1307* (London).

Cobban, Alan B. 1988. *The Medieval English Universities: Oxford and Cambridge to c. 1500* (Aldershot).

Coleman, Janet. 1981. *Medieval Readers and Writers: 1350–1400* (New York).

Coleman, Joyce. 1990a. "The audible Caxton: Reading and hearing in the writings of England's first publisher," *Fifteenth-Century Studies*, 16, 83–109.

1990b. "The solace of hearing: Medieval views on the reading aloud of literature," *ARV: Scandinavian Yearbook of Folklore*, 46, 123–34.

1995. "Interactive parchment: The theory and practice of medieval English aurality," *Yearbook of English Studies*, 25, 63–79.

Cressy, David. 1980. *Literacy and the Social Order: Reading and Writing in Tudor and Stuart England* (Cambridge).

Crosby, Ruth. 1936. "Oral delivery in the Middle Ages," *Speculum*, 11, 88–110.

1938. "Chaucer and the custom of oral delivery," *Speculum*, 13, 413–32.

Curtius, Ernst Robert. 1953. *European Literature and the Latin Middle Ages*, trans. Willard R. Trask (London).

De Laborde, A. 1909. *Les Manuscrits à peintures de la "Cité de Dieu,"* vol. I (Paris).

De Looze, Laurence. 1991. "Signing off in the Middle Ages: Medieval textuality and strategies of authorial self-naming," in Doane and Pasternack, eds., *Vox Intexta*, pp. 162–78.

Diamond, Arlyn. 1977. "Chaucer's women and women's Chaucer," in Diamond and Lee R. Edwards, eds., *The Authority of Experience: Essays in Feminist Criticism* (Amherst), pp. 60–83.

Doane, A. N., and Carol Braun Pasternack, eds. 1991. *Vox Intexta: Orality and Textuality in the Middle Ages* (Madison).

Dorson, Richard. 1968. *The British Folklorists* (London).

Doucet, Roger. 1920. "Pierre du Chastel, Grand Aumônier de France," *Revue historique*, 133, 212–57; 134, 1–58.

Doutrepont, Georges. 1909. *La Littérature française à la court des ducs de Bourgogne* (Paris).

Duggan, Joseph J. 1989. "Performance and transmission, aural and ocular reception in the twelfth- and thirteenth-century vernacular literature of France," *Romance Philology*, 43, 49–58.

Eagleton, Terry. 1984. *The Function of Criticism: From "The Spectator" to Post-Structuralism* (London).

Edwards, A. S. G. 1983. "Lydgate manuscripts: Some directions for future research," in Derek Pearsall, ed., *Manuscripts and Readers in Fifteenth-Century England: The Literary Implications of Manuscript Study* (Cambridge), pp. 15–26.

and Derek Pearsall. 1989. "The manuscripts of the major English poetic texts," in Jeremy Griffiths and Derek Pearsall, eds., *Book Production and Publishing in Britain 1375–1475* (Cambridge), pp. 257–78.

Ferrier, Janet. 1956. *French Prose Writers of the Fourteenth and Fifteenth Centuries* (Oxford).

Fichte, Jörg O. 1988. "Hearing and reading the *Canterbury Tales*," in Willi Erzgräber and Sabine Volk, eds., *Mündlichkeit und Schriftlichkeit im englischen Mittelalter* (Tübingen), pp. 121–31.

Finnegan, Ruth. 1973. "Literacy versus non-literacy: The great divide? Some comments on the significance of 'literature' in non-literate cultures," in Robin Horton and Finnegan, eds., *Modes of Thought: Essays on Thinking in Western and Non-Western Societies* (London), pp. 112–44.

1988. *Literacy and Orality: Studies in the Technology of Communication* (Oxford).

1994. "Literacy as mythical charter," in Deborah Keller-Cohen, ed., *Literacy: Interdisciplinary Conversations* (Cresskill, N.J.), pp. 31–47.

Fisher, John H. 1965. *John Gower: Moral Philosopher and Friend of Chaucer* (London).

1985. "Chaucer and the written language," in Thomas J. Heffernan, ed., *The Popular Literature of Medieval England* (Knoxville), pp. 237–51.

Frese, Dolores Warwick. 1991. "The marriage of woman and werewolf: Poetics of estrangement in Marie de France's 'Bisclavret,'" in Doane and Pasternack, eds., *Vox Intexta*, pp. 183–202.

Gaspar, Camille, and Frédéric Lyna. 1944. *Philippe le Bon et ses beaux livres* (Brussels).

George, Kenneth M. 1990. "Felling a song with a new ax: Writing and the reshaping of ritual song performance in Upland Sulawesi," *Journal of American Folklore*, 103, 3–23.

Giffin, Mary. 1956. *Studies on Chaucer and His Audience* (Hull, Quebec).
Ginsberg, Warren S. 1988. Notes to "Clerk's Prologue" and "Clerk's Tale," in Geoffrey Chaucer, *The Riverside Chaucer*, ed. Larry D. Benson, 3d ed. (Oxford), pp. 879–84.
Goetsch, Paul. 1991. "Der Übergang von mündlichkeit zu schriftlichkeit," in Wolfgang Raible, ed., *Symbolische Formen medien Identität, ScriptOralia*, 37, 113–29.
Goodall, Peter. 1992. "Being alone in Chaucer," *Chaucer Review*, 27, 1–15.
Goody, Jack, ed. 1968a. *Literacy in Traditional Societies* (Cambridge; rpt. 1981).
1968b. "Introduction," in Goody, ed., *Literacy in Traditional Societies*, pp. 1–26.
1977. *The Domestication of the Savage Mind* (Cambridge).
1986. *The Logic of Writing and the Organization of Society* (Cambridge).
1987. *The Interface Between the Written and the Oral* (Cambridge).
and Ian Watt. 1963. "The consequences of literacy"; rpt. in Goody, ed., *Literacy in Traditional Societies*, pp. 27–68.
Gough, Kathleen. 1968. "Implications of literacy in traditional China and India," in Goody, ed., *Literacy in Traditional Societies*, pp. 69–84.
Green, D. H. 1984. "On the primary reception of narrative literature in medieval Germany," *Forum for Modern Language Studies*, 20, 289–308.
1990. "Orality and reading: The state of research in medieval studies," *Speculum*, 65, 267–80.
1994. *Medieval Listening and Reading: The Primary Reception of German Literature 800–1300* (Cambridge).
Green, Richard Firth. 1980. *Poets and Princepleasers: Literature and the English Court in the Late Middle Ages* (Toronto).
Grudin, Robert. 1991. "Humanism," *Encyclopedia Britannica*, 20, 665–77.
Guenée, Bernard. 1976. "La Culture historique des nobles: Le Succès des *Faits des Romains*, XIIIe–XVe siècles," in Philippe Contamine, ed., *La Noblesse au moyen age XIe–XVe siècles: Essais à la mémoire de Robert Boutruche* (Paris), pp. 261–88.
Habermas, Jürgen. 1989. *The Structural Transformation of the Public Sphere: An Inquiry into a Category of Bourgeois Society*, trans. Thomas Burger (London).
Hallmundsson, May N. 1970. "A collection of materials for a study of the literary scene at the end of the fourteenth century" (Ph.D. thesis, New York University).
Halverson, John. 1991. "Olson on literacy," *Language in Society*, 20, 619–40.
Harris, William V. 1989. *Ancient Literacy* (Cambridge, Mass.).
Harwood, Britton J. 1990. "Dame Study and the place of orality in *Piers Plowman*," *ELH*, 57, 1–17.
Havelock, Eric. 1963. *A Preface to Plato* (Cambridge).
Hoggart, Richard. 1957. *The Uses of Literacy: Aspects of Working-Class Life with Special Reference to Publications and Entertainments* (rpt. Harmondsworth, 1966).
Hohendahl, Peter Uwe. 1982. *The Institution of Criticism* (Ithaca).
Howard, Donald R. 1976. *The Idea of the Canterbury Tales* (Berkeley).
Hymes, Dell. 1962. "The ethnography of speaking," in T. Gladwin and W. Sturtevant, eds., *Anthropology and Human Behavior* (Washington, D.C.), pp. 15–53.

Irvine, Martin. 1985. "Medieval grammatical theory and Chaucer's *House of Fame*," *Speculum*, 60, 850–76.

Jardine, Lisa, and Anthony Grafton. 1990. "'Studied for action': How Gabriel Harvey read his Livy," *Past and Present*, 129, 30–78.

Jennings, Margaret. 1986. "To *Pryke* or to *Prye*: Scribal delights in the *Troilus*, Book III," in Julian N. Wasserman and Robert J. Blanch, *Chaucer in the Eighties* (Syracuse), pp. 121–33.

Johnson, A. F., ed. 1923. *Francisci Petrarchae Epistolae Selectae* (Oxford).

Kellogg, Robert. 1977. "Oral narrative, written books," *Genre*, 10, 655–65.

Kenny, Anthony, and Jan Pinborg. 1982. "Medieval philosophical literature," in Norman Kretzmann, Anthony Kenny, and Jan Pinborg, eds., *The Cambridge History of Later Medieval Philosophy* (Cambridge), pp. 11–42.

Kenyon, Frederic G. 1932. *Books and Readers in Ancient Greece and Rome* (Oxford).

Kingsford, Charles Lethbridge. 1913. *English Historical Literature in the Fifteenth Century* (Oxford).

Kinney, Arthur F. 1986. *Humanist Poetics: Thought, Rhetoric, and Fiction in Sixteenth-Century England* (Amherst).

Kittay, Jeffrey. 1988. "Utterance unmoored: The changing interpretation of the act of writing in the European Middle Ages," *Language in Society*, 17, 209–30.

Kolve, V. A. 1984. *Chaucer and the Imagery of Narrative: The First Five Canterbury Tales* (London).

Krynen, Jacques. 1981. *Idéal du prince et pouvoir royal en France à la fin du Moyen Age (1380–1440): Etude de la littérature politique du temps* (Paris).

Lambert, Mark. 1975. *Malory: Style and Vision in "Le Morte Darthur"* (New Haven).

Lawton, David. 1987. "Dullness and the fifteenth century," *ELH*, 54, 761–99.

Leclercq, Jean. 1962. *The Love of Learning and the Desire for God: A Study of Monastic Culture*, trans. Catharine Misrahi (New York).

Lewis, C. S. 1964. *The Discarded Image: An Introduction to Medieval and Renaissance Literature* (Cambridge).

Lindahl, Carl. 1987. *Earnest Games: Folkloric Patterns in the "Canterbury Tales"* (Bloomington).

Lord, Albert. 1960. *The Singer of Tales* (rpt. New York, 1973).

Lovatt, Roger. 1981. "John Blacman: Biographer of Henry VI," in R. H. C. Davis and J. M. Wallace-Hadrill, eds., *The Writing of History in the Middle Ages: Essays Presented to Richard William Southern* (Oxford), pp. 415–44.

Luria, Alexander. 1976. *Cognitive Development: Its Cultural and Social Foundations*, ed. Michael Cole, trans. Martin Lopez-Morillas and Lynn Solotaroff (Cambridge).

Mangeart, Jacques. 1860. *Catalogue descriptif et raisonné des manuscrits de la Bibliothèque de Valenciennes* (Paris).

Mann, Jill. 1991. "The authority of the audience in Chaucer," in Piero Boitani and Anna Torti, eds., *Poetics: Theory and Practice in Medieval English Literature* (Woodbridge), pp. 1–12.

McKenna, Steven R. 1988. "Orality, literacy, and Chaucer: A study of performance,

textual authority, and proverbs in the major poetry" (Ph.D. thesis, University of Rhode Island).
McKitterick, Rosamond. 1989. *The Carolingians and the Written Word* (Cambridge).
Mehl, Dieter. 1974. "The audience of Chaucer's *Troilus and Criseyde*," in Beryl Rowland, ed., *Chaucer and Middle English Studies in Honour of Rossell Hope Robbins* (London), pp. 173–89.
Middleton, Anne. 1978. "The idea of public poetry in the reign of Richard II," *Speculum*, 53, 94–114.
1980. "Chaucer's 'new men' and the good of literature in the *Canterbury Tales*," in Edward W. Said, ed., *Literature and Society* (Baltimore), pp. 15–56.
Minnis, A. J. 1988. *Medieval Theory of Authorship: Scholastic Literary Attitudes in the Later Middle Ages*, 2d ed. (Philadelphia).
Monks, Peter Rolfe. 1990. *The Brussels "Horloge de Sapience": Iconography and the Text of Brussels, Bib. Royale, MS. IV 111* (Leiden).
Muscatine, Charles. 1966. "The *Canterbury Tales*: Style of the man and style of the work," in Derek Brewer, ed., *Chaucer and Chaucerians: Critical Studies in Middle English Literature* (London), pp. 88–113.
Narasimhan, R. 1991. "Literacy: Its characterization and implications," in Olson and Torrance, eds., *Literacy and Orality*, pp. 177–97.
Nelson, William. 1976/77. "From 'Listen, lordings' to 'Dear reader,'" *University of Toronto Quarterly*, 46, 110–24.
Olson, David R. 1977. "From utterance to text: The bias of language in speech and writing," *Harvard Educational Review*, 47, 257–81.
and Nancy Torrance, eds. 1991. *Literacy and Orality* (Cambridge).
Olson, Glending. 1982. *Literature as Recreation in the Later Middle Ages* (Ithaca).
O'Neill, Barry. 1994. "The history of a hoax," *New York Times Magazine* (March 6), pp. 46–49.
Ong, Walter J. 1965. "Oral residue in Tudor prose style"; rpt. in Ong, *Rhetoric, Romance, and Technology*, pp. 23–47.
1967. *The Presence of the Word: Some Prolegomena for Cultural and Religious History* (New Haven).
1971. *Rhetoric, Romance, and Technology: Studies in the Interaction of Expression and Culture* (Ithaca).
1982. *Orality and Literacy: The Technologizing of the Word* (London).
1984. "Orality, literacy, and medieval textualization," *New Literary History*, 16, 1–12.
Orme, Nicholas. 1973. *English Schools in the Middle Ages* (London).
1984. *From Childhood to Chivalry: The Education of the English Kings and Aristocracy 1066–1530* (London).
Owst, G. R. 1961. *Literature and Pulpit in Medieval England*, 2d ed. (Oxford).
Painter, George D. 1976. *William Caxton: A Biography* (New York).
Parkes, M. B. 1973. "The literacy of the laity," in David Daiches and Anthony Thorlby, eds., *The Mediaeval World* (London), pp. 555–77.
1976. "The influence of the concepts of *ordinatio* and *compilatio* on the development of the book," in J. J. G. Alexander and M. T. Gibson, eds., *Medieval*

Learning and Literature: Essays Presented to Richard William Hunt (Oxford), pp. 115–41.

Patterson, Lee. 1989. "'What man artow?': Authorial self-definition in *The Tale of Sir Thopas* and *The Tale of Melibee*," *Studies in the Age of Chaucer*, 11, 117–75.

Payne, Robert O. 1963. *The Key of Remembrance: A Study of Chaucer's Poetics* (rpt. Westport, Conn., 1973).

Pearsall, Derek. 1976. "The English romance in the fifteenth century," *Essays and Studies*, 29, 56–83.

1977. "The *Troilus* frontispiece and Chaucer's audience," *Yearbook of English Studies*, 7, 68–74.

1985. *The Canterbury Tales* (London).

1989. "Gower's Latin in the *Confessio Amantis*," in A. J. Minnis, ed., *Latin and Vernacular: Studies in Late-Medieval Texts and Manuscripts* (Woodbridge), pp. 13–25.

1992. *The Life of Geoffrey Chaucer: A Critical Biography* (Oxford).

Prevost, M., and Roman d'Amat, eds. 1956. *Dictionnaire de biographie française*, vol. VII (Paris).

Rashdall, Hastings, and Robert S. Rait. 1901. *New College* (London).

Raynaud, Gaston. 1903. *Introduction* (vol. XI of Eustache Deschamps, *Oeuvres complètes*) (Paris).

1905. "Introduction," in Jean le Seneschal et al., *Les Cent Ballades*, ed. Raynaud (Paris), pp. i–lxx.

Reid, Joyce M. H., ed. 1976. *The Concise Oxford Dictionary of French Literature* (Oxford).

Renoir, Alain. 1986. "Oral-formulaic context: Implications for the comparative study of mediaeval texts," in John Miles Foley, ed., *Oral Tradition in Literature: Interpretation in Context* (Columbia, Mo.), pp. 416–39.

Robinson, James Harvey, and Henry Winchester Rolfe. 1898. *Petrarch: The First Modern Scholar and Man of Letters* (New York).

Root, Robert K. 1913. "Publication before printing," *PMLA*, 28, 417–31.

Rowland, Beryl. 1981. "Chaucer's speaking voice and its effect on his listeners' perception of Criseyde," *English Studies in Canada*, 7, 129–40.

1982. "*Pronuntiatio* and its effect on Chaucer's audience," *Studies in the Age of Chaucer*, 4, 33–51.

Saenger, Paul. 1982. "Silent reading: Its impact on late medieval script and society," *Viator*, 13, 367–414.

1991. "The separation of words and the physiology of reading," in Olson and Torrance, eds., *Literacy and Orality*, pp. 198–214.

Salter, Elizabeth. 1978. "The 'Troilus frontispiece,'" in Geoffrey Chaucer, *Troilus and Criseyde: A Facsimile of Corpus Christi College Cambridge MS 61* (Cambridge), pp. 15–23.

Sanders, Barry. 1991. "Lie it as it plays: Chaucer becomes an author," in Olson and Torrance, eds., *Literacy and Orality*, pp. 111–28.

Schibanoff, Susan. 1988. "The new reader and female textuality in two early commentaries on Chaucer," *Studies in the Age of Chaucer*, 10, 71–108.

Schlauch, Margaret. 1963. *Antecedents of the English Novel* (London).

Scribner, Sylvia, and Michael Cole. 1981. *The Psychology of Literacy* (Cambridge).

Severs, J. Burke, ed. 1967. *A Manual of the Writings in Middle English, 1050–1500*, vol. I (New Haven).

Seymour, M. C. 1974. "The manuscripts of Hoccleve's *Regiment of Princes*," *Transactions of the Edinburgh Bibliographical Society*, 4, 253–71.

1981. "Introduction," in Thomas Hoccleve, *Selections from Hoccleve*, ed. Seymour (Oxford), pp. xi–xxxiii.

Sherman, Claire Richter. 1969. *The Portraits of Charles V of France (1338–1380)* (New York).

1971. "Representations of Charles V of France (1338–1380) as a wise ruler," *Medievalia et Humanistica*, n.s., no. 2, 83–96.

1995. *Imaging Aristotle: Verbal and Visual Representation in Fourteenth-Century France* (Berkeley).

Spearing, A. C. 1972. *Criticism and Medieval Poetry*, 2d ed. (London).

1976. *Medieval Dream-Poetry* (Cambridge).

1985. *Medieval to Renaissance in English Poetry* (Cambridge).

1987. *Readings in Medieval Poetry* (Cambridge).

Spiegel, Gabrielle M. 1991. Review of Brian Stock, *Listening for the Text*, in *Speculum*, 66, 480–82.

Spielmann, M. H. 1900. *The Portraits of Geoffrey Chaucer*, Chaucer Society 2d ser., no. 31 (London).

Stock, Brian. 1983. *The Implications of Literacy: Written Language and Models of Interpretation in the Eleventh and Twelfth Centuries* (Princeton).

Street, Brian V. 1984. *Literacy in Theory and Practice* (Cambridge).

Strohm, Paul. 1971. "Jean of Angoulême: A fifteenth-century reader of Chaucer," *Neuphilologische Mitteilungen*, 72, 69–76.

1989. *Social Chaucer* (Cambridge).

Strouse, Jean. 1981. *Alice James: A Biography* (London).

Taylor, Andrew. 1992. "Fragmentation, corruption, and minstrel narration: The question of the Middle English romances," *Yearbook of English Studies*, 22, 38–62.

Thomas, Rosalind. 1989. *Oral Tradition and Written Record in Classical Athens* (Cambridge).

Thrupp, Sylvia L. 1948. *The Merchant Class of Medieval London: 1300–1500* (Chicago).

Troyan, Scott D. 1990. "Rhetoric without genre: Orality, textuality and the shifting scene of the rhetorical situation in the Middle Ages," *Romanic Review*, 81, 377–95.

Tucoo-Chala, Pierre. 1981. "Froissart dans le Midi pyrénéen," in J. J. N. Palmer, ed., *Froissart: Historian* (Woodbridge), pp. 118–31.

Turville-Petre, Thorlac. 1977. *The Alliterative Revival* (Cambridge).

Vaughan, Richard. 1962. *Philip the Bold: The Formation of the Burgundian State* (Cambridge).

Vinaver, Eugène. 1971. *The Rise of Romance* (Oxford).

Vitz, Evelyn Birge. 1987. "Orality, literacy and the early Tristan material: Béroul, Thomas, Marie de France," *Romanic Review*, 78, 299–310.

Waldron, Ronald. 1957. "Oral-formulaic technique and Middle English alliterative poetry," *Speculum*, 32, 792–804.

Watson, Andrew G. 1984. *Catalogue of Dated and Datable Manuscripts c. 435–1600 in Oxford Libraries*, vol. I (Oxford).

Weiss, R. 1957. *Humanism in England During the Fifteenth Century*, 2d ed. (Oxford).

Windeatt, Barry. 1990. "Chaucer and fifteenth-century romance: *Partonope of Blois*," in Ruth Morse and Barry Windeatt, eds., *Chaucer Traditions: Studies in Honour of Derek Brewer* (Cambridge), pp. 62–80.

Wright, Louis B. 1931. "The reading of Renaissance English women," *Studies in Philology*, 28, 671–88.

Yeager, Robert F. 1984. "Preface," in Yeager, ed., *Fifteenth-Century Studies: Recent Essays* (Hamden), pp. vii–ix.

1990. *John Gower's Poetic: The Search for a New Arion* (Woodbridge).

Zumthor, Paul. 1987. *La Lettre et la voix de la "littérature" médiévale* (Paris).

Index

Index

CAMBRIDGE STUDIES IN MEDIEVAL LITERATURE

Titles published

1 *Dante's "Inferno": Difficulty and dead poetry*, by Robin Kirkpatrick
2 *Dante and Difference: Writing in the "Commedia,"* by Jeremy Tambling
3 *Troubadors and Irony*, by Simon Gaunt
4 *"Piers Plowman" and the New Anticlericalism*, by Wendy Scase
5 *The "Cantar de mio Cid": Poetic creation in its economic and social contexts*, by Joseph Duggan
6 *The Medieval Greek Romance*, by Roderick Beaton
7 *Reformist Apocalypticism and "Piers Plowman,"* by Kathryn Kerby-Fulton
8 *Dante and the Medieval Other World*, by Alison Morgan
9 *The Theatre of Medieval Europe: New research in early drama*, edited by Eckehard Simon
10 *The Book of Memory: A study of memory in medieval culture*, by Mary J. Carruthers
11 *Rhetoric, Hermeneutics and Translation in the Middle Ages: Academic traditions and vernacular texts*, by Rita Copeland
12 *The Arthurian Romances of Chrétien de Troyes: Once and future fictions*, by Donald Maddox
13 *Richard Rolle and the Invention of Authority*, by Nicholas Watson
14 *Dreaming in the Middle Ages*, by Steven F. Kruger
15 *Chaucer and the Tradition of the "Roman Antique,"* by Barbara Nolan
16 *The "Romance of the Rose" and its Medieval Readers: Interpretation, reception, manuscript transmission*, by Sylvia Huot
17 *Women and Literature in Britain, 1150–1500*, edited by Carol M. Meale
18 *Ideas and Forms of Tragedy from Aristotle to the Middle Ages*, by Henry Ansgar Kelly
19 *The Making of Textual Culture: Grammatica and literary theory, 350–1100*, by Martin Irvine
20 *Narrative, Authority, and Power: The medieval exemplum and the Chaucerian tradition*, by Larry Scanlon
21 *Medieval Dutch Literature in its European Context*, edited by Erik Kooper

22 *Dante and the Mystical Tradition: Bernard of Clairvaux in the "Commedia,"* by Steven Botterill
23 *Heresy and Literacy, 1000–1530*, edited by Peter Biller and Anne Hudson
24 *Virgil in Medieval England: Figuring the "Aeneid" from the twelfth century to Chaucer*, by Christopher Baswell
25 *Sciences and the Self in Medieval Poetry: Alan of Lille's "Anticlaudianus" and John Gower's "Confessio Amantis,"* by James Simpson
26 *Public Reading and the Reading Public in Late Medieval England and France*, by Joyce Coleman